I0730705

THE

MODERN TRAVELLER.

A

POPULAR DESCRIPTION,

GEOGRAPHICAL, HISTORICAL, AND TOPOGRAPHICAL,

OF THE

VARIOUS COUNTRIES OF THE GLOBE.

PERSIA AND CHINA.

VOL. II.

LONDON:

PRINTED FOR JAMES DUNCAN;

OLIVER AND BOYD, EDINBURGH; M. OGLE, GLASGOW;
AND R. M. TIMS, DUBLIN.
1827.

LONDON:
Printed by WILLIAM CLOWES,
Stamford-Street.

CONTENTS

OF THE SECOND VOLUME.

PERSIA.

CHINA.

iv   CONTENTS.

DIRECTIONS FOR PLACING THE PLATES.

THE
MODERN TRAVELLER,

&c. &c.

PERSIA.

PERSEPOLIS.

Out of Egypt, there are few monuments of remote antiquity so intrinsically interesting, or which have employed so much learned speculation, as the ruins in the plain of Merdasht, which are supposed to mark the site of the far-famed Persepolis. They are found at the distance of four and thirty miles N.E. of Shiraz, in the route to Isfahan, and have consequently been described by almost every European traveller who has visited Persia. Yet, they still remain an enigma, their history, date, and object being involved in venerable mystery. Their very name has passed away; their founder is unknown; and the obscure tradition which assigns them to king Jemsheed, serves only to prove, that of nothing are the Persians more entirely ignorant than of their own history and that of their ancient monuments.

Sir W. Ouseley,* who has devoted nearly half of his second volume to the historical illustration of these

* While Sir Gore Ouseley was detained at Shiraz in June and July 1811, several of the gentlemen attached to the embassy were despatched in various directions to explore the country. Sir Wm. Ouseley, his Excellency's brother, went to Fassa and Darab; the Hon. Mr. Gordon undertook a dangerous journey to Shouster;

PART III.   B

remains, and Sir Robert Ker Porter, who has furnished the best description of them, will be our chief
guides on this occasion, while we shall avail ourselves
of the additional information furnished by Mr. Morier,
Lieut. Alexander, and the older travellers.

The road from Shiraz passes through the *Tengui-
állah-akbar*, and, for about three miles, winds along the
course of the Roknabad, to a *rahdári* or guard-house,
called the tower (*burje*) of *Khelaut-poushoon*,* from
its being the place to which the governors of Fars
proceed in state, in order to be invested with the *khe-
laut*, or dress of honour, sent by the Shah, as the insignia of office. Near the gateway of the pass, some
new sculptures have been executed by order of the
prince-governor, on the face of a rock on the left hand
side of the road, past which the stream flows. The
subject of the first is, his majesty, Futteh Ali Shah,
seated on his throne, with the heir-apparent near him.
The second exhibits Roustum, the hero of Persian
romance, on horseback, in the act of transfixing with
an arrow a tiger, who has a man under him. The
workmanship, Lieut. Alexander says, is by no means
despicable. The country through which the road
passes, is hilly and open. Scarcely a shrub enlivens
the brown, arid mountains, which, here and there, are
varied, by the capricious directions of the strata, into
the most remarkable forms. At seven miles, the road
lies over the *Kutul-i-bajgah* (hill of the custom-house),
so named from a *rahdári*, where a transit duty is
levied upon merchandise. A little further are remains

Col. D'Arcy proceeded to Ferouzabad; Major Stone, by a new
route, to Shapour; and Mr. Morier to Persepolis, where he was
subsequently joined by Sir W. Ouseley.

* From *khelaat*, the dress, and *pushan*, investing, &c. Similar
towers, bearing the same name, are found near every capital.

of an ancient edifice, which, according to tradition, bore the name of *Gumbed-i-Sabz*, the Green Villa, being one of the seven summer-houses erected by king Bahram Gour. Near this is the small stream called *Ab-i-Barik* (narrow water).[*] About seven miles further, over a rugged and stony road, lead to the town of Zargoon, distant from Shiraz, according to the reckoning of the natives, five *farsangs*, but Sir W. Ouseley ascertained it to be rather more than seventeen miles and a half.

Zargoon (Zarkan) is described as " a considerable village," and an " insignificant " town. It consists of from 300 to 400 houses, built at the foot of a rocky mountain, which intercepts the air, and renders the heat extremely oppressive. The thermometer (in July) rose, at three o'clock, to above 109° in the shade. The moskitoes (*pashehs*) here are innumerable. The town contains some linen-manufactories, but is chiefly remarkable for mules, of which it furnishes great numbers. The inhabitants, Mr. Morier says, looked really the victims of oppression ; and they confirmed the impression produced by the misery of their appearance, by stating that, owing to the excessive extortion of their governors, upwards of a hundred families had recently migrated to Tehraun. The mule-drivers (*katirjees*) of the southern provinces, a " sturdy and obstinate race," are mostly of Zargoon. A snowy peak of the distant mountains, called the *Koh Shish-peer*, is seen bearing N. 42° W. Near it are some celebrated springs ; and not far from the mountain is a town of about 300 houses, called Ardekan.

[*] This would seem to be either the Roknabad, or one of its sources. Mr. Morier speaks of the ruin as a caravanserai.

At two miles from Zargoon, the traveller enters on the plain of the same name, a tract of excellent soil, and partially cultivated, extending nearly 15 miles E. and W. Three miles further, crossing the Bundemir, he enters the plain of Merdasht. A high bridge, called the *pul-i-khân*, has been thrown across the river, immediately behind a projecting foot of the mountain; but it is so much out of repair as not to be passed without danger, owing to a considerable chasm in it, not by any means recent. The river is here exceedingly rapid, and pours along through steep, rocky banks, with a tremendous noise for a stream scarcely twenty yards across.

The great plain of Merdasht (Marvdasht) or Istakhr, is one of the most fertile in Persia, being watered in all directions by rivulets and artificial drains, which ultimately unite in the Bundemir. The older travellers bear testimony to the richness of its products and to its former populousness. Eight hundred and eighty villages might once be counted on the plain, and more than 1500 within a compass of twelve leagues round the ruins * Such a situation might seem to have been admirably adapted for the site of the capital. Of the many streams which intersect the plain, two only have been dignified by either classical or oriental geographers with the name of rivers; the Kour or Araxes, now called the Bundemir, and the

* The plain of Merdasht is described by Della Valle as the most fertile that he had seen in any province of Persia. Chardin eulogizes it as "*fertile, riche, abondante, belle, et délicieuse.*" Kæmpfer praises its fertility, and Le Brun makes the statement relative to the number of its villages, adopted above. See Ouseley, vol. ii. p. 307, *note*. It appears to be the plain referred to by Strabo under the name of Cœlo-Persia, or hollow Persia, through which flowed the Cyrus or Kuros.

Faruáb or Farwár, the Sewund river, which is supposed to be the Medus of Strabo.* The former takes
its modern appellation from a dike (*bund*) constructed,
in the tenth century, by the Emir Azzad ad Douleh,
near the junction of the two streams, where there is a
village of the same name. Rising in the mountains
of Kilar (or Gilar), in Fars, it runs southward, collecting the waters of the *Shaáb Bavan* and other
smaller streams, till, after a course of 113 *farsangs*, it
falls into the great salt lake of Bakhtegan, a little
below Gawakoon, between 30 and 40 miles from Bundemir. Several dikes have been at different periods
constructed upon this river, in order to detain its
waters for the purposes of irrigation. The first is the
bund of Ramgard, or Fakhristan; " an ancient structure which, under the Seljoukian dynasty, having fallen
into decay, was repaired by the Attabeg Fakhr ad
Douleh Chaveli." The second is the *Bund Azzadi*, or
Bund Emir, by which the territory of the Upper Kurbal
is watered. The third is the *Bund-i-Kassar*, at Gawakoon, which, being also in a state of ruin, was re-

* The various names applied to these rivers, have been an occasion of much perplexity to geographers. D'Anville supposed the
Bundemir to be the Araxes, and the Medus to be the *Kûr.* Lieut.
Alexander, misled probably by his authority, says: " A small
stream, dignified by the appellation of the Cyrus, and which Strabo
mentions that Alexander crossed in going to Persepolis, joins the
Bundemir stream at the village." But that the Bundemir is the
ab-i-Kur of the oriental geographers, on which the *bund* was erected,
is certain, and it apparently answers to the Cyrus of Strabo. On
the other hand, the Araxes which Alexander is stated to have
crossed in advancing towards Persepolis, and into which Strabo
represents the *Medus* as falling, must also be the Bundemir, which
receives the Farwar or Sewund stream. We must therefore regard
the Bundemir, Kur, and Araxes as one river. Such is the conclusion to which Sir W. Ouseley conducts us by a careful collation of
authorities (vol. ii. pp. 326—34), and he may be said to have fairly
exhausted the subject.

paired by the Attabeg Chaveli : by this the district of Lower Kurbal is irrigated.

The village of Bundemir, which takes its name from the second of these, is about sixteen miles from Zargoon, at the further extremity of the plain of Merdasht.* A large and strong stone dam has been carried across the stream, which descends, through numerous sluices and arches, in a fall of between 18 and 20 feet, turning several mills by means of the canals which divide, and in some places undermine the village. The bridge which has been raised upon the dam, is a very substantial structure, without parapets, and does credit both to the architect and' his munificent employer. † By this noble work, we are told, " an arid and barren tract of considerable extent was fertilized, and the blessings of plenty diffused among several hundred villages : some of these, but mostly deserted and in ruins, yet exist, a monument of his glory, and a reproach to his degenerate successors." To the same enlightened sovereign is ascribed the formation of a reservoir in the castle of Istakhr ; on which occa-

* Mr. Morier says : " Bend Emir, called by the Persians two *fursungs* distant from Zergoon, is about *seven miles* by my calculation. Its exact bearing from the ruins of Persepolis is S. 15° W." Lieut. Alexander, however, found it a day's journey of 16 miles from Zergoon ; but possibly there may be a nearer route. Bundemir belongs to the large *boloök* or district of Kurbal (improperly written Corbal), from which comes the greater part of the wine known under the name of Shiraz.—MORIER, vol. ii. p. 74. Kurbal is generally transposed by the natives into Kulbar or Kulvar.

† " The *Bend*," says Mr. Morier, " has been built immediately upon the superior angle of what must originally have been a natural fall, and consists of a straight bridge of thirteen arches : to this bridge the river flows in a slow current, but, immediately on passing through the arches, it falls abruptly over the inclined wall.... into a new and more extensive bed." The height of the fall, he represents to be 30 or 40 feet. Sir W. Ouseley says, 18 or 20.

sion he is stated to have exclaimed : " I have erected a mountain in the midst of a lake, and a lake on the summit of a mountain." * From this expression it would seem, that the Kour had previously formed a lake in the adjacent plain. Azzad is stated to have turned its course at an incalculable expense, and by confining its waters within their present channel, rendered them the source of fertility to the whole district.†

The *Faruab*, or Sewund river, is said to issue from a mountain near a village called Farwab, in the district of Huberkan. After passing Sewund, it winds S.W. through the narrow vale into the plain of Mer-dasht ; and flowing by Istakhr, falls into the Bend-emir or Kour, somewhere above Fhatabad. The extent of its course is eighteen *farsangs*. ‡

The village of Bendemir is picturesquely situated ; §

* Ouseley, vol. ii. p. 183.

† Emir or Amir is stated by some writers to have been the proper name of the engineer, " a stranger who, being on his travels, voluntarily undertook the work." This derives plausibility from its being called also the Bund Azzadi ; and yet, it is more likely that it should refer to the title of the prince, who never assumed any higher style than *ameer*. He died A.D. 983· The Persians naturally rank among their greatest benefactors, those who have contributed to obviate the distress occasioned by the paucity of springs and rivers Similar works have immortalized many ancient princes. Thus, Hezekiah entitled himself to the grateful remembrance of the Jews.—See 2 Chron. xxxii. 30.

‡ See Morier, vol. ii. p. 115. Ouseley, vol. ii. p. 328. According to Ibn Haukal, " at the gate of Istakhr, it flows under the Khu-rasán bridge, whence it proceeds until it falls into the river Kur." Edrisi, the Nubian geographer, says : " Istakhr is situate on the river Faruab, and has a bridge called the Khurasán bridge "—from its leading in a north-easterly direction towards Khorasan. The proper name of the river is Parvab or Paruab, pronounced Faruab ; and this has been corrupted into Palwar, Farwar, and Peleuar. Morier says, it is called Polbar, and written Ferbar.

§ Houses and trees are prettily disposed all around, which,

the Author of Lalla Rookh has, however, attributed to this celebrated stream, more scenic beauty than appears now to adorn its banks, when he sings :

> " There's a bower of roses by Bund Emir's stream,
> And the nightingale sings round it all the day long."

" We neither saw rose-bowers," remarks Lieut. Alexander, " nor heard the soft warbling of the bulbul. Weeping willows hung over and dipped into the stream, which dashed with a loud, rushing noise through the arches of the bridge, sending up clouds of vapour from the white spray and foam of its broken waters......Fish are here so numerous, that ten thousand grayling were caught in a few hours, in nets ; many of a large size. Several pelicans were seen here, though I was not fortunate enough to obtain the sight of one." Like most streams in this country, Sir W. Ouseley says, it abounds with tortoises, but the Persians never eat them. He saw many in it, and two of large size were shot by his party. Several bullets were discharged, but in vain, at water-snakes of various colours. Although the water " had not a very tempting appearance," it was found pleasant, and is deemed salubrious.*

Bundemir is not, however, in the direct road from Shiraz to the *Takht-i-Jemsheed,* from which it is

---

backed by the wild-shaped rocks of the *Nokara Khoneh,* produce a picture seldom seen in the monotonous landscape of Persia. The falling river, with its foam and impetuosity, has all the effect of a cascade; while there is a strong contrast kept up by the tranquillity of the village scenery around it."—MORIER, vol. ii. p. 73.

* Ouseley, ii. 179. Alexander, p. 136. Sir W. Ouseley came upon the river in his route from Darab to Persepolis, where it falls into the lake. "From this spot," he says, " during the remainder of our day's journey (to Gawakoon), we rode along the left bank of that greenish, deep, and dirty-looking stream, which resembles in many places a broad English canal,"—Vol. ii. p. 178.

fourteen miles distant. From the *Pul-i-khan* to the extremity of the plain, where the Persepolitan remains are situated, is a distance of between ten and eleven miles (nearly seventeen miles from Zargoon). Their first appearance is thus described by Lieut. Alexander.

" On awaking, we observed the pillars of the palace of Persepolis, rising grey in front of a dark hill, and about a *fursung* off. We quickly mounted, and attempted to ride towards them; but it was a couple of hours before we reached them, being impeded by the swampy ground. The ruins, from the plain, have a very imposing appearance, rising on a platform 50 feet in height, which is built of huge stones. The length of the platform is 1500 feet. Towards the north end is a double flight of easy steps of blue marble veined with quartz. At the top are four walls, two pillars between them, and the bases of two others. On the walls are the figures of winged bulls of colossal size. The whole may have formed part of a gateway. Near it is a stone cistern. Proceeding onwards is another double flight of steps, on the front of which are sculptured an immense number of figures with high caps, in procession. Having surmounted the few steps leading to the highest part of the platform, we got amongst the pillars, thirteen of which only are now standing: there are the traces of forty.* Those which exist, are very elegant and lofty, with a fluted shaft: they exhibit the appearance of very great antiquity, and are composed of greyish marble, which takes an excellent polish, and yields easily to

* Hence the name of *Chehel Minareh* (Forty Steeples), or *Chehel Sutun* (Forty Columns), by which these ruins were formerly distinguished. But they have been much more numerous. Another name given to them, was *Hezar Sutun* (Thousand Columns).— OUSELEY, ii. 302.

the hammer. Proceeding southward, are seen the remains of apartments: they are square inclosures; the sides of the doors are sculptured. Near the hill, there is an immense square inclosure, which seems to have been the principal residence. Through different parts of the platform run narrow, subterranean passages; originally, perhaps, aqueducts. The marble of the square inclosures is jet black. In many parts of the ruins are square tablets, inscribed with the arrow-headed characters, which have hitherto defied interpretation. Behind the ruins, on the platform, are two sepulchres on the hill, a considerable portion of which has been scarped, and the smooth rock sculptured. At the bottom of the scarp is an opening into the rock, into which having crawled, I entered a small apartment, wherein I perceived oven-shaped recesses, which probably contained the bodies. There is a third round to the southward, which has never yet been entered. All along the crest of the hill above the ruins, are seen the remains of fortifications consisting of dilapidated stone walls. Many travellers assert, that there could have been no city of any size within many miles of the palace, from there being no remains of buildings on the plain; but the peasants are constantly turning up immense quantities of bricks in every part of the valley, from the hill-fort of Istakhar northward as far as Bundemir: consequently, there must have been an immense city here." *

This general sketch will scarcely, however, satisfy our readers; and we shall therefore proceed to give them the substance of the minute and copious description furnished by Sir Robert Ker Porter, who devoted

* Alexander, pp. 137—9.

above a week to the examination of these interesting remains.*

" The artificial plain on which the ruins of this immense royal citadel or palace stand, is of a very irregular shape. The following is the extent of each face : that to the south, 802 feet ; to the north, 926 ; and to the west, 1425. The level on which the buildings have been erected, is become exceedingly uneven, being raised in parts by the accumulation of fallen ruins. To the N.W., considerable masses of the native rock shew themselves without incumbrance, and still bearing the marks of the original implements with which the higher pieces had been hewn down to the level required. In the same direction, just beyond the face of the artificial plain, the rock protrudes itself in vast, abrupt cliffs, but still shewing traces of not having quite escaped the pickaxe. In deeper cavities, the progress of a quarry is visible, part of the rock in some places being half hewn through, and, in others, lying in completed slabs ready for removal. Indeed, there are plain indications that this superb structure was not deemed entirely finished. The steep faces of the rocky terrace are formed of dark grey marble, cut into gigantic square blocks exquisitely polished, and, without the aid of mortar, fitted to each other with closeness and precision. The encroachments of ruins and vegetation at its base, have raised hillocks against all the sides, making rough slopes where once were perpendiculars. At a spot near the groupe of columns, its present perpendicular line is 30 feet ; but there can be no doubt that, might we clear away all that hides this beautiful wall, we should find an additional depth of 20 feet. The southern

* This Author gives the latitude of the ruins, 29° 59′ 39″.

side, at this time, does not rise higher than 18 or 20 feet, and I think, never could have exceeded 30. To the north, it varies from 16 to 26. This spacious artificial platform consists of three separate terraces. The first, or lowest, embracing the whole length of the southern face, is 183 feet in width. Along the edge, large masses of stone remain in different spots, with fragments of a parapet. On the edge of the third or highest terrace, to the south, are decided marks of a strong range of railing or palisadoes. These marks cease at the top of the flight of steps connecting this terrace with the one beneath. At the top of the steps we find two large holes, cut deeply in the stone, which received the pivots of the gates that anciently closed this ingress.

" There is but one way by which the summit of this platform is attained, and that consists of an ascent by steps, situated in its western face (961 feet from the southern face, and 208 from the northern). The approach is on a scale so magnificent, that it fully prepares the mind for the forms of vastness and grandeur that are met with above. A double flight of steps, on a very gentle ascent, rise N. and S. : they measure 22 feet in width ;* each step is $3\frac{1}{4}$ inches in height; and in all, they number fifty-five. The masons have not required many blocks of marble in their construction, each block being so large as to allow ten or fourteen steps to be cut into its solid mass. The base these cover, is 67 feet by 22. On ascending the first flight, an irregular landing-place presents itself, 37 feet by 44, whence springs a second flight of forty-eight steps, covering 59 feet by 22. A couple of corresponding staircases terminate on the

* According to Morier, 26 feet, 6 inches.

grand level of the platform, by a landing-place occupying 64 feet, and 29 feet above the lower one. I invariably rode my horse up and down these steps
during my visits.

" On reaching the platform, the first objects that
strike the astonished traveller are, the lofty sides of
an enormous portal, the interior faces of which are
sculptured into the forms of two colossal bulls. They
look towards the west, their head, chest, and fore-leg
occupying almost the whole thickness of the wall in
that direction; the rest of the body is left in relief.
A pedestal formed of two blocks, elevates them 5 feet
above the level of the platform. At a considerable
height above their backs (on the sides of the portal),
are three small compartments filled with inscriptions
in the arrow-headed character. Whatever may have
finished the top of the walls, is so totally destroyed,
that not a vestige remains. The heads of the bulls
are entirely gone; but enough is left of the animals,
to shew distinctly what they are. Round the necks
of these bucolic sentinels are broad collars of roses,
executed with the most critical nicety; and over the
chest, back, and ribs extends a kind of decoration resembling short curling hair,* cut with a correctness
and delicacy peculiar to Persian sculptures of antiquity. The proportions of the animals are admirable,
and although the manner of their execution is dry,
there is a grandeur in their forms, which perfectly
accords with the prodigious scale on which all around
them is designed. The breadth of the wall, facing
the west, is 5 feet; its length, 21; its height, 30.
The one wall (of the portal) is distant from the other
about 12 feet: the intervening space is flagged with

* Some have taken these " spiral knobs" for bosses of armour,

beautifully polished slabs cut from the neighbouring rocks. On both sides, I found a cloud of initials, and names, and dates of former visitants.

" Proceeding onward to the east, at the distance of 24 feet from the portal, once stood four magnificent columns. They were all erect at the time Sir John Chardin visited Persepolis. Two only remain, and not a relic of their companions. They were placed equidistant from each other, at 22 feet. The accumulation of ruins mouldered into earth, has nearly buried the bases of those yet standing. Their capitals are singular and beautiful, consisting, as it were, of three combined into one. The shaft gradually narrows towards the top, varied by thirty-nine flutings near the cincture; each of which is 4 inches in width. The tor is 13 feet 10 inches in circumference; and thence to the top of the capital is about 45 feet. The surface is perfectly smooth, and I should be led to imagine that, when the four stood erect, they might have sustained the pedestal of some sculptured image. A space of 24 feet separates them from a second portal, differing in no way from the preceding, either in form or in dimensions, except that its length is 18 feet, instead of 21. The inner sides are sculptured in like manner, but the animals represented are monstrous. They have the body and legs of a bull, ornamented with trappings similar to those already described; but an enormous pair of wings project from the shoulders, extending high over the back, and covering the breast, whence they might seem to spring, as the whole chest is cased with the plumage. The huge feathers which compose the wings, are exquisitely cut. The heads of the animals look direct to the mountain, which is due east, and shew the faces of men; but the blind zeal of the khalifs, if not some later hand, has terribly

mutilated the features. The expression of the countenance is severe, and a long and carefully curled
beard adds to the majesty of the general air. The
ears are those of a bull, and from them hang large
drop ear-rings of a very elegant form. On the head
is a cylindrical diadem, on both sides of which,
horns are clearly represented, winding from the brows
upwards to the front of the crown ; the whole being
surmounted with a sort of coronet, formed of a range
of leaves like the lotus, and bound with a fillet beautifully carved in roses. We find the hair ranged over
the forehead in the usual style of the ancient Persian
kings ; the beard also is disposed in the way peculiar
to royalty ; but the hinder hair lies in long and close
curls round the back of the neck, totally differing from
any of the bas-reliefs in other parts of the ruins.
From the top of the crown to the hoof, the animal
measures 19 feet. Three compartments of inscription are cut in the wall over his body.

"This is the only specimen known to exist in
Persia, of the human and bestial form conjoined.*

* An agate seal, brought by Niebuhr from Basrah, and supposed to be of the highest antiquity, exhibits the winged-bull with
a human head. A similar device appears on a carnelion brought
by Sir W. Ouseley from Shiraz, as well as on many Greek medals,
gems, and bronzes ; but "the temple of Persepolis is the only place
in which such a representation is known to exist in marble." A
learned French antiquary (M. d'Hancarville) infers from this circumstance, the "prodigious antiquity of this symbolic figure,"
which, he thinks, must be anterior to any Grecian statue, "since
it must have been executed at least 600 years before Inachus, the
most ancient of the kings of Greece." Travellers have been much
embarrassed by these sphinxes. Della Valle describes them as composed of the body of a horse, with a human head, and the wings
of a griffin. Herbert fancied one to be like an elephant, another
a rhinoceros, and a third, "like unto Pegasus," or the "volant
griffin" in the Orlando Furioso. Mandelslo describes the first two
as "horses with harness and saddles very antique:" of the others,

Various opinions have been conceived of its meaning. Mons. Anquetil du Perron advances very cogent reasons for supposing it to be a symbolic representation of Noah!   Mons. de Sacy considers it to be the emblem of Kaiamurs, the first sovereign of the Paishdadian dynasty, and he derives the name Kaiamurs from *Gaw-i-mird*, bull and man.   But it is interesting to observe, how this singular hieroglyphic might be attributed to Cyrus himself, whose empire over the East was prophesied by Ezekiel under almost the same figure, upwards of fifty years before his accession. (Ezek. i. 7–10.)   Daniel foretels the empire of the same prince under a similar union of the human with the bestial form, describing it as "a lion with eagle's wings," and "a man's heart was given to it." (Dan. vii. 4.)   Commentators have explained the human attributes as prophetic of the wisdom and clemency of Cyrus's character.   But, whatever be the real intention in the bull-man which is here placed in the ancient seat of the earliest monarchs of the East, in the gate of his palace, his attributes fully answer to the general idea of an emblematic reference to a just sovereignty.

" On turning to the right of the portal, an expanse

the hinder part, he says, resembles that of a horse, but the crowned head resembles that of a lion.   Chardin describes the latter as a *winged horse* with the head of a man: in the first two, he discovered something of the horse, the lion, the rhinoceros, and the elephant. Kæmpfer knew not whether they represented "a camel-lion" or some other monster.   Le Brun assigns them the body of a horse, the short thick paws of a lion, and the head of an *ape*.   Niebuhr considers the winged-figures as Persian sphinxes, and the others as representing the imaginary unicorn.   D'Hancarville declares the winged figures to be bulls, and the other two to be composed between the bull and the lion.   For these curious details, we are indebted to Sir W. Ouseley's diligence.—Vol. ii. pp. 246—8.

of 162 feet lies between it and the magnificent terrace that supports the multitude of columns from which it takes its name. One object alone arrests attention in our progress towards them: this is a fine cistern, hewn out of the solid rock, 18 feet by 16. It is now only 3 feet above the level of the rock, or rather, the earth that has collected over it. Subterraneous aqueducts filled it with water, and, as another of these channels runs in a parallel line to the west, a corresponding reservoir may have been in that direction.

" On drawing near the *Chehel-minar* or Palace of Forty Pillars, the eye is riveted by the grandeur and beautiful decorations of the flight of steps which lead up to them. This superb approach consists of a double staircase, projecting considerably before the northern face of the terrace, the whole length of which is 212 feet: at each extremity, east and west, rises another range of steps; and again, about the middle, projecting from it 18 feet, appear two smaller flights rising from the same point. Here, the extent of the range, including a landing-place of 20 feet, amounts to 86. The ascent, like that of the great entrance from the plain, is extremely gradual; each flight containing only thirty-two steps, (none exceeding 4 inches in height,) in breadth 14 inches, and in length 16 feet. The whole front of the advanced range is covered with sculpture. The eye at first roves over it, lost and bewildered by the multitudes of figures; but I took time to distinguish every one, and to copy them as distinctly as I could.

· " The space immediately under the landing-place is divided into three compartments. The centre one has a plain surface, as if intended for an inscription: probably, writing may have been there, which is now obliterated. To the left of it, are four standing

figures about 5 feet 6 inches high, habited in long
robes, with brogue-like buskins on their feet. They
each hold a short spear in an upright position,
with both hands. The fluted, flat-topped cap is
on their heads; and from the left shoulder hang
their bow and quiver. The nicety with which
all the details are executed, renders these sculptures particularly interesting to the historian, and
to the historical painter: they mark the costume
of the time and the people, and their progress in
the form, variety, and use of arms. In the latter
instance, I cannot omit noticing the clearness with
which they shew the ancient method of stringing
the bow, and the manner of attaching the leather
cover to the quiver, which protects the feathers of the
arrows from damage. Being an old bowman myself,
these peculiarities of archery were more readily observed by me.

" On the right of the vacant tablet are three figures
only. They look towards the opposite four, and differ
in no way with respect to their robes and fluted helmet; but they have neither bows nor quiver, carrying
the spear only, with the addition of a large shield on
the left arm, something in the shape of the body of a
violoncello; or rather, I should say, exactly in the
form of a Bœotian buckler. It appears extraordinary,
that none of these armed figures wear any thing like
a sword or dagger; but, on examining all the sculptures throughout, I did not find the representation of
what we call a sword, on any one of them. As this
seems to have been the grand approach to the entrance
of the palace above, doubtless the spear-men just described must have been intended to portray the royal
guards: the fashion of their dress accords perfectly
with the account given of it by Herodotus, (b. v.

c. xlix.) who states, that ' they were armed with a bow and a short spear, and habited in long robes, with their hair flowing full behind.'   When describing the army of Xerxes, he writes : ' The Persians defend their heads with a small helmet called a tiara ; their bodies are covered with sleeved tunics of various colours ; upon these are plates of steel, like the scales of a fish ; their thighs are protected in the same way. They are armed with large bows and arrows, the shafts of which are reeds.   They carry a short spear ; and for defence, use a shield denominated *gerra* ; beneath it is the quiver ; and on their *right side* is a dagger hung from a belt.'—In neither of these descriptions do we find a sword mentioned ; but Xenophon, in his Cyropedia, particularly names it, whenever the arm of the Persians are noticed.   From all this, and from never finding the vestige of a sword on any of these most ancient bas-reliefs, I am led to think, that when the authors of greatest antiquity speak of the Persian sword, they can only intend this dagger-like weapon, the ἀκινάκης of the Greeks, and the *acinaces* of the Romans, the poniard, so accurately delineated by Herodotus, being invariably worn on the right side. We find another weapon of the kind mentioned by writers as having been in use amongst the Persians ; such as the *copis* of Quintus Curtius. (b. viii. c. xiv.)   But I should regard this latter as the short falchion peculiar to certain tribes immediately border-ing on the shores of the Euphrates and the Persian Gulf, who would, at times, serve in the Persian armies.   It is described as curved, like the dagger of the present day, which is in use amongst their de-scendants.*

---

* Xenophon ascribes to Cyrus the first introduction of the long Median robe among his Persian followers.—*Cyrop.* b. viii.

" Two angular spaces on each side of the corresponding groupes of spear-men, described on the surface of the staircase, are filled with duplicate representations of a fight between a lion and a bull, a most spirited and admirable performance. The bull is decorated with the same kind of curled hair over its chest, back, and tail, which ornaments his similitude at the gate of the first portal, but with this difference in the additional ornaments : the collar of the animal in the combat is perfectly plain, and there is no radiated form on his breast; here, the head is perfect, and we find a single horn projecting over his forehead. The circumstance of a collar round the neck of the bull, proves him to be no wild one, and that we are not to understand the combat as accidental. But, whether it may be received as a proof, that such conflicts were brought forward before the Persian people, is another question. That wild animals of the untameable sort were not merely hunted by these Eastern princes, but preserved near their palaces, is evident, from the lion's den which we find at Babylon after its conquest by Cyrus; but by no accounts that I can recollect, does it appear, that the beasts so immured were ever used for sport of any kind after their first capture. The question remains, are they, like the bulls on the portals, allegorical figures ? In this bas-relief, we find the bull is in the grasp of a lion, the usual symbol for only the most royal virtues ; and, as Cyrus himself was typified in the East under the form of a lion with a man's heart, and the Assyrian empire under the form of an ox or a bull, it does not seem improbable, that the conquest of Cyrus over the two great empires of Assyria and Babylonia, united at Babylon, should be typified on each side of this ingress to his palace, by the lion's seizure of the one-horned bull, the single horn being so large and twisted as well to symbolize the union of a double power. The fire, beauty, and truth with which these quadrupeds are hewn, may appear hardly credible to one who has not beheld them on the spot ; for no artist of Greece or Rome could have been more faithful to the proportions of nature, or have shewn more knowledge of the anatomy of their forms.

" On the inclined planes corresponding to the slope of the stairs, runs a kind of frieze, on which is cut a line of figures, 1 foot 9 inches in height, answering in number to the steps, each one of which appears to form a pedestal for its relative figure. The figures themselves appear a lengthened rank of those already described on each side of the blank tablet ; and a similar range runs up the opposite slope. As the lines of figures are so disposed as to face each other, both looking towards one centre-point, those on the right present their left sides to the spectator, by which the whole of the bow and quiver they carry, are more accurately seen. A narrow border of open roses, closely set, finishes the upper edge of the frieze, while an equal number of figures ornament the interior face of the same staircase. We can have no doubt, in casting our eyes over the numbers, the uniform dresses, arms, and positions of these men, that they are the stone effigies of the vast body-guard, the *Doryphores*, which once held an actual station on these very spots. Cyrus, after the conquest of Babylon, chose ten thousand spear-men from amongst his faithful Persians, for this very purpose ; and Xenophon adds, that in his day, the royal guard was still kept on the same footing. These men had already received the distinguishing mark of honour, the Median robe, (the *kaliaut* of that time, and probably the origin of the

custom,) and also the high cap worn by Cyrus himself. His description of the Great King's munificence,
and his equalising his general appearance with that
of his immediate followers, fully accounts for the
similitude of the caps and robes, in these ranges of
figures, to the head-dress and raiment of the royal
personage in several of the bas-reliefs. But, with
regard to the high cap, or tiara, when mentioned as a
universal costume with the Persians, we should recollect, that it was of many varieties, and is not always
to be considered as resembling the royal turban, or
tiara. On examining the bas-reliefs, it will be found,
that none of the figures wear the same high cap
as the sovereign's, but those who are distinguished
by the same full robe; hence, all who appear in that
garb, though stationed where modern refinement would
only place a guard of rank and file, may be esteemed
the kinsmen and friends of the king, to whom alone
he gave the privilege of wearing the form of the royal
tiara.* At the extremity of the spears of the least
mutilated, I observed an ornamented ball, which recalled
to my mind the *Melophores*, or thousand guards of
Xerxes, who bore at the end of their lances, apples or
pomegranates of gold. (Herod. vii. 61.)

" I now proceed to the objects on the face of the
next flight of stairs, first taking the left wing, which
stretches to the east. Here again, in the triangular
space formed by the slope of the steps, we find a repetition of the contest between the lion and the bull,

---

* The head-dress of Cyrus, as described by Xenophon, consisted
of two parts; the tiara, or high cap, and the diadem, *i.e.*, the
cydaris or *wreath;* but the materials alone were held sacred to the
regal dignity. Probably, remarks Sir Robert, the curved tiara or
cyrbasia, originated with Darius Hystaspes, when he, as well as his
six associates in the death of Smerdis the Magian, bent forward
their high caps to distinguish each other.

occupying a length of 23 feet. It is divided by a tablet, on which may be traced an almost obliterated inscription, which reaches nearly from top to bottom, at
present 6 feet 10 inches deep, and in width 4 feet
10 inches; whence begin the lines of three rows of
sculpture, all sadly defaced, but covering an expanse
of 68 feet, and terminating at the top of the steps of
the outward approach. Of the upper row of figures,
the lower extremities alone remain, appearing no
deeper down the surface of the wall than 12 inches;
the rest having risen above the level of the terrace, to
form a kind of parapet; but it is now totally broken
away, and vestiges of it may be seen thickly scattered
over the ground below.

"This deplorably mutilated row of figures commences with a chariot drawn by two bulls; a second
follows it; then comes a horse, with the feet of a
man appearing on its opposite side, as if in attendance
on the animal; again, two others in succession; then
five figures habited in short vests; and after them
comes an uninterrupted suite of forty-four long-robed
spear-men. It is curious to observe, how the rotation
in this procession resembles that of Cyrus to his first
great royal sacrifice; the chariots, and the bulls, and
the led horses for sacrifice to the sun, the spear-men,
&c. &c. A border carved with roses divides each
row of bas-relief from the one below it. By the fre-
quency of these ornaments, we see how indigenous
the rose has ever been in this country, and how much
admired from the earliest times.

"The next begins with a range of thirty-two figures,
of which every alternate one is clothed in a long robe,
its full, loose sleeves reaching to the wrists, and its
flowing skirts to the ancles. In front, about the
centre of the waist, the robe appears gathered up,

both for convenience and grace of drapery; for there, connected with a girdle, it falls in regular folds over each thigh; and where the knots of the belt are tied, is stuck a dagger, the handle of which exactly resembles that worn by the Persian of the present day. What is discoverable of the upper part of the sheath, shews a very singular form, not unlike that of the Malay *creesse*. These figures in the flowing robes, always have ear-rings and collars, and some, the addition of bracelets. On their heads they wear the high fluted tiara, covering a bushy fulness of hair, profusely curled upon the neck, and combed up from the forehead, with a termination of curls there also. The beard partakes of the same taste, and is not long, but ending rather square. The feet are enveloped in the sandal buskin. And in this range, we find the figures so habited always holding the hand of the person immediately before them, or of the one immediately behind; a circumstance which would imply their belonging to the establishment of the king, and so leading forward persons, comparatively strangers, to the presence. With the exception of one or two, they all hold in their right hands a flower resembling the lotus; and several of them have a cased bow hanging on the left hip.

"The other alternate figure is attired in a short tunic, reaching to the knees, with long tight sleeves; indeed, the whole of the dress seems so close, that not a fold appears. His lower extremities are covered by trowsers, meeting at the ancles a high shoe, at the top of which they seem to be tied; and yet there is something in their form and smoothness that gives one the idea of jack-boots. On his head is a round-topped cap, projecting at the top a little over the brow. This style of coiffure differs entirely from the fluted cap or

tiara, and resembles what we call the Phrygian bonnet. I should be led to suppose, from its simplicity,
and the corresponding plainness of the habit almost
invariably worn with it, that the entire dress presented by the figure who wears it, is the genuine Persian habit ; I mean the dress of the people of Persia
Proper, not of the empire in general. The robe and
tiara described above, are evidently the Median
fashions. The strap which binds the body of this
ancient Persian, is very distinctly marked. He wears a
second, from which depends, on the right side, a dagger
of a quite different shape from that of the robed cour-
tier. This is very broad in the blade, and the point
of its sheath seems fastened to the right thigh, near
the knee, by a thong. Though not much larger than
the common dagger of the time, used by other nations,
still I look upon this stout little weapon to have been
the actual Persian sword of that early age ; which all
the ancient accounts describe as ' extremely short, and
worn on the right side.' Some of these figures carry
the cased bow, some are decorated with ear-rings, collars, and bracelets, and others have a long cloak hanging from their shoulders, and attached by strings to
the breast. All carry the lotus. Twenty-eight robed
Persians, armed with spears, and every one in the
same attitude, close this line. These do not wear the
fluted cap, but have each a fillet round his head, on
which are the traces of leaves. Ten or a dozen sculptured cypress-trees complete this bas-relief, and terminate near the stairs. The height occupied by the
line of figures, is only 2 feet 10 inches.

" The third and lowest bas-relief presents the same
procession of robed and tiara-capped Persians, alternately arranged with their tunicked brethren, to the
number of thirty-two ; and, in like manner as above,

followed by a train of twenty-one guards, in the same uniform as those in the upper bas-relief. Time, assisted by the destroying mallets to which I have referred before, has cruelly defaced the middle series, after having entirely demolished the best part of the row above; but this lowest range, happily for the antiquary, has till very lately been concealed, probably for ages, under heaps of ruins at its base. In Le Brun's time, the heads only of the figures were visible; but some of the gentlemen belonging to one of our late embassies to Persia, set men to work, and were successful in bringing this more perfect specimen to the eye of observation.

. " The opposite wing of this magnificent approach is, like the other, divided into compartments by a large cypress-tree. Vast fragments of this also lie on the ground beneath; the higher range of figures, like those opposite, presenting no more than 12 inches of their original surface; but enough is left to shew, at the commencement of the procession, the lower parts of men and horses. The number of groupes which occupy the spaces in this range between the cypresses, is six. The figures are exceedingly broken, but still, I could discern that every man carried something in his hand like an offering, and that almost all the parties had a horse in their train. From most eastern historians we learn, that that animal was as valuable a present to the monarchs of Persia in those days, as it is considered at present. A continuation of these remnants, becoming more explicable, but not increasing in height, completes the line along the slope of the stairs, forming its parapet till it meets the ground, and the figures appear to be as follows. The feet of several men are traceable, and the last leads a bull; then intervenes a tree; five more men follow, the fifth leading another bull; then occurs the cypress; again five men appear, one bearing a round shield, the remainder carrying spears; then come a couple more; after whom are two bulls drawing a kind of chariot covered with lozenge ornaments; the suite is closed by a figure leading an animal resembling the ibex.

" The row on the second line begins with a robed Persian, armed with a dagger at his belt. In his right hand he carries a staff, apparently the ensign of his office, whilst his left holds the hand of a person behind him, whom he appears to be leading forward. This person precedes four others, as being their chief; three of them bear on both their hands different articles of dress; the fourth, in a similar way, carries a couple of large cups. The style of carrying any thing, as well as presenting it to a superior, appears to have been the same then as it is now; the most trifling offering being always given with both hands. The whole of this groupe of five behind the robed Persian, are uniformly habited in short tunics, bound round the waist with a simple buckle and belt. Their legs and feet are covered with a sort of hose, of the jack-boot appearance I mentioned before; and, as a long pair of stockings is amongst the raiment borne, we may conclude that this under-garment is of that character. The upper parts of the figures are too much defaced to shew any thing of a head-dress. A tree divides these from the second groupe. In this, the leading personage is habited in the old Persian tunic, with the same simple belt as belongs to the dress in the opposite wing, and without a dagger. He bears a staff, though not so long a one as the robed personage of the same apparent office in the preceding groupe; he has a collar also, to mark his consequence. With his left hand he leads forward the first figure in a groupe of six. This suite are habited in a sort of wrapping surtout, the arms naked from the hand to the elbow, where they meet a short sleeve; a kind of cape with a tasseled end hangs over the shoulder, down on the breast. A helmet-like cap covers the head, from which depends a bag, very similar to what is worn in some parts of Kourdistan at the present day: shoes are on the feet. The little that is left unbroken away of the hair, appears in the bushy style of the Medes. Two of these men carry basins, and a third, something like a piece of stuff; the fourth holds a staff in his right hand, and the end of a halter in his left, by which he leads a large bull; the fifth walks by the side of the animal, with his left arm over the back, carefully guiding it; he also holds a staff. The bull is admirably sculptured, and the usual heavy, sullen step of the animal is shewn to perfection. In this, the artist has displayed the earthly creature, having copied his original of the pasture with the most masterly fidelity; while the colossal bulls, at the portals, present a contrast which fully shews his design in each. A glance at them conveys to the mind an image of the same animal, but of some supernatural order; making the like distinction between them and the natural bull, as the Greeks accomplished, when the gigantic Hercules was hewn from the quarry, giving more than mortal dignity to the common proportions of man. The same *beau idéal* is displayed in the forms of the lions; and this very distinction, so happily shewn on the same platform, may be another argument for supposing a symbolical meaning is couched under all the animals exhibiting such supernatural elevation of character.

The third groupe in rotation is preceded by a robed Persian, leading by the left hand the first man

of six in suite; the heads of the whole are totally demolished, but in other respects they are not much
damaged. A tight gabardine sort of dress, with short
sleeves, reaches below the calves of the legs; on their
feet are short boots, neatly tied upon the instep. Their
waists are bound with sashes, with fringed ends tastefully disposed on the left side. The second man carries
a couple of basins ; he is followed by one bearing in
each hand two regular-shaped forms, evidently the skins
of some small animal ; the third holds a piece of stuff.
Two others come forward, attending a couple of sheep
with very huge horns and fine curled coats ; which
corroborates the idea of the foregoing skins being probably the beautiful fleeces of the young lambs. Such
fleeces, from a peculiar breed, are still in great request
in these countries ; particularly those of the grey curled
lamb of Bokhara, which, both in Persia and Russia,
bring the greatest prices.

" The introducer in the fourth groupe, is one of the
tunic-dressed Persians. The person he leads by the
hand, seems in all things habited like himself, if we
except his staff and collar of office, and the appearance
of a cap falling low in the pole of the neck of the led
personage. The cap has a peculiarity of curving
backwards at its high top, instead of forwards, as we
have usually seen on figures wearing the short tunic.
On the left side of this man, hangs a cased bow, the
only one in the groupe. The next person, dressed in
the same way in all respects excepting the bow, appears walking by the side of a horse, which he holds
by its bridle ; the mane and tail are nicely tied up,
and the peculiarity of its form, no doubt, marks the
particularity of its breed. The succeeding four figures
carry articles, apparently of horse-furniture, one of
them holding a sort of saddle-cloth and stirrup at-

tached. The usual intervening cypress separates this
last groupe from the fifth ; and here we find a robed
conductor, (indeed, throughout these bas-reliefs, this
duty seems to be alternately exercised by the Median-
robed Persian, and the Persian in the genuine habit
of his country,) leading a person in a different costume
from any of the former. The hair, as we may judge
by his followers in the same general raiment, is bound
by a fillet, and projects a little behind in small neat
curls ; the beard is very short. Both arms and legs
are naked, the feet being defended by a sandal. A
short tunic comes to the knee, and is open at the side,
being bound at the waist by a very broad belt. A
tight mantle, through which passes the arms, hangs,
almost like a modern European coat, to near the calf
of the leg ; a tasseled end falls between the arm and
the vest. Two persons in this garb conduct a bull,
not at all inferior in spirit and beauty to the former ;
and he, likewise, is meant for a beast of earthly pastures. He is followed by three spear-men, dressed
precisely like their three preceding unarmed compeers ;
but the foremost of these warriors carries a spear in
his right hand, and a large round shield on his left
arm, covering his person from the chin almost to the
knee. His two followers have no shield, but each
carries a spear in either hand. The cypress concludes
the groupe. Along this line may be seen the extent
of the native artist's skill in portraying the uncovered parts of the human figure. The fine management of these naked limbs, the truth of the muscles,
and the spirit of their action, might lead one to think,
that the same hand that executed them, did not touch
the stiff, wooden-like legs belonging to some of the
figures more completely covered ; and, probably, this
was really the case, the master-chisel only applying

itself to the general sketch and perfecting finish of the most scientific parts of the art.

" The sixth groupe is led forward by one of the old tunicked Persians, with his staff and collar of consequence. The front of his cap has been a little knocked off, else his head might be called in excellent preservation; the face is perfect, and shews a fine physiognomy. The man in his charge has not been so fortunate; the whole of his face is gone, having left only the beard, which is much larger than any I had seen in the other bas-reliefs, excepting those which represent royalty; but the hair in this beard is perfectly straight, and cut square at the end. The hair of the head behind appears to be turned up smooth over a roll, surmounted with a kind of skull-cap helmet, bending forward in the Phrygian point over the forehead; two flaps proceed from the helmet, guarding the ears. The dress of this man and his five followers, is exactly alike; and all sharing the same progress, more or less, towards decapitation. Their upper garments are tight, with sleeves to the wrist, and flying off slopingly behind the thighs, in a point still more like a modern coat than the one I mentioned before. A large buckle and strap confine the waist; but what makes this garment look most like a European dress, are two or three lines from the shoulder down the front of the breast, which have the appearance of lapels or facings. The first, who is led forward by the conductor, wears a cased bow at his side. The four who follow him, have a similar appendage; but the first of them carries in addition, a dagger, or short sword, held up by both hands, with the sheath and fastenings to the belt attached to it. Hence, I should suppose, from that being the only weapon of the kind which we see on these sculptures

that its steel original answered indiscriminately to the
name of sword or dagger, according to the ideas of the
ancient writers who described it ; for, perhaps, it is as
much too large for the common fashion of the one, as
it is too small for the usual size of the other. The
next figure carries a couple of immense bracelets or
fetters, like those in a preceding bas-relief ; and the
two succeeding men are armed with war-hammers,
holding one in each hand. The last person in the
groupe wears the same dress as the others, with the
exception of the belt and cased bow ; his occupation
is to lead a very fine horse, of a totally different description from the former. The tree terminates this
line of sculpture, by the side of an inscription.

" We now commence the lower range, which is clear
all the way to the very feet of the figures ; at which
point, I am inclined to think, the ornamented part of
the stairs finished ; leaving only a few feet of plain
surface below, now hidden by the mouldered ruins,
before we come to the original level of the top of the
first terrace.

" The conductor of the first groupe in the lower
row, is one of the robed Persians, with his short
sword, and Median fluted cap. He is the only
one whose staff of office has retained its rounded
top. The three figures which immediately follow
him, wear high pointed tiaras, seemingly formed of
rolled linen, and answering in shape to the descriptions we have of the priests' mitres. Neither
their hair nor their beards differ in any way from
the common fashion of the time, excepting, that
behind the ear hangs a long single braid, terminated by two large beads ; their under-garments reach
nearly to the ancle. Over them is a shorter vest,
and a mantle with a deep cape, which falls loosely

down the back, and over the naked arms; tassels are
at each corner. Sock-like boots are on their feet.
After the chief of the party, who is led as usual, follow the two other mitred persons, carrying a bowl in
each hand. Then comes a third figure, in the same
dress as the foregoing, but without a cap of any kind;
he bears a couple of immense bracelets in his hands,
whose circular form is connected by the heads of serpents. The one on the right hand is perfect; but the
other, in the left, can just be discerned as having
been. The two remaining persons of the groupe are
in charge of a chariot, which is drawn by a pair of
magnificent horses. One of the men, in ampler garments than his compeers, and bare-headed, holds the
bridles of the horses. His companion in the rear,
dressed more like the man with the bracelets, follows,
leaning his left hand on the backs of the animals, and
holding a long wand in the other. The horses are
without trappings; but the details of their bits, and
the manner of reining them, are executed with the
nicest care. The pole of the car is seen passing
between the horses, projecting from the centre of the
carriage, which is in a cylindrical shape, elevated
rather above the line of the animals' heads. The
wheel of the car is extremely light, and tastefully put
together. In fact, the whole of this chariot-groupe is
portrayed and finished with a beauty and accuracy
that alike excite our wonder and admiration.

" The second party consists of five persons, exclusive
of the tunicked Persian, who is their master of the
ceremonies. The heads of these men are covered with
a very extraordinary kind of bonnet, pointed and inclining forward, and appearing something cloven at
the top, where an interior cap shews through the cleft.
Two large corners from each side of the bonnet are

drawn back and fastened up behind; evidently to be
let down at pleasure, and drawn forward for the protection of the ears and chin, like the bashlicks of the
mountaineers, who use them as a defence from the
wind and snow. The peasantry of the plains, too,
frequently case their heads in the same manner.
In all other respects, the dress of the men in this
groupe, resembles that of their conductor; only, he
wears the low common Persian cap, with his collar and
staff of office; and in addition to their simple tunic,
they have a short, scanty mantle, fastened on the left
breast with a clasp or buckle in the form of a bow.
Tassels ornament the corners of the mantle. The
second figure which follows the leader of the groupe,
is attendant on an almost gigantic horse, whose ardour
he seems to check, by the tightness with which he
holds the bridle. Round the animal's neck are a collar
and a bell; his mane is hogged, though enough has
been left on the forehead to form a tuft, which is tied
like a brush; apparently a favourite ornament with
these people from a very early time. The three following figures bear articles of dress; the last is almost
obliterated.

" The approaching line of persons which compose
the third groupe, consists of eight, all bare-headed, and
in one attire; the same precisely with the unbonneted
men who precede the chariot, excepting that the
texture of the under-garments of these is carved in
waving stripes; with the others, it is plain. Three of
these persons carry variously formed bowls; two others
follow, holding some folded substance in their hands,
not unlike the bread of the country; two more close the
party, each charged with a couple of globular forms,
probably melons. The conductor of these is a robed
figure.

" In the fourth groupe, we return to a succession of
five persons, who are led by a tunicked Persian. They
are clothed in tight vestures of the same kind, with
long sleeves like his ; but their waists are bound by a
cord, knotted in front. They wear very full and
loose trowsers, hanging in wavy masses over the tops
of their boots, which reach to the calf of the leg, and
are a little turned up at the toe. Their heads have
neither cap nor bonnet, but are tied with a fillet.
The hair and beard are quite smooth and uncurled ;
and these, and the groupe which follows, are the only
people with the same sort of ring in their ears. Three
of these persons carry bowls ; the fourth supports himself by a long staff, and leads by the bridle, with his
left hand, a dromedary, whose neck is decorated with
a collar and bell. In comparing the general character
of this animal, particularly those I have seen since my
arrival in Persia, with its delineation here on stone,
I found it a most faithful copy ; the head is finely
marked, and the bunches of hair behind his ear and
below his throat, with the large, round protuberances
above his knees, are accurately placed ; the muscles of
the limbs are so well cut, as to give an appearance of
almost actual movement to the animal. The drome-
daries most in use amongst the northern tribes of the
empire, are commonly natives of the ·country about
Bakou ; they are valued, for size and strength, far
above the camel. Some, to improve the qualities of
the latter, cross the breed with a dromedary.

" The fifth and last groupe of the procession is conducted by the robed introducer, who leads forward the
chief of the party, a dignified-looking person, enveloped in a large folded cloak, which is thrown care-
lessly over the left shoulder, and reaches nearly down

to his sandalled feet. His hair is uncurled, and bound with a fillet. The rest of the party are almost naked, their only covering being a small piece of garment resembling a short petticoat, which is confined on the hip by a thick roll of some sort of stuff or linen. The first of them bears on his shoulders a pair of large scales, which contain four small bottles. The next man brings four more bottles, set in two basins. He is followed by one who guides an animal, which I immediately recognised to be the gour or wild ass. Another attendant stands behind it, while the last person in the groupe brings up the rear with a pair of implements like mallets in his hands.

" Here end all the remains of the bas-reliefs on this division of the edifice, from which we may collect any idea of what might have been the subject of the whole representation. Having already noticed a considerable resemblance between certain objects in these successive groupes, and the first grand procession of the great founder of the empire, I shall offer an abstract of Xenophon's account of the solemnity, before I proceed to my own remarks on the subject.

" ' But now,' says the historian, ' we will relate how Cyrus first marched in grand procession out of the palace; for the majesty of this procession seems to have been one of the means by which he held his government in such high consideration. First, therefore, he arrayed himself, and his commanders, and other chosen officers, in the splendid robes of the Medes, that they might all appear beautiful and noble. There stood first before the gates, four thousand guards, drawn up four in front, with lances in their hands; two thousand on each side of the gates. The Persians stood on the right hand, and the other allies

on the left of the way. When the gates of the palace
were thrown open, first came forth certain bulls, very
goodly beasts, four abreast, devoted to paternal Jove,
and to such other of the gods as the Magi directed.
Next to the bulls, horses were led, for a sacrifice to
the sun. After these proceeded a white chariot, very
costly, its seat of gold adorned with a crown, and
sacred to Jove. Then came another white chariot,
sacred to the sun, and decorated in the same manner.
After that, a third chariot, with horses in scarlet
housings; and behind it, followed men, bearing fire
upon a large altar. After these, Cyrus himself appeared, clad in his royal robes and diadem. When the
chariot of Cyrus advanced, the four thousand guards
led on before, and two thousand attended on each side;
the chief officers of his person, gallantly mounted and
finely clothed, with javelins in their hands, to the
number of three hundred, followed after. Then were
led the noble horses maintained for Cyrus himself,
with their bridles of gold, and caparisoned in housings
wrought with raised stripes; and these horses were
two hundred. After them marched two thousand
spear-men. Then came the first formed body of
Persian horse, to the number of ten thousand, marshalled a hundred deep, under Chrysantes. After
these, marched a second ten thousand, under Hystaspes. They were followed by the like number, in the
leading of Datarnas. Then came the Median, the
Armenian, the Hyrcanian, the Caducian, and the
Sacian horse. And after these troops, went the
chariots, ranged four abreast, under the command of
the Persian Artabates. Upon this occasion, Cyrus
established equestrian and other games amongst his
chiefs and followers; and to the victors he gave oxen,
and cups, that they might sacrifice and feast. The

method of this procession, then settled by Cyrus, continues to this day; excepting only that the victims make no part in it when the king does not sacrifice. Every nation thought they did themselves an injury, if they did not send Cyrus the most valuable productions of their country, whether they were the fruits of the earth, or creatures bred there, or manufactures of their own: and every city did the same.' (Cyrop. b. viii.) We are told, that Cyrus received such presents in the way of tribute from the nations at large; but from the Persians alone he took them as free gifts. In the preceding quotation, we may trace some affinity between its solemn procession and bringing of presents, with the series of subjects just described in the bas-reliefs on the palace-walls. I do not mean to say that they were intended as a commemoration of this, or perhaps any other of Cyrus's personal solemnities of the kind, but my reference shews the antiquity of the custom and its details. He was much less likely than his successors, to erect that sort of monument to the honour of his conquests and institutions; and nothing is more probable, than that these magnificent registers of a great empire were chiselled from the rock, by the command of his not unworthy successor, Darius Hystaspes. He mounted the throne of Persia hardly ten years after the death of Cyrus. Ctesias asserts, that the tomb which Darius ordered to be made for himself, was excavated in the mountain near Persepolis; but, whether he chose his last rest to be there, or in the sacred caves at Nakshi-Roustam, does not affect the probability of his having devoted some part of his long reign, and the labours of his numerous artists and artisans, to the embellishment of this ancient metropolis. Cambyses, the son of Cyrus, had begun many public works, both here and at Susa, employing the captives he had brought from Egypt, in the decoration of his two favourite cities. The usurper Smerdis, who followed the short reign of Cambyses, had hardly time to seat himself on the throne, ere he was dispossessed and slain by the son of Hystaspes, the friend and kinsman of Cyrus. Drawing his claim to the sceptre, or rather confirming his hold of it, by that affinity, what is more likely, than that the avowed restorer of the ancient royal line should thus embellish the native palace of his great predecessor, by commemorating on marble, the very institutions which he had made the principles of his own government? The length of his reign allowed him ample time for the prosecution of the most elaborate works, and the extent of his resources afforded him liberal means of carrying the most magnificent plans into execution.

" That the design of the artist who composed the bas-reliefs, was not to display a religious procession, seems clear from the nature of the articles borne by the different groupes of the train; and as Darius adopted the style of Cyrus in receiving presents from his own conntrymen, instead of tribute, I am not diffident in assigning the sculptures in question entirely to Darius; supposing them to represent the feast at the vernal equinox, when the Persians would present their gratuities, and the governors of provinces, with their delegates, would bring in the annually collected tax from each, with a due proportion of offerings.*

* For this ingenious idea, the Author acknowledges himself to be indebted to M. Heeren, a French writer. This custom is still perpetuated in the festival of the *Noo-rooz*, which is supposed to have had its origin in the reign of Jemsheed; and there is a remarkable passage in the book of Job, which has been thought to allude to a similar ceremony.—See Job i. 6; ii. 1.

" We learn from Xenophon, how the usual attendants on the Persian sovereigns were disposed ; and we
find that a certain number of the chosen guard were
always stationed at the different doors of the palace.
The seven figures grasping spears, and standing as in
front of the outer flight of steps, probably represent
these favourite sentinels ; their appearance being military, and their situation perfectly unconnected with
the train of groupes drawn along the line of the left
wing of the staircase. All the groupes face that part
of the stairs which leads on to the terrace ; and therefore, we must consider this approach as pointing immediately to the presence of the Great King. The
procession of personages on the left wing appear to be
nobles and high officers of the empire : those in the
Median robe and fluted tiara were probably of the
highest order, (that which Cyrus denominated the
alike honoured,) while collars, bracelets, &c. were
dispensed to those whose situations might claim less
conspicuous distinctions. Not one among this succession of persons carries the short staff, the badge of
royal ushers, as we see it held in the hands of their
compeers in the opposite wing. Hence I should consider these to be nobles and great officers of the empire present at court, but not (officially) assisting at
its ceremonies. In this train, the tunicked and the
robed have all the cased bow or the dagger at the belt ;
which appears to have been as indispensable to the
dress of ceremony in those days, as the sword is in
our own times, both in Persia and in every court of
Europe. In the bas-relief upon the tomb at Nakshi-
Roustum, we see that, even at a religious solemnity,
arms were not excluded, for the principal personage .
who stands before the altar of fire, leans on a bow.
Almost every one in this procession holds in his hand

a figure like the lotus, to which the early Persians attached a peculiar sanctity.*

" The very mutilated range of figures above these lotus-bearing nobles, and on the upper line of the staircase, is preceded by a file of military'; and being in part composed of horses, chariots, bulls, and other objects likely to be selected as fit oblations at the vernal feast, I have no doubt that a continuation of a similar train went along the exterior inclining wall of the steps, in the manner of the corresponding bas-reliefs still existing down those to the west. It would be a vain task to attempt assigning to the particular parties divided by the marble avenue of cypress-trees, each its separate country, according to its different costume. Sufficient variety, however, presents itself in the several groupes, to make it evident, that they came from parts of the empire as distinct in climate as different in the fashion of their garb ; some being so lightly clothed as merely to wear what decency demands, and others covered up from the sock to the chin......We find the most valuable animals the tributary countries would produce; the horse, the sheep, the bull, the dromedary, and the *gour* or wild-ass, so precious in the eyes of a Persian prince as an object of chase. Others present specimens of manufactures in articles of dress and arms, and some carry vessels of honey, perfume, and spices. Yet, it is likely that all the vases and bowls were not appropriated to hold-

---

* This flower was alike sacred in Persia, India, and Egypt. It was an emblem of fecundity, of beauty, and of purity. The Egyptians introduced it into the architecture of their temples, where it is seen forming the varied capitals of their vast columns. It is the *fleur-de-luce* of the arms of France; and Sir R. K. Porter remarks, that, in all pictures of the salutation of the Virgin, this flower is introduced. " It has, in fact, been held in mysterious veneration by people of all nations and of all times."

ing these lighter kind of oblations, but were masses of
gold or silver. Herodotus mentions (lib. iii. 96.) its
having been a custom in the East, to melt the precious
metal, and pour it into earthen vessels: when the
liquid gold or silver cooled, the mould was broken, and
the metal came out in the shape it had received.
Counting the number of groupes which fill the space
between every two cypresses, I found eighteen on this
face of the wall, and two at the commencement of the
slope on the steps, which makes up exactly the twenty
governments into which Darius divided his empire; a
coincidence we may regard as an additional corrobora-
tion of the idea, that these bas-reliefs represent the
delegated tributaries of that partition.[*]

" On ascending the platform on which the palace of
Forty Pillars once stood, nothing can be more striking
than the view of its ruins, so vast and magnificent, so
fallen, mutilated, and silent,—the court of Cyrus, the
pavilion of Alexander's triumph, and the memorial of
the wantonness of his power! This immense upper
platform stretches N. and S. 350 feet, and from E. to
W. 380 feet. The greater part is covered with broken
capitals, shafts of pillars, and countless fragments of
building, some of which are richly ornamented with the
most exquisite sculpture. The distribution of the pillars comprised four divisions; consisting of a centre phalanx of six deep every way, an advance body of twelve

[*] " Two of the cuneiform inscriptions on this part of the platform, have been so far translated by Professor Grottefund as to
shew that Darius is the subject of both. One (on the wall at the
entrance) runs thus: ' Darius, the brave king, the king of kings,
the king of nations, the son of Hystaspes, the descendant of the
sovereign of the world in the constellation of Môro.'" Another is
to a similar effect; the sovereign of the world is Jemsheed. If
this rendering may be depended upon, the date of these sculptures
is no longer matter of hypothesis. .

in two ranks, and the same number flanking the centre. The advanced division, composed of a double line of six columns, is 20 feet from the landing-place, and meets the eye immediately on ascending. One only is now standing; the shattered bases of nine others still remain, but the places only are left of the other two which completed the colonnade. About 38 feet from the western edge of the terrace, appears the second double range of columns, the most northern of them being 100 feet from that face of the height; but, on the western side, they seem on the brink of a precipice; for there, the upper terrace rises stupendously from the plain. Five of the twelve columns in this western division are still erect; the capitals are in tolerable preservation, and the bases of the whole are equally perfect. From hence to the eastern range, of a similar number, is a distance of 268 feet. Four of these are standing, and the pedestals of four more are yet undemolished; but the rest have been totally destroyed, or lie buried under masses of ruin, which become hillocks at this point; spreading very far, and indeed so deep, as to form a regular slope to the walls of a spacious edifice, standing further eastward on the great platform; by which circumstance, the face of the terrace in this quarter is almost completely lost.

" The form of the columns which compose the three distinct colonnades, is the same in all. Besides the admiration which the general elegance of their form and the exquisite workmanship excited, I never was made so sensible of the impression of perfect symmetry. The total height of each column is 60 feet; the circumference of the shaft, 16 feet; and its length, from the capital to the tor, 44 feet. The shaft is finely fluted in fifty-two divisions. · At its lower ex-

tremity begin a cincture and a torus ; the former,
two inches in depth, the latter, one foot ; whence de-
volves the pedestal in the form of the cup and leaves
of a pendent lotus. It rests upon a plinth of 8 inches,
and in circumference measuring 24 feet 6 inches ; the
whole, from the cincture to the plinth, comprising a
height of 5 feet 10 inches. The capitals which remain,
though much injured, are yet sufficient to shew that
they were all surmounted with the double demi-bull.
The heads of the bulls forming the capitals, take the
direction of the faces of the respective fronts of the
terrace ; and I think there can be no doubt, that the
wide hollow between their necks received a beam,
meant to support and connect an entablature, over
which has been placed the roof. I do not see the
purpose of these three distinct colonnades at equal
distances from the grand central quadrangle of pillars,
unless they were covered piazzas. That pillars so
terminated were intended to be connected, is made
evident by those on the fronts of the tombs at Nakshi-
Roustam. But, as the ruins that lie scattered near
these divisions, seem, by far the greater part, to consist of fragments of the fallen columns themselves, I
should be of opinion, that the superstructure was of
different materials ; probably some sort of timber with
a thin coating of stone.*

* In the general disposition of these colonnades, the Author supposes that a considerable degree of resemblance may be detected
to the plan of the palace of Solomon, called, " the House of the
Forest of Lebanon;" and at all events, the description given of
that building proves, that different sorts of timber were used in
the connecting parts of the noblest structures, long before the era
of Cyrus. The account, especially in the Authorized Version, is
somewhat obscure ; but thus much is clear ; that " the foundation
was of costly stones, even great stones, stones of ten cubits and
stones of eight cubits ; and above these were costly stones, squared
to a measure" (Boothroyd's Version), " and cedars. And the great

" At a distance of 60 feet from the eastern and western colonnades, stood the central phalanx of columns, in number thirty-six; but no more than five at present exist entire. Therefore, adding these to those still standing in the three other groupes, there are just fifteen remaining erect among the fallen host which lie in all directions, broken or mouldering to dust.* This central groupe is arranged in rows of six deep on all sides, forming an exact square. They are placed at the same distance from each other as the columns in the other divisions, and their dimensions are similar in point of circumference, and in the depth of the pedestal, as also in the general particulars of their ornaments; but they are only 55 feet in height. Their shafts, which are fluted like the others, are about 35 feet in length; the capitals are of a quite

court round about was of three rows of hewn stones and a row of cedar beams, both for the inner court of the house, and for the porch of the house."—1 Kings vii. 10—12.

* If Lieutenant Alexander be correct in his statement, two have since fallen. Sir W. Ouseley has collected in a note, the various accounts of their number given by former travellers, which, could they be depended upon, would shew the progress of dilapidation. When Della Valle visited these ruins in 1621, 25 columns were standing. Herbert, in 1627, and Mandelslo, in 1638, saw but 19. Kæmpfer, in 1696, and Niebuhr, in 1765, 17. Francklin, in 1787, counted only 15, which still remained on their pedestals in 1818. Lieutenant Alexander, in 1826, saw only 13. " One column, of many that stood on the plain, not far from the terrace, and opposite its southern angle," had been pulled down a few years before Sir W. Ouseley's visit, by some Eelauts, in the hope of finding any iron or lead that might have been used in the joinings of the blocks. (Ouseley, vol. ii. p. 236.) Of the total number of columns originally included in the palace, every traveller gives a different calculation. Don Garcias de Silva Figueroa, in 1619, calculated that there had been six rows, of eight columns in each. Sir T. Herbert says, 100; Thevenot, 108; Chardin, 12 rows of 10 each; Kæmpfer and Le Brun, 72; Niebuhr, 71; Francklin, 54; Morier, 72; Sir W. Ouseley, " at least 84;" Sir R. K. Porter, 60.

different character, being of the same description with that in the great portal. The two lower divisions are evidently constructed of the hallowed lotus : the upper compartment has only two volutes. The middle compartment (which is one division of the lotus) appears to have had some extraneous body introduced into the opening between it and the lower part ; and the angular and unfinished state of that side of the capital seems to testify the same. Here, then, the connecting line must have run, whence the roof could spring. I remarked another circumstance, which may corroborate the idea of a roof having been here : there is a manifest appearance of some immense body having fallen against the interior of the capitals, and fractured them to a very ruinous degree, while their outward faces are nearly without a scar. Hence I would conclude, that the whole of these central columns have been attached to the support of some covering.

" But there is one peculiarity observable in the middle range of twelve, pointing N. and S., that gives support to a very interesting idea. All their pedestals rise some feet higher than any of those by which they are surrounded ; the stone work being rough and unfinished, and projecting in strong unshaped blocks, as if to sustain an additionally elevated pavement. To an eye which had lately witnessed a vernal procession to the foot of a Persian throne, the present scene seemed well adapted for a similar celebration ; and as the sovereign is now, and by every account always has been, seated above the level of his courtiers, on this very marble pavement, or flooring of some costly wood, which I have supposed formerly covered these rugged pedestals, probably stood the throne.*

* " It is curious," remarks the Author, " to turn again to the Book of Kings, to compare this supposed site of the throne of Jemsheed,

" The nearest building (now standing) to the palace just described, appears on an elevation of about seven or eight feet above the level of the plane of the colonnades, and occupies a length of 170 feet by 95. We approach it from the west by a double flight of stairs, which are almost in complete ruin; but fragments on and near them shew that they also have been decorated with sculptured guards and other figures. The side to the east is so heaped with fallen remains, covered up with the earth of centuries, that it is impossible to find any trace of a corresponding range of stairs there. To the south, the whole face of the terrace which supports this building, is occupied with another superb flight, the landing-place of which embraces nearly 48 feet by 10. Its front is divided by a tablet bearing an arrow-headed inscription, on each side of which stand spear-men of gigantic height; their heads and shoulders alone are now visible above the accumulated rubbish round the base of the edifice.

" To the north of this building, after ascending its terrace, we find an open space of 65 feet in width, on

with what is said of the situation of the throne of Solomon." The passage referred to is thus rendered by Dr. Boothroyd: " He then made a porch with pillars: its length was fifty cubits, and its breadth thirty cubits; and the (area of the) porch was before those pillars, and over them were thick planks. He next made a porch for the throne, where he might judge, (hence called) the judgement-porch; and it was covered with cedar from the floor to the ceiling. And his own apartment where he sat, was a court-hall behind the porch, of like workmanship." 1 Kings vii. 6—8. " Moreover, the king made a great throne of ivory, and overlaid it with pure gold. And the throne had six steps, with a footstool of gold, fastened to the throne, and arm-stays on each side of the seat, and two lions standing by the arm-stays; and twelve lions, on either side (six), stood upon the steps. The like had not been made in any kingdom." 2 Chron. ix. 17—19. This display of royal magnificence was several centuries before the era of Darius, and might well excite the emulation of a Persian monarch.

which appear the foundations of some narrow walls, probably belonging to what had been the front of the edifice, now fallen and swelling the heaps below. On each side of this space, 40 feet towards the S., stand two lofty entrances, composed of four solid upright blocks of marble nearly black: within the portals, two guards are sculptured on each side in bas-relief. They are habited in the Median robe, armed with a long spear, and, instead of the fluted tiara, their heads are bound with a broad band, which I should suppose was metal. In front of the foremost guard appears a long cylindrical form, which he seems to grasp behind with his left hand: it is constructed of perpendicular rod-like shapes, capped at the top with a flat surface, which is parallel to the chin of the figure. It seems possible, that this questionable object may be intended for the ancient shield called the *gerra*, which is universally described as formed of the osier or branches of the willow. On the immediate verge of the landing-place from the western flight of steps, we enter a portal of these long-shielded guards, and, at a very few paces onward, pass through a second into a room 48 feet square. Two other doors open from it to the north, two to the west, one to the south, and originally two to the east: but one only remains on that side, fragments alone of the second marking where its frame-work had been. On three sides of the room, we found several niches, each excavated in one solid stone to a depth of 3 feet, 5 in height, and 6 in width. They appear to have been exquisitely polished within, while upright lines of cuneiform characters run along their edges. Four windows, 10 feet high, open to the south; they embrace the whole thickness of the wall, namely, 5 feet; and at present, from the accumulation of ruins on the floor, are hardly a foot above it. The doorways have all, on each side, duplicate bas-reliefs of a royal personage with two attendants, one holding an umbrella. Compartments with inscriptions are over the heads of all the gruupes. Three other bas-reliefs exhibit a single combat between a man and a lion, a man and a griffin, and a man with a non-descript creature.

" There is another division (apartment) of the same building, 30 feet by 48, open to the south, and terminating, on each side towards that point, on the landing-place of the superb stairs, by a couple of square pillars, of one block of marble, about 22 feet high: these are covered with a variety of inscriptions, cuneiform, Kufic, Arabic, and Persian. The Arabic was written, A.H. 881. The whole of the ground within the shell of this building, is greatly raised by the crumbled masses of its fallen roof. Faint traces of a double colonnade are still visible along the open space between the western brink of the greater terrace and the western face of this building.

" I have now mentioned an ascent of three terraces from the plain; first, the grand platform which supports all the others; secondly, the *Chehel Minar* terrace; thirdly, the terrace that sustains the edifice just described. A fourth elevation of the same kind, presents itself at about 96 feet to the south of the preceding; its summit is on a level with that of the third terrace, but three of its sides are much obscured by the mounds at their base. Along its northern verge, parallel to the before-mentioned structure, rise the heads of a line of figures equal in size to those on the stairs of the terrace of the double chamber: these figures seem to be armed with the bow and quiver only, no trace of a spear being to be seen. A flight of sadly mutilated steps, in two ascents of fifteen

each, is found at the north-western corner: on these
are vestiges of much fine bas-relief decoration.
Having reached the plane of the terrace, I saw a
square of 96 feet: 38 feet of the western side was
occupied by the depth of the approach just described,
whence ran along, in two direct lines, the bases of ten
columns, 3 feet 3 inches in diameter. Were the hillocks of buried ruins removed, I doubt not we should
find the remnants of a piazza along every side. At
the south-western angle of this terrace, is an additional square elevation, the whole depth of which,
from the summit to the base, is 62 feet: along its
upper surface are the lower parts of twelve pillars in
three rows, of the same diameter as those in the
neighbouring colonnade.

" Immediately beyond this comparatively small
terrace, rises a fifth and much more extensive elevation. But, before I commence the details of this
fifth terrace, I must hazard a few suggestions on one
of the most interesting spots of the whole magnificent
platform.

" From the southern extremity of the eastern
colonnade on the terrace of the *Chehel Minar*,. and
over all the heaped fragments which slope from that
point down to the great platform, is an expanse of
315 feet, measuring in a direct line from the colonnade to the northern front of a building on the fifth
terrace. The whole of this space lies open without a
wall or pillar; but its level is interrupted by an immense mound of ruins....I would hazard the opinion,
that this immense heap covers the mouldered relics of
a division of the palace answering to that immediately
to the south (on the fifth terrace); probably, the more
magnificent of the two, as it would be so much nearer
the great hall of audience, and likely, from that cir-

cumstance, to have contained the banqueting chambers. Here, in that case, may have stood the very
palace which fell a sacrifice to the drunken revelry of
the Macedonian conqueror....Certainly, not a trace of
fire is discernible on any of the adjacent walls ; and
it may be alleged that, if so considerable a building in
their vicinity had been consumed to ashes, the ravages
of the flames must have reached and marked some of
them. But, on perceiving how unconnectedly all the
edifices stood, not merely separated by spacious areas,
but divided by detached terraces, we might easily
imagine how one of them might be burned to the
ground, without a spark reaching any of the others.
Besides, the solidity of the walls of these palaces is
calculated to confine the fire as in a furnace, while it
continued to devour all that was combustible within.
The internal materials of the destroyed palace, according to Quintus Curtius, were cedar and other con-
sumable substances : these, with the splendid hangings * and carpets, would, when once the brand was
set to the building, hasten its destruction. The next
objection might be, that no trace of such solid walls is
left. But the stone would be so injured by the action
of the fire, that we may readily conceive of its rapidly
crumbling to decay, and falling in upon the already
prostrated roof. Besides, we learn from Plutarch,
that the madness of Alexander's intoxication sub-
sided almost as soon as the wanton act was committed,
and that he made every effort to extinguish the flames,
or prevent them from spreading. In this attempt, it
is likely that part of the edifice itself might be battered in to smother the fire. The foundation of the
mound would thus be raised at once, and the casualties

* See Esther I. 6.

of successive ages could not fail to heap it with earth, till it assumed the rounded form in which it now appears.*...That the ruin was not cleared away for the purpose of rebuilding, is not a surprising circumstance, when we consider the brevity of Alexander's life and the periods of confusion which followed his death. The city gradually fell into neglect and consequent decay. A long succession of strange princes, Greek and Parthian, naturally inclining to prefer any city as their residence before the capital of the ancient race, promoted the abandonment of these walls and towers, which the cruel devastation of the Arabs in after ages utterly accomplished. Hence, it is probable, that this very spot has remained in almost the same state, from the night of the destruction of the stately palace, which took place 329 years B.C., to the present day.

" On the terrace to the south of this mound, (the fifth in the order of description,) stand the remains of one of the most regularly planned structures of the whole platform. Its site is also the most elevated, shewing, even now, upwards of twenty feet above the level of that vast foundation. From its dimensions, and the disposition of its numerons apartments, with its contiguity to the destroyed part which I suppose to have contained the festival halls, and the passages

* Quintus Curtius, with his customary exaggeration, represents Alexander as burning to the ground *the whole city*, not leaving a vestige to mark where it stood, and which was only, he affirms, to be traced by the course of the Araxes! So far from this being correct, (and its absurdity has brought the whole story into question,) we learn from both Strabo and Arrian, that Alexander inhabited the royal palace of Persepolis after his return from India. A hundred and sixty years afterwards, Antiochus Epiphanes formed a project to pillage the city of Persepolis and its temple.—See 2 Maccabees, ix. 2.

leading to the high court of ceremonies (the *Chehel-minar*), I am induced to believe this the dwelling quarters of the monarch. Hence, it is deeply to be regretted, that its state is nearly the most ruinous; though enough remains to allow the ground-plan to be traced with the greatest precision, and also to shew the bases and plinths of its pillars, with fragments of beautiful sculpture scattered about in sad confusion. The principal doorways and huge marble window-frames are yet in their places: their lofty sides and ponderous lintels resemble, though with the finest workmanship, our Druidical monument at Stonehenge. Beginning at the southern side of this terrace, we find, at the eastern and western ends, two flights of narrow steps, descending to a lower level of 30 feet. These ways of ingress appear, from their style, to have been private; probably appropriated only to the inhabitants of the place. The several faces of the building are at present marked only by their founda-tions, with the exception of one window to the west, and three to the east. They open from a couple of corresponding wings, which divisions are each subdi-vided into three spacious apartments; the outer ones alone communicating with the pillared courts. In the centre of those courts or quadrangles stand the plinths of four small columns, not more than 2 feet 6 inches in diameter, but placed at the distance of 6 feet from each other, and 16 feet from the door; this leads into a noble hall, 90 feet square, the pavement being marked with the sites of thirty-six pillars, 3 feet 3 inches in diameter. A door on the opposite side of the hall corresponds to the one already mentioned, both conducting into similar open quadrangles of four pillars. Another portal leads to the south, and a fourth and fifth to the north, into a large vestibule, the whole width of the hall, which was supported by eight similar columns, as their plinths still remain to testify. Two doors from the vestibule, pointing east and west, lead into six smaller rooms ; and, from similar foundations, I 'conclude that they joined others still more to the north.

" The windows are each formed of four large blocks of marble, six feet thick, (which is the depth of the walls,) four feet eight inches in height, and three feet six in width. On the inner faces of those that give light to the rooms, are duplicate bas-reliefs, occupying the whole surface, and consisting of two figures in each. The first figure is clothed in the long robe and buskins ; on his head is a kind of cowl, which passes over his mouth, and hangs down upon his chest and back. His face is much mutilated, and so are his hands, in which he appears to be carrying a cup. He is followed by a man in a short tunic and a singularly shaped cap, which comes over his mouth and beard: with his left hand he grasps the horn of an animal resembling the mountain goat of the country, but the horn issues from the middle of the forehead, in form like that of the ibex....The leading person in all the groupes is dressed exactly like the man with the cup ; and those that follow are in the habit of the man who holds the goat. One of these leaders supports a tray on both hands, on which rests a shape not unlike a skin of wine : the persons following him carry each a covered vessel, resembling dishes now in use for *kabobs.* This suite of apartments, I should think, might have been originally appropriated to the private table of the sovereign and his family. On the broken remnants of other windows are found similar lines of figures. Among the least defaced, I found two habited in the Median robe, their visages uncovered ;

one holds in his right hand a sort of censer, and in the other, a vessel resembling a pail, probably to contain the aromatic gums ; the man who follows, has a little glass bottle in the palm of one hand, and in the other, carries a piece of linen.

" The frames of the doors have all one bas-relief ; namely, a royal personage, followed by two attendants bearing an umbrella and a fly-chaser. Wherever this is found, there are three small compartments of inscription over it. The outer doors and those in the wings are ornamented with the two guards armed with the spear only. In this part of the building may be seen, in various places beneath the pavement, what was the subterraneous aqueduct: it passes in a direct line under the centre of the great hall due East, where it received its supply of water from an immense tank, yet visible at the foot of the rocks in that quarter. From the same centre, the great hall, it strikes out again in a northern direction, being traceable to the cistern near the grand portals of the bulls on the first platform ; and doubtless it has many other branches, now lost under the accumulated ruins. This channel is very ruggedly hewn out of the solid rock ; and it is this dark way which some former travellers, not apprehending its real purpose, have described as a secret passage communicating with other mysterious excavations in the body of the mountain, and leading to subterranean entrances into its tombs. A close examination of its channel appeared to me to leave no doubt of its (real) use.*

* " I made an attempt to pierce into the great subterranean passages that traverse the ground on which Persepolis is built, and of which Chardin has given so full an account; but I was not more successful than he seems to have been in his first trial. I had several people with me with candles and lanterns, but we found our-

" At the sides of the open court stand the remains of its once magnificent approaches. Near that to the east, ten or twelve feet from the landing-place of the stairs, rise, from a hollow beneath to a level with the pavement, four enormously large and strong supports, not unlike roughly-formed pedestals. The flight of steps they face, is a double ascent: they are in a state of almost complete decay, having a scarcely legible inscription and bas-reliefs of guards, with duplicates of the combat between the lion and the bull, all in the same broken condition.

" About sixty feet further to the north, appear several colossal masses of stone, formerly the sides of large portals leading into a square edifice, small in proportion to the size and number of its entrances; for, from the situation of the four doors, it could not have been more than ninety-six feet square. Three of the doorways are pretty entire. On the interior face of the one to the east, are three figures twelve feet in height, a repetition of the king and his two attendants. The face of his majesty is mutilated, but his air is singularly stately and majestic. A long beard is disposed with the nicest care upon his breast, and the abundant mass of hair which covers his neck, is not less scrupulously curled. His tiara has a smooth surface, but partakes of the general shape worn by his

selves stopped short by a very narrow passage, after having walked some forty paces upright. We then crept through this on our hands and knees, and again came to a higher part. Again we proceeded, and then were obliged to crawl, until there was only room to put one's head through, when we thought it time to return. This is so much like Chardin's account of his first adventure in the dark passages, that I am inclined to think we did penance on the same spot. Of this I am certain, that it is not the famous passage in which he walked at his ease for near an hour, and then came out for fear of losing his way."—Morier, vol. ii. p. 78.

robed nobles and guards. In his right hand, he carries a long staff with an ornamented top; in his left, a lotus. The broad belt and Median robe complete his raiment. His attendants are clad in the long robe, with the metal fillet round their heads, and rings in their ears: one is carrying in both hands an umbrella over the head of the great personage, while the other waves the fly-chaser in the same direction, grasping in his left hand what probably is intended for the royal handkerchief. The fine finish of this bas-relief redoubled my regret at the demolished state of the faces and hands. One large stone, 16 feet by 8 or 9, contains the groupe. Another block of smaller dimensions surmounts it, on which is seen a figure whose dress and outline of form resemble those of the personage below. His left hand holds a ring; his right is raised and open. He issues from a circle, whence diverge two floating forms, something like serpents, with their heads hidden behind the figure. A pair of immense wings spread themselves on each side of the circle; in that respect differing from the radiated vehicle of the aërial being so often seen on the tombs of Nakshi-Roustam....On the portals are duplicate representations of the same royal personage; but here, he is seated on a chair of state, holding a staff in one hand, and a lotus in the other. An attendant is waving the fly-chaser over his head, and the aërial figure above described, hovers near him. These portals open opposite to each other in the four sides of this quadrangular building: in the centre, I found the plinths of four columns, ten feet equidistant from each other, and four feet in diameter. From their smoothness, it does not appear that they have been surmounted with any other materials....This place seems very likely to have been dedicated to religious uses, and was probably the private oratory of the king. I should suppose, that between these four pillars stood the altar that contained the sacred fire.

" At about 160 feet to the S. E. of this little building, upon the level of the great platform, appears another pile of ruins. On drawing near, I found not only foundations and scattered fragments, but the frames of doors and windows, and niches in the walls, some upright, and all distinctly traceable. A quadrangular building of 48 feet constitutes its chief structure : another, separated from it only by a wall, extends 30 feet towards the S., where it is completely open. These two apartments would appear to have comprehended the whole edifice, did we not see a continuation of the foundation of walls along the southern front, with the fragments of columns, architraves, and other architectural adjuncts to the support of a roof. At the extremities of the walls which point to the S., are two single stones, 18 feet in height, 5 in thickness, and $3\frac{1}{2}$ in width, with large square holes near the top, as if for the reception of a beam. A couple of doorways have bas-reliefs of the double guard, and a portal of considerable width leads from the southern apartments into the inclosed quadrangle, on which we found the walking figure of the king, with one attendant carrying a parasol. The square apartment has received its light from a range of lofty windows : the casements of three are tolerably perfect, as well as several niches in the solid wall. Two entrances from the east and west are ornamented with bas-reliefs of a combat between a man and a lion. Two others perforate the wall to the north, but one portal only is standing ; its sides are sculptured with the spear-men. The ground within these apartments, as well as that without, is raised and rendered very uneven by the fallen fragments of their more ruined parts. No trace of any inscription is to be found in the building, nor does it appear to stand, like those to the west, on any terrace of its own.

" At 190 feet to the north, stands a structure next in extent, as a single building, to the *Chehel Minar*. It is a perfect square of 210 feet. Two doors enter it from every side ; but those from the north have been the grand portals, being 13 feet in width, whereas all the others are only 7. Between them are seven large windows, whose side blocks measure 10 feet, the original depth of the walls : on the other sides, between the doors, is an immense niche. At 40 feet from the northern front, almost parallel with its east and west corners, rise the mutilated forms of two colossal bulls on pedestals, 18 feet long by 5 feet in height : these face the north. At 270 feet from them, in the same direction (but not the same line), appear two others, looking due S., which have formed the sides of a grand gateway, the style and dimensions much like those of the great portal on the first platform : it was probably the entrance into some spacious outer court. A little further north, we see an enormous insulated column terribly broken.

" To return to the square building. The sides of the principal doors are richly adorned with sculpture; and in the most elevated compartment, we find the kingly personage seated on his chair of state, his feet resting on a footstool. Over his head are remains of a bas-relief, representing a canopy supported by slender pillars, the whole profusely decorated with fretwork, fringes, and borders of lions and bulls. There can be little doubt, that the attendant spirit had, as usual, surmounted the groupe, but it was entirely broken away. In this representation of the royal personage, his dress is particularly simple, having neither collar nor bracelets : in his right hand, he holds the long staff or sceptre, and in his left the lotus. Behind him stands the usual attendant with the fan and handkerchief, his face muffled. A second figure, in the short Persian tunic, follows, bearing the royal bow and battle-axe. A third person stands behind, on the other side of the pillared recess which incloses the king. His dress is the Median robe and fluted tiara, and he holds in both hands a long wand. Before the foot of the throne are two gracefully shaped censers, with chains to their covers ; and a muffled attendant approaches, bringing a small pail, which probably was to contain the prepared aromatics. Immediately behind the censers, and in front of the sovereign, appears a man in the short tunic and plain bonnet, his left hand grasping the short staff of office, and his right held to his mouth, to prevent his breath exhaling on the august personage before whom he bends.* Beneath the royal groupe, and divided from it by a long horizontal border studded with roses, are five ranges of attendants, (ten in each,) and separated from each other by a similar border. A frame of this rose-work incloses the whole bas-relief like a picture. ......These five ranges of guards placed over each other, gave me an impression, that the platform on which the royal chair stood, was placed on an elevation of five steps.

" Just beyond the great northern front of this building are two portals, pointing E. and W., their

* " Xenophon mentions, that, in addressing a superior, the speaker generally held his hand to his mouth, that his breath might not be disagreeable to his auditor. Possibly, the serving-men have their faces muffled up, that the royal viands might not be breathed upon."

sides sculptured with the double guard : were the earth cleared away from the base, these figures would be 12 feet high. The whole way between these portals is thickly scattered over with fragments of columns, architraves, &c., which leave no doubt that a covered colonnade overshadowed this principal face of the building. The doors that open from the southern side, have the same sculptures as those on the northern side. Here also, on the higher compartments, sits the royal figure in the usual garb, but attended by the fly-chaser alone. The canopy over his head is quite entire, displaying the most exquisite workmanship in its fretted fringe, roses, and other ornaments. Lions and the unicorn bull fill two rows of it, the first range being separated by the serpent-winged emblem, as in the mutilated canopy on the other side. The aërial figure surmounts the whole ; but, instead of a ring, the *ferwer* * holds the lotus. Three rows of figures, with a broad frieze between each row, fill the space between the royal seat and the ground : the first consists of four persons upholding the platform on which the throne is placed, in the manner of caryatides ; the second row, of five men, uphold the intermediate frieze in the same way ; of the third, one figure only, an Ethiopian, is visible. The whole is enclosed in a frame-work of double pillars, to which the canopy is attached, bearing a close resemblance to the royal elevation on the tombs at Nakshi-Roustum.

" On the four portals pointing east and west, is repeated the bas-relief representing a single combat between a human figure and various animals. The scale is colossal. The man who contends with the

* The attendant spirit.

animals is usually called the pontiff-king; a title
which, in my mind, forms a clear text for the explanation of the whole. He is represented as a personage
of a singularly dignified mien, clad in long robes, but
with the arms perfectly bare; his hair, which is full
and curled, is circled with a low diadem, and his
sweeping, pointed beard is curled in the style worn
by royalty alone. He is in the act of grasping with
his left hand the strong horn that grows out of the
forehead of his antagonist, while he thrusts his short
sword composedly into the animal's body. In the
first bas-relief, the creature is a monstrous combina-
tion of the body and limbs of a lion with the head and
neck of an eagle, covered, half way down its back,
with immense plumage like scale-armour. In the
corresponding sculpture, the head seems to be that of
a wolf, the fore legs and body those of a lion, and the
hinder legs are certainly those of an eagle: the neck
is scaled or feathered with a prickly mane, and it has
wings stretching nearly to its tail, which is extremely
long, and formed of a chain of bones like the *vertebræ*
of the back. The remaining adversaries, exhibited
on the other two doors, are of a more natural appearance, being a horned lion and a unicorn bull......A
Persian standing at our side, pointed to these combats as representations of actual combats between
Jemsheed, or Roustum, or Isfundeer, and the emis-
saries of evil in those hideous forms. The hero, I
suppose to be intended for Darius Hystaspes, or his
son and successor, Xerxes. In consequence of the
death of Zoroaster, who had been massacred in the
great sacerdotal city of Balkh, by Argasp the Scythian
king, Darius took on himself the title of archimagus;
and after avenging the murder of his prophet on the
Scythian nation, we are told by Porphyry, that he

commanded that the name of that sacred distinction should be inscribed on his tomb.[*]

" Going out at the eastern portal, where the king and the tailed monster keep guard, the mountain itself was before me. The slope commences at 200 feet from the side of the edifice, rising from the platform which has been cut from its base. Ascending the height for above 600 feet, I arrived at one of the excavated tombs, which stands in a direct line with the great building of the pontiff king....Another excavation is seen more to the south, and higher up the mountain.... Near the south-eastern angle of the platform, and on the slope of the hill, I found the extensive reservoir which formed the grand fountain for the reception of the waters of the mountain, whence they flowed in a variety of subterranean channels through the body of the platform to the cistern, and diverging thence again, supplied the buildings on the several terraces....Before I took my final leave, I rode over the ground round the base of the great platform, to search for relics of the city beyond its lines. Few remain. The first that presented itself was a stately doorway or porch, standing singly on the plain, at a short distance from the rocks :

---

[*] See vol. i. p. 60. In all the Persian legends, Sir R. K. Porter remarks, " the countries N. of Elbors are typified under the figures of the simourg, eagle, or griffin; and it is not improbable, that the monster with the skeleton tail, and which is very like the martichorus of Ctesias, may be the *ghoul* of Isfundeer." In his expedition against the capital of Argasp, he is stated to have had to pass through seven enchanted gates. " The first was defended by two wolves; the second, by two enormous lions; the third, by a dragon; the fourth, by a *ghoul*, or demon devourer of the dead; the fifth by a griffin; the sixth, by an ever-flowing cataract; the seventh, by a lake and boundless mountains; all which marvellous impediments he surmounted, and having gained the city, killed Argasp the king."

the inner faces of its sides are sculptured with figures
in long robes, now nearly broken away.   To the S.W.
of the platform is a heap of beautiful fragments, apparently the ruins of a temple or some structure of consequence, which the views of Chardin and Le Brun
have distinguished by a noble and solitary column,
standing up from amid its fallen companions, like a
hero over his mighty dead.   But it is now laid beside
them ; and the long grass alone waves its green banner
above the prostrate pillars.*   The last object of any
consideration is an unfinished tomb in the base of the
mountain southward of the platform, and not far from
the ruin just described. The architectural character of
this sepulchre is precisely the same as the others above;
but its situation is singular in being so near the
ground : had its lower divisions been completed, they
would have risen hardly more than four feet from the
level of the plain. I found some difficulty in approaching it, scattered masses of rock blocking up the
way ; and when I surmounted them, and stood by
the half-hewn work, which appeared as if the sculptor
had just taken away his tools to come again to-morrow,
I could scarcely believe that what I looked upon had
been so left nearly 2000 years ago. The upper compartment alone has been finished, containing the bas-
relief of the king, the altar, and the hovering figure....
Full of the recollections of Cyrus who had planted
this empire, and of Alexander who had torn it from
its rock, I turned from the tenantless tombs and
desolated metropolis. All were equally silent,—the
monuments of a race of heroes whose spirits live in
their actions, and of two princes at least whose

---

* This is probably the column referred to by Sir W. Ouseley.—
See *note* at p. 45.

existence was foreshewn, and their names stamped on the imperishable tablets of Holy Writ." *

Little requires to be added, from the pages of other travellers, to this clear and satisfactory account of the field of ruins; but the learned diligence of Sir W. Ouseley has supplied some historical illustrations which deserve notice in this place.

The whole of the magnificent platform is now ordinarily styled by the Persians, *Takht-i-Jemsheed*, Jemsheed's Seat or Throne; a term often used to denote a royal palace, as the *Takht-i-Kajar* at Shiraz, the *Takht-i-Sulieman* near Mourghaub, and the *Takht-i-Rustum* near Isfahan. This popular name seems to have superseded only within the last century, that of *Chehel Minareh* or Forty Pillars, by which they had been commonly designated. Chardin refers to authors who had styled them *Takht-i-Kai-Khosrau*, the Throne of Cyrus; while Kæmpfer and Le Brun speak of them as bearing the denomination of *Khaneh-i-Dárá*, the Mansion of Darius. The names of *Chehel Sutún* and *Hezar Sutún*, applied to them by some oriental writers, have already been referred to. To this title is sometimes added the name of Istakhr, as that of the city and territory. There can scarcely be a doubt, Sir W. Ouseley thinks, that the author of the Dabistan alludes to these Persepolitan remains, when he mentions an idol temple at Istakhr, called *Haft Súr*, the Seven Walls or Ramparts.† The word

* Porter's Travels, vol. i. pp. 582—683. In giving the contents of 100 quarto pages, we have found it necessary to prune, in some degree, the luxuriance of the Author's style, but have adhered to his language.

† "A name," remarks the learned Traveller, "which Kæmpfer's plan would seem to justify; for it represents the *Takht* as comprising only seven distinct edifices, whereas even now there are vestiges of more."

Istakhr is of very doubtful etymology. According to one tradition, that city was founded by Caiumers or Kaiomurs, or, according to another, by his son, whose name was Istakhr. Hyde and Kæmpfer derive the word from an Arabic root, which would make it signify, the Marble Palace; * but a Persian lexicographer explains it as signifying a pond, lake, or reservoir. Istakhr, we are told, "was the name of a castle in the province of Fars, so called from an immense cistern which it contains;" it signifies also, "that castle in Fars which was the royal residence of Darai (Darius), the son of Darab." The name occurs repeatedly in the *Shah Nameh* of Ferdousi; it appears under the form of *Stahr* in the Armenian History of Moses Choronensis; and Istakhr is noticed as a most ancient city by the early Mussulman, writers. On the other hand, no such name as either Istakhr or Persepolis has been discovered throughout the Zendavesta; but Sir W. Ouseley hazards the conjecture, that this city is referred to under the names of *Var-jem-gird, Jem-gird,* or *Jem-kand,* the City, Fortress, or Mansion of Jem (Shem ?) surnamed Sheid, the luminous or splendid.† Had the capital borne the

* " *E rupe desumptum* seu *rupe constans,* saxeum palatium, nomine deducto ab octava conjugation eradicis *Sachr, i.e.,* rupes."— HYDE.

† " Ferdousi, having mentioned the jewels which profusely decorated the throne and person of Jemshid during the great festival called *Nawruz,* compares him, when seated in royal state, to the sun shining amidst the heavens. According to the *Zein-al-Akhbar,* it was on the *Nawruz,* or vernal equinox, that Jemshid, having triumphed over the blacks and the *dives,* or demons, caused immense quantities of jewels obtained as spoils from the enemy, to be piled upon his throne so that all might behold them. As the sun shone through the windows on those jewels and the gold, his whole palace was illuminated by their reflected brilliancy; and on this account he was surnamed *Sheid,* which, in the Parsi dialect, signifies splendour; and the sun, for this reason also, is called

name of Istakhr in the time of the Macedonian conqueror, it is not likely, he contends that they would have rejected it for the compound appellation of Persepolis, "the City of the Persians," which looks like a translation of the native name. That original name, Sir W. Ouseley conceives to have been *Parsagarda*, the City of Pars, the Son of Pahlav; or rather, the City of the Parsees or Persians; and he has laboured to shew that Persepolis and Parsagarda were the same city.* Against this ingenious hypothesis, however,

Khúr-sheid.... Thus, Theophilact, an historian who flourished about six centuries after Christ, relates that the Persian king Hormisdas, sitting on his throne, astonished all spectators by the blazing glories of his jewels; and King Agrippa, as we learn from Josephus (Ant. lib. xix. c. 7.) was almost regarded as a god, so powerfully did his ornamented dress reflect the morning sunbeams."—OUSELEY, ii. 15, 16. See also a curious paper on glories, in App. No. 2.

* Both Persepolis and Pasargadæ, the learned Traveller argues, were situated on the river Kûr, and if not absolutely identical, must have been very near each other. Mr. Hoeck supposes that they were the names of places so near, as to be, in fact, parts of the same city, Pasargadæ lying eastward, and Persepolis westward of the river. Strabo states, that Alexander, having burned the palace of Persepolis to avenge the Greeks, immediately went to Pasargadæ; and Arrian says, that Alexander, having visited the tomb of Cyrus at Pasargadæ, returned to the palace which he had destroyed. There is strong reason to suppose, however, that the site of Pasargadæ and the tomb of Cyrus are correctly fixed by Mr. Morier at Mourg-aub, distant from Istakhr about thirty miles. Pasargadæ is said to have owed its origin to a camp which remained on the spot where Cyrus, with his Persians, conquered Astyages the Mede; (a similar origin is assigned to Grand Cairo, and many other cities in the East;) and the word has been explained as signifying Πιρσων στρατοπιδον. This, remarks Sir W. Ouseley, will be the meaning, whether we read *gadæ*, with Strabo, Arrian, and others, or *gardæ* with Pliny; *gadah* or *kadah* signifying in Persian, a house or dwelling, as *mei-kadah*, a wine-house; *atesh-kadah*, a fire-temple. He prefers, however, as the proper reading, *gardæ*; *gard*, or *gerd*, signifying in Persian, as in many other languages, a walled city, e.g. *Darabgerd*, *Ramgerd*, &c. So, we have Stuttgard, Belgrad,

there lie many objections not easily disposed of; and it is certain, that the native historians speak of this ancient capital under no other name than that of Istakhar, or Istarakh.

At what era a city was first founded here, can only be conjectured; but we may safely conclude, that the natural advantages of the situation would recommend it, in the earliest ages, as the seat of empire; and there is nothing improbable, therefore, in the supposition that King Jemsheed himself held his court at Istakhr.[*] An Arabian writer of the ninth century, (Tabri,) gravely states, that King Solomon occasionally left the holy city of Jerusalem, to reside at Istakhr of Pars, where the vestiges of his palace yet remain. Ibn

Novogrod, *Gardiki*, *Karth*-age, &c. In the first member of the word, Πασας is supposed to be a mistake for Παρσας, as it is sometimes written. Yet, it is scarcely credible, that Strabo and Plutarch should not know how to spell the national appellative. According to this hypothesis, Persepolis was a Greek translation of Parsa-gardæ; although the original word was not understood by the Greeks! It seems more probable, that Pasa is a different word, erroneously confounded with Parsa. Ptolemy places a *Pasacarta* in Parthia. See Ouseley, vol. ii. pp. 316—334. May not Persepolis have been a dedicatory title bestowed upon Istakhr by the Macedonian conqueror in honour of Perseus?

[*] It has been mentioned above, that some of the Persian writers cited by Sir W. Ouseley ascribe its foundation to Caiumers. Thus, in the *Nizam-al-Tuarikh,* a work of the 'thirteenth century, it is said, that Caiumers "founded two cities: one Istakhr, wherein he chiefly resided; the other Damavand. Istakhr was the capital of his grandson Hushang, and was so considerably enlarged by Jemshid, that it extended from the borders of Khafreg to the extremity of Ramgerd, a space of twelve *farsangs;* and there he constructed an immense edifice, of which the columns and other vestiges remain to this day; and they are called *Chehil Minarah.*" The same story is repeated by Fazlallah Casvini, who adds Balkh to the cities said to be founded by Caiumers, but represents Istakhr as his chief residence. Hamdallah, the Persian geographer, repeats the tradition, interposing the name of Istakhr, the son of Caiumers, between that monarch and Hushang.

Haukal, in his Oriental Geography, speaks of Istakhr
as the most ancient and celebrated city in Pars, where
the sovereigns of that region always resided, until
King Ardasheer removed the seat of his empire to
Júr or Gúr (Feroozabad). Solomon, the son of David,
he tells us, came in one day from Tabereah (Tiberias),
as tradition relates, to Istakhr, where was a *masjed*
which still bore his name. Among the chief wonders
of Pars, he enumerates several lofty structures which
tradition assigned to Solomon and the Dives; and
here, he adds, " are sculptured figures and columns ;
and the forms of those mansions once occupied by the
tribe of Aad are, even 'now, presented to our view in
this edifice, which resembles, in magnitude, that visible at Baalbek."

Ferdousi states, that, when Kai Kobad was called
to the imperial throne, he set out from his northern
residence near Mount Elborz, and proceeded towards
Pars, in which was " the key to the treasures.
Istakhr then became his dwelling-place; it was the
glory of his nobles." Here also, King Kai Kaús is
said to have received Kai Khosrau on his arrival from
Isfahan, and afterwards resigned to him the throne.*

* In the *Mejmaa al Insab* (Collection of Genealogies), written in
A.D. 1332-5, Istakhr is said to have been founded by Kai Káús,
who "lived in the time of Solomon, with whom he observed terms
of peace; and he was safe from the sword of Solomon; and he
requested of him that the *dives* should, at his command, be employed on works in the city of Istakhr ; and all those edifices which
now remain in the territory of Fars, are vestiges of Káús; but
some attribute them to Jemshid." (OUSELEY, ii. 377). A similar
account is given by a Persian writer of the thirteenth century, the
author of the *Mujmel al Tuarikh*, who cites from the Chronicle of
Tabri, the tradition, that these structures were erected for Káús
by the *dives* at the command of Solomon. " But Solomon," he
adds, " was contemporary with Khosrau, according to another account; and Hamdallah Isfahani denies to this edifice (the throne

When, in the reign of Dara (Darius), the Persian dominions were invaded by Sekander (Alexander), " armies so numerous went forth from Istakhr, that their lances obstructed the wind in its progress;" but these being defeated, the conqueror is described as entering in triumph, " Istakhr of Pars, the royal crown, the glory of that country." Shapoor II. is stated to have made Istakhr his residence, although he occasionally visited Teisfun (Ctesiphon); here, also, was the court of Yezdejird I. Hormuz III., who reigned towards the close of the sixth century, passed two months of every year at Istakhr, " when the nights were shortest, the air of the place being so cool and pure that he could not prevail on himself to leave it." But early in the seventh century, it had apparently ceased to be a royal residence, since Khosrou Purveez is stated to have bestowed the government of Istakhr on one of his chiefs.

of Solomon) the origin above assigned; for it exhibits many figures of *hogs* sculptured in stone, and there are not any living creatures more odious than swine to the children of Israel. And he further says, that it contains inscriptions in Pahlavi, which a certain *mûbed* (priest of the fire-worshippers) was once brought there to read; and among those inscriptions, some declared, that *the edifice had been constructed in the time of Jem,* on such a month and day." (*Ib.* 358). Záb, the father of Kai Kobad, it is subsequently stated, died at Istakhr, and was entombed at the mountain foot; also Kai Kobad himself, although some accounts make him to have died at Balkh. Kai Káús died at Istakhr, and was there deposited in the sepulchre of his father; also Ardashir, son of Babek, and his son Shapoor, and the last Darius. (*Ib.* p. 361.) It is remarkable, that Kai Khosrau, who is supposed to be the Cyrus of the Greeks, was *not* buried at Istakhr. " According to some traditions," says the *Nizam al Twarikh,* " Solomon, on whom be the peace of God! attacked Kai Khusrau, who fled from Istakhr to Balkh, where he was slain." But the same historian mentions, that Kai Khusrau resigned the throne to Lohrasp, and retired from public life. (*Ib.* p. 371). Lohrasp himself is stated by Mirkond to have abandoned Istakhr through fear of Solomon, and to have resided at Balkh! (*Ib.* 393).

According to the author of the *Nisam-al-Tuarikh*, when Zerdusht, in the reign of Gushtasp, invited mankind to renounce the Sabian, and to adopt the Magian worship, he resided on *Nefisht*, a mountain of Istakhr. " In that mountain and its vicinity," it is added, " are the sculptured figures and tombs of most of the ancient Persian kings. Among the Persians prior to Islam, there were three kinds of sepulture : some bodies were interred in (natural) caverns ; some in *dakhmahs* formed in mountains ; and others, the bones being separated, were placed in jars or urns under ground. Then Gushtasp, having become a disciple of Zerdusht, went to Istakhr, and established his residence on that mountain." From another chronicler we learn, that Gushtasp, on his return from Balkh to Istakhr, caused a *dakhmah* (vault) to be made, in which he deposited, with much reverential ceremony, the book Zend, and appointed a body of persons to guard it. " This book, according to Mirkhond, consisted of twelve thousand ox-skins, so tanned as to resemble thin leaves of paper, on which the doctrines of Zoroaster were written in letters of gold and silver." The place at Istakhr where these sacred writings were deposited, is by other historians called *Der Nebisht* or *Zerbisht*, " that is to say, the library ;" and when Sekander (Alexander) arrived at Istakhr, he commanded translations of all the books to be made, and sent into Greece, and they were deposited in Macedonia, and the *Dernebisht* was burned.*

" When the grandson of Gushtasp, King Bahman, bequeathed the crown to Khumáni or Humai, who was both his daughter and his wife, his son Sásán re-

* Ouseley, ii, pp. 344, 370, 374, 410.

tired from court, and in the vicinity of Istakhr led an obscure pastoral life." It was into the river Kour in the territory of Istakhr, (although some accounts transfer the scene of the transaction to a river in Balkh,) that Khumani threw the box or ark that contained her infant son Dara (Darius), who was saved and brought up by a miller. To this same queen is ascribed the erection of some of the structures at Istakhr: according to some writers, she built the palace of *Chehel-minar*, while others make her to have rebuilt the whole city. Among other edifices, she is stated to have built a great mansion that stood in the midst of Istakhr, which the Mussulmans converted into a *masjed* or mosque; but this mosque had fallen into decay in the thirteenth century.[*]

When Ardasheer Babegan raised the standard of revolt against the Parthian monarch, Istakhr is stated to have been the residence of a king, probably a viceroy, named Jauher, (some make him to have been the son of Ardavan or Artabanes,) who was put to death by order of Ardasheer. The seizure of Istakhr made him master of all Fars, and he was soon able to gain possession of Kerman and Isfahan. On one occasion, having gained a great victory at Merve, he sent the heads of some of his vanquished enemies to be placed over the gate of the fire-temple at Istakhr. In the fourth century, twelve thousand families were removed, partly from Istakhr, and partly from Isfahan, by Shapoor II., to repeople the deserted city of Nisibis. Yezdijerd, the last of the Sassanian dynasty, is stated to have been concealed at Istakhr, when called to the throne A.D. 632; but the territory of Istakhr is meant, in which the castle of Fahender might be in-

---

[*] See authorities in Ouseley, ii. p. 344, 371, 374, 391.

cluded.* In the year 644, Istakhr capitulated to the Mohammedan forces; but four years after, the people revolted and slew the Arabian governor. In consequence of this insurrection, the Khalif·Othman sent troops from Basrah to Istakhr, and great multitudes of the inhabitants were massacred. In this same century, Shiraz was founded, and soon became, what Istakhr had been, the capital of Fars.† Frequent mention is subsequently made by the Mohammedan writers, of the castle of Istakhr, which appears to have been used as a state prison so late as the year 1501, when the ex-governor of Shiraz was confined in it; but that fortress must not be confounded with the city, which, after having long been on the decline, was ultimately destroyed by the fanatical Arabs.

Such is the sum of the information laboriously compiled by Sir W. Ouseley from the oriental writers, with regard to this interesting site. Little stress as can be laid on the confused traditions which they agree in reporting with regard to its early history, there can be no doubt, we think, that the foundation of Istakhr must be referred to the Kaianian dynasty. Its embellishment was, doubtless, the work of different successive princes. To no one would the sculptured palaces be with more probability referred, than to Cambyses, the conqueror of Egypt. Yet, Susa continued to be the favourite residence of the Persian monarchs in the reign of Bahman or Ardisheer Dirazdust,‡ B.C. 461. To this monarch and his daughter Homai, we should be inclined to ascribe the principal edifices. The subject of the principal sculpture, there can be little doubt, is the institution of the *Noo-rooz*, which dates from the time of Jemsheed or

---

* See vol. i. pp. 123, 349.　　† Ouseley, ii. pp. 346, 7, 371.
‡ See vol. i. p. 64.

Cyrus, who is probably the monarch intended in the first bas-reliefs; * but the pontiff-king is more likely to be Darius Hystaspes, the buildings being doubtless of a later date than the original *takht* or platform.†

The two tombs excavated in the mountain immediately behind the *Takht-i-Jemsheed*, are between 300 and 400 yards apart. The front of each, finely sculptured, consists of two compartments. In the lower one, which is about 70 feet wide, is carved a

* That the Cyrus of Xenophon is the Jemsheed, or rather one of the Jemsheeds, of Persian tradition, seems in the highest degree probable. It has already been remarked (vol. i. p. 43), that, in the Kai Khosrou of the Persian annals, it is impossible to recognise the character of the hero of Xenophon and the restorer of Jerusalem. It is difficult to imagine that, of so beneficent a sovereign, no traditional vestige should be left in the country over which he reigned; but yet, unless Cyrus be Jemsheed, his existence has left no trace behind. Nor is it less unlikely that the Jemsheed of tradition should be a personage altogether fabulous, like the Jemsheed of Ferdousi. The fact seems to be, that the name is titular, not personal; and we are strongly inclined to believe the words *Jem-sheid* and *Kour-sheid* (from which the Hebrew Koresh seems derived) to have similar meaning; *Jem* being perhaps the same word as the *Shemsh* or *Semes* of the Hebrew Scriptures (but foreign from the Hebrew) which signifies, the sun.

† With a view to assist in determining the true era of the *Takht-i-Jemsheed*, the learned Author offers the following " negative observations," subject to correction from future travellers. Among these ancient monuments he did not perceive, 1. any object appearing to be a vestige of the Arsacidan kings; nor, 2. any vestige of the Sassanian dynasty, besides two Pahlavi inscriptions; 3. nor any representation of a long or crooked sword; 4. nor any human figure with a full face; 5. nor any human figure mounted on horseback; 6. nor any figure of a woman; 7. nor any sculpture representing ships, or alluding to naval affairs; 8. nor any arches; 9. nor any human figure sitting cross-legged; 10. nor any human figure in a state of nudity, nor any object in the slightest degree indecent; 11. nor any vestiges either of wood or of brick; 12. nor any remains of gilding; 13. nor any insulated statue or figure in full relief; 14. nor any figure that has ever actually been an object of idolatrous veneration.—Ouseley, vol. ii. pp. 273—296. Most of these negative remarks are strong indications of high antiquity.

false door between two columns surmounted with capitals of the double unicorn; from which issues a beam supporting an architrave, frieze, and cornice. On this entablature rests, in the upper compartment, " a kind of stage, not unlike the Israelitish ark of the Covenant," on which is placed a blazing fire-altar. Before it stands the pontiff-king, or some officiating priest, his right hand uplifted, and his left hand grasping a bow; and between this person and the altar, hovers the mysterious *ferouher*, or attendant spirit, issuing from the winged globe or circle. " As the same subject is repeated in seven different places, and always on the fronts of tombs, we may," remarks Sir W. Ouseley, " with some reason conjecture, that it related to those whose bodies were therein deposited,—in their general character, regal or pontifical. The king appears with the same countenance and dress, and in the same attitude, on all the seven tombs; and each contains receptacles for three bodies. It can, therefore, scarcely be supposed, that the royal figure was designed to represent, like a portrait, any particular personage. It is not impossible, that these excavations were prepared by some ancient monarch as sepulchral monuments for his descendants during many generations." * Each chamber is about 30 feet wide, 15 or 18 feet deep, and 10 or 12 feet high: the most southern was found deeply covered with stagnant water.

About three quarters of a mile southward, is the third tomb, (first described by Niebuhr,) which has never been finished, although apparently the most ancient. " On inspecting the first projection of the mountain (in that direction), my eye," says Mr. Morier, " was

* Ouseley, ii. p. 268.

attracted by some square, loose stones, evidently cut
for the purposes of masonry, that were strewed on the
acclivity; and, on turning the angle of the projection,
I was surprised to see a tomb, similar to the two on
the mountain, except that it was much more decayed,
not so much ornamented, and without any appearance
of an entrance. The upper part of the front is built
with square stones, similar to those which first caught
my eye; the remainder is cut into the rock. What
makes it most remarkable, is a collection of large
stones, which seem to have been purposely so placed
before it in intricate avenues, as to form a labyrinth,
which, there is reason to suppose, from the many
fragments in its vicinity, was roofed with stone, and
then covered over with earth. No other part of the
monument, therefore, was intended to be seen, except
the square front on which the figures are sculptured;
and we may thence conclude, that these tombs were
never entered but in a secret manner, and that the
avenues to them were through subterraneous passages,
but so constructed, that none but the privileged could
find their way through them." *

In many parts of the great plain of Istakhr, are seen
fragments of marble columns, doorways, and other
vestiges of structures, similar in style to those of the
Takht-i-Jemsheed; together with small niches cut in
the rock at such a height that it is difficult to imagine, how or for what purpose they were executed.
At length, after proceeding northward for a mile and
a half or two miles, the traveller arrives at what now
bears the name of *Naksh-i-Rejeb* (the portrait of Re-
jeb or Rajab). This is a chamber cut in the rock, but
open at top; on the face opposite its entrance, and on

<hr>

* Morier, vol. ii, p. 86,

each side, are sculptured numerous figures, one of which is supposed to represent the imaginary hero, Rajab; but the subjects of all the tablets relate to the early monarchs of the Sassanian dynasty, particularly Ardasheer and his son Shapour. One large tablet has been supposed to represent Ardasheer resigning the symbol of empire into the hands of his son, as seen at Shapoor; * and another apparently alludes to the same participation of empire between two equestrian figures. Several inscriptions in Pahlavi are found here.

About four miles from the *Takht* are the sculptured tombs absurdly called (like many similar monuments) *Naksh-i-Rustam* (the portrait of Rustam). The tombs, which are four in number, are all contained in the space of about 200 yards, on the surface of the steep and craggy rock. The top of the rock has been levelled, so as to form a platform about 20 feet square, on which is an elevated seat or throne, 9 feet by 6; it is ascended by five steps. The shaft of a column 6 feet high, stands upon the summit of the rock, at the angle towards the N.W., nearly over the first and most northern piece of sculpture. The entrances into the tombs appear to be from 30 to 40 feet above the level ground: Sir R. K. Porter says, 60 feet. They were excavated, Sir W. Ouseley is of opinion, by the same race of kings who constructed the *Takht;* but the chisel has been actively employed to commemorate princes of the Sassanian dynasty.+ The figures on the tablets are, like those at *Naksh-i-Rejeb*, larger than the natural size, and in spirited relief, though

. * See vol. i. pp. 95, 324.

' + " To these tablets, the earliest date that I would assign, is the third century, while the four tombs above them appear to me coeval with the *Takht*, and by many hundred years more ancient than the Sassanian sculptures."—OUSELEY, ii. 205.

some are much injured. The subjects are much the same
as those at Shapoor. The supposed Ardasheer again
appears on horseback, delivering the circlet of royalty
into the hands of his illustrious son; and there is an
exact copy, on a larger scale, of the conqueror bestow-
ing mercy on a suppliant captive, supposed to be a
Roman. The names of *Artashetr* and *Shapuhri* are
sufficiently conspicuous in some Greek and Pahlavi
inscriptions at this place, which have been deciphered,
after Niebuhr's copy, by M. de Sacy. One very remarkable inscription, of at least 120 very long lines,
presents, legibly expressed in Pahlavi characters, the
name of Varahran.

The fullest account of these sculptures is given by
Sir R. K. Porter, to whose pencil the public are indebted for spirited copies of the whole. In the first
which presents itself towards the east, the personage
on the left is, he says, undoubtedly a woman; and
the correspondence of the design to a Sassanian silver
coin in his possession, enabled him to identify the personages represented, with Baharam Gour and his
favourite queen. Another of the bas-reliefs, in which
the same monarch appears with huge tassels or bags
attached to his shoulders, as well as to a staff behind
him, he supposes to refer to Baharam's stratagem in
his encounter with the khakan of Tatary: he had
ordered his troops to provide themselves with bladders
filled with stones, the noise of which threw the enemy
into confusion.* The bas-relief supposed to represent
Ardasheer delivering the circlet to Shapoor, Sir Robert
would assign to a Greek chisel; which the Greek inscriptions render not improbable. That which ap-

* See vol. i. p. 106. The battle is said to have been fought near
Rhey; and an unfinished bas-relief on the rocks above that city,
appears to refer to the same event.

pears on the horse of the supposed Shapoor, is thus translated by M. de Sacy: "This is the figure of the Servant of Ormuzd, the God Ardasheir, king of the kings of Iran, of the race of gods, son of the god Babek, king." On the shoulder of the horse bearing the personage who bestows the circlet, is an inscription which the same learned professor translates: "This is the figure of the god Jupiter;" * the word Διος being substituted for Ormuzd, the supreme deity of the Persians. It would therefore seem, that this bas-relief is designed to represent Ormuzd delivering the *cydaris*, or wreathed symbol of empire, to Ardasheer, the restorer of the native monarchy and the Magian faith. But for the inscriptions, Sir R. K. Porter admits, that the explanation usually given would seem more probable, as the equestrian figure designed to represent the god Ormuzd, has nothing about it that suggests the idea of deity; but, clumsy as is the allegory, the inscriptions must be supposed to tell the real design of the artist, unless we suppose them to be of later date than the sculpture. †

The tomb least difficult of access, is the last on the left, over a tablet representing an equestrian combat. "Up to the low and narrow doorway of this tomb," says Sir W. Ouseley, "we were, not without much trouble, dragged by our servants; for they, climbing circuitously, had ascended to the summit of the mountain, and thence let down a rope, to which was fastened the long silk sash of Colonel D'Arcy, who first entered the excavation.‡ I followed by the same

* Ταυτα το πρεσωπον Διος Θεου.

† Porter, vol. i. pp. 530—561.

‡ Capt. Sutherland had previously entered one of the tombs in 1808, the one furthest to the northward, (Morier, i. 128) which he found to be 37 feet in length and 9½ in height. This appears to be the

means, and found myself in a chamber 35 feet long, 7 feet broad at each end, and 8 feet in the middle. This measurement does not include the depth of three arched recesses, hollowed, like the chamber itself, in the solid rock, and forming sepulchral vaults 9 feet long by 5½ feet broad. Immense slabs of the same rock cover the vaults: these it would have been impossible to lift, or even move, without the assistance of several men. There is a fracture in one vault, made probably by the violators of these tombs, who, we may suppose, while taking out the body in search of treasure, raised and propped the stone cover, until, having accomplished their object, they let it fall in its original situation. Through the aperture it was easy to ascertain, that this vault contained nothing more than some pieces of stone. Within this chamber, of which the ceiling is arched, like the recesses, and about 10 feet where highest, all parts are of the plainest execution: we could not discover one letter of an inscription, not one figure, nor even a stroke of the chisel that might be reckoned ornamental.

same that Sir W. Ouseley describes. The second and third, according to his Persian companion, had also been explored'; but the fourth (the last on the right of a person approaching the mountain) was believed to have escaped violation from its inaccessible height, and was supposed to be still replete with treasure. Chardin bribed a servant to climb up and examine one of these tombs, but did not himself venture: he says: " *Nul Européen n'y est jamais entré, que je sache.*" Neither Le Brun nor Niebuhr had sufficient courage. Sir R. K. Porter, however, in 1818, performed the ascent. He describes the chamber he entered, as blackened all over by smoke either from lamps or fires. Every one of the covers of the tombs, he says, has been broken near the corners. He had a light introduced into all three, by which he was enabled to ascertain that they were alike empty, not containing even any loose dust. The entrance of the chamber appeared to have been originally closed by a stone door, the deep holes which received their pivots being still visible.—PORTER, l. 521—3.

" The next object of our examination was a remarkable edifice opposite to this tomb. It is a square
of about 23 (24) feet, and nearly 30 feet (Sir R. K.
Porter says 35 feet) high, constructed of white marble
in a most substantial manner. Of the flat roof, one
great stone has been dislodged from its place by the
violence of man or an earthquake, and now projects
near a corner of the front wall facing the mountain.
Some violence has also effected a fissure in the lower
part of that wall, immediately under a small door-way,
up to which we climbed, about 11 feet from the ground,
and introduced ourselves into a square chamber, 12
feet 3 inches square, and probably 20 feet high. The
ceiling is composed of two immense marble slabs. The
walls are without any sculptures or ornaments whatsoever. In the front wall, externally, are many small
oblong perpendicular niches; and a multiplicity of
niches of the same size, besides a few of larger dimensions, appear in each of the other three faces;
but none sink deep into the stone, nor can they ever
have admitted light or air. For this extraordinary
building, as for most of their ancient monuments, the
Persians readily find a name : our guide called it the
Kerennái Khaneh, or Station of the Trumpets; ano-
ther-man, the *Nakareh Khaneh*, or Kettle-drum
House; and a third assured me that it was the Kaabah of Zaratusht (Zoroaster)." * Mr. Morier does

* This edifice, Sir W. Ouseley remarks, would naturally suggest
to a Mohammedan the idea of the *Kaabah* at Mekka, which is so
called from its cubical form, the word signifying a die. There is
another place called the *Nokara Khaneh ;* a rock of very singular
shape near Kurbal, but without sculptures. The designation appears to rest upon no other foundation than the tradition, that the
drums and trumpets of king Jemsheed in his palace of *Chehel
Minar* could be heard at that place, distant nine geographical miles
in a straight line !—MORIER, ii. 73.

not hesitate, indeed, to call it a fire-temple; and he
says, that the inside exhibited signs of fire. Sir R. K.
Porter describes the walls as black with smoke. The
larger niches, resembling windows, are described by
the former Traveller as " closely fitted with a stone."
" A cornice, enriched with dentils, passes round the
summit; and in the lines where the stones have been
fitted, oblong, perpendicular incisions are made at
regular intervals. The people call it a pigeon-house."
Sir R. K. Porter describes it as " built with marble
from the adjacent rocks, each block being 3½ feet in
width, but varying in length. One single slab forms
the cornice of the northern face, which is 22 feet 8
inches long; an amazing mass to have been placed
where it now is. Accumulated earth and rubbish
have doubtless diminished the visible height of the
building. Ten layers of marble blocks are now all
that we see, which give the edifice an elevation of 35
feet. The portal is 5 feet wide and 6 feet high, leading
through a wall of 5 feet 3 inches thick. The grooves
for the pivots of its doors are deeply cut, both at the
bottom and the top, where they were fastened to the
sides of the wall; so that the ponderous stone divisions must have met in the middle, and shut close.
*The circling marks of their movement are strongly
worn in the marble floor."*

Not far distant, following the abrupt turn of the
rocks towards the East, are " two fire-altars," † four
feet and a half square, and between five and six feet

* Porter, vol. i. p. 562. This is probably the *mesjed*, or " temple of Solomon," referred to by Casvini (Ouseley, ii. 367), which
was at the foot of a mountain, and " *within the city.*"

† Morier, i. 128. Ouseley, ii. 298. Kæmpfer supposes them to
have served as beacons, and Della Valle styles them pedestals. See
a view of them in Porter, i. 566.

in height, narrowing upwards: they are formed from a protuberance of the rock. On the top of each is a square cavity, eight inches deep, supposed to be the receptacle of the sacred fire. The eminence on which they stand, is called *Sang-i-Sulieman*, Solomon's Stone. Further on, in the recess of the mountain, are twenty holes or windows of different sizes, but all of the same pattern, with inscriptions over them, differing apparently in character, Mr. Morier says, from all that he had previously seen. About a mile from *Naksh-i-Rustam* in an easterly direction, is seen a large rock, about 200 feet in circumference, which has been divided into two channels as if designed to form part of an aqueduct; but it is evidently an unfinished work. From this rock, Mr. Morier crossed to the other side of the plain, which is here intersected by numerous artificial water-courses, and came to some ruins called *Takht Taous* (the peacock throne), and *Harem Jemsheed*. " They are situated in the centre of an extensive spot, which, from the configuration of the land around, in elevated terraces and mounds, appeared an artificial inclosure. The wall, indeed, in many parts could be distinctly traced on the summit of the mounds. On arriving at the ruins, I found them to consist of a solitary pillar with a double-headed sphinx for its capital, besides, strewed on the ground, a great quantity of shafts, bases, and capitals of the same dimensions, and all of the same description as those at Persepolis. Several large blocks are arranged about it, as the fragments of some building. The column is fluted like the Doric, but with lines more closely connected: it is 1 foot 8 inches in diameter at the bottom, and 6 inches less at the top, a little above 17 feet in height, and the base, including a torus, 2 feet more. A little further on is

the ruin of a large pillar not fluted, and the fragments
of a sphinx-capital. *Naksh-i-Rustam* bore N. 50 W.
from this place." *

Sir R. K. Porter says : " The height of the pillar,
judging by its (seven) fallen companions, is 20 feet 6
inches. The capital is in the form of the head, breast,
and bent fore-legs of a bull, richly ornamented with
collars and trappings, united at the back to a corresponding bust of another bull, but leaving a cavity
between sufficient to admit the end of a square beam."
They are of a dark grey marble, beautifully fluted. " A
few yards to the N.E. are found remains of thick walls
and the yet unmutilated marble work of several door-
frames. Indeed, the whole surface of this immense
terrace is covered with mounds of ruins and noble
architectural fragments. It appears evident that two
distinct edifices have stood here ; apparently a temple
and a palace ; and we perceive it to have been a fortified place. Its situation admirably adapts it for such
a post, commanding the entrance into the great valley,
and the foundations of the walls and towers are yet
standing. Its northern bank is washed by the Kur-
aub, and at the foot of its southern slope, between it
and the mountain, passes the road, which was formerly
closed in upon the present fortress of the valley, by
an enormous gate ; the architecture and solidity of the
walls shew the antiquity of the structure and the importance of the situation." †

All the way from this place to Persepolis, the rock
bears marks of the chisel : in some places, it is intersected by long channels as if for water-conduits, and
in others, carved into various shapes as if it had
been fitted to the purposes of habitation ; but Mr.

* Morier, vol. 1. pp. 141, 2.   † Porter, vol. 1. pp. 514, 15.

Morier was unable to discover any sculptures in this direction.

Other caverns and sculptured rocks are found, however, near the village of Hajji-abad, situated close to the foot of that range of mountains, at the eastern extremity of which are the sculptures of *Naksh-i-Roustam.** The place is called *Zendan Jemsheed*, the prisons of Jemsheed. The first cave is apparently natural, not of any great depth, and exhibits no traces of art. The second to the left of this, is a deep indentation into the mountain, at the entrance of which, the rock has been smoothed and cut into five tablets, on three of which are Pahlavi inscriptions. The third cavern to the right of this, is celebrated for its great depth, but appears to have nothing artificial about it.†

In the plain of Merdasht, to the northward, are several conspicuous masses of rock, insulated from the surrounding mountains. On the top of one of these are the remains of the fortress which still retains the name of Istakhr. It is visible to the eye from the *Takht ;* but, owing to the numerous dikes and canals which intersect the plain, Mr. Morier found the distance between three and four *farsangs.* After proceeding nearly three miles southward to cross the Polbar (Farwar)

---

* " The valley, or rather dell, of Hadjee-abad cannot be more than two miles from end to end ; the most *western* extremity being formed by the rocks of Nakshi Roustam, which stretch from the village of Hadjee-abad in a direction N. 68° W. The whole of the northern side of the valley is one succession of perpendicular cliffs, pile above pile, almost entirely of white marble, their uneven summits taking the boldest and wildest forms, broken into yawning chasms, and divided by deep rents, torn by the rushing waters."—PORTER, vol. i. p. 513.

† Morier, vol. ii. pp. 80, 81. Two of the inscriptions are given by Sir R. K. Porter, vol. i. p. 513.

river at a bridge, he came to a village situated at the foot of the insulated mountain called *Koh Ramgerd,* where he obtained a guide to the " Rock of Istakhr." The rock rises abruptly to the height of about 500 feet from a steep conical hill, which appeared to be itself nearly 700 feet in height. Mr. Morier ascended on the N.W. side, winding round the foot of it, through more shrubs than are to be seen in any other part of the surrounding country.* The path is narrow, steep, and intricate, but might be ascended, he thinks, by mules or asses. The remains at the summit con- sist of part of a gate, the ruins of several turrets, four reservoirs, and the wrecks of many walls. The rock has, at its summit, a gradual inclination from both sides towards the centre, forming a furrow, in which the reservoirs have been constructed. Near the largest of these is a solitary fir-tree, with a few scanty shrubs.

The view from this eminence commands a great extent of country. The range of mountains bounding the plain of Shiraz to the south, are seen bearing S. 10° W., and the Peera-zun bearing S. 35° W. West- ward, the eye wanders over a region of high moun- tains, of which the snowy summit of the *Koh Shishpeer,* bearing N. 75° W. is the most prominent feature. In

* In ascending the hill of Istakhr, Mr. Morier remarked, that his old guide placed, here and there, a stone on a conspicuous bit of rock, or two stones upon one another, uttering, at the same time, a prayer for their safe return. "This action appears," he remarks, "to illustrate the vow which Jacob made, when he tra- velled to Padan Aram, in token of which he placed a stone and set it up for a pillar." Gen. xxviii. 18—22. It is common in many parts of the East, we are told, particularly on a high road to a great town, when the town is first seen, for the traveller to set up his stone, with a devout exclamation, in token of his safe arrival.— MORIER, ii. 84.

the foreground rises another insulated rock, similar to that of Istakhr, on which are the ruins of the castle of Shahrek, looking like an immense square turret on a tumulus.[*]

This latter castle is evidently so called after the viceroy or governor of Istakhr, named Shahreg or Shahrek, who was slain in defending the city against the Arabs in the seventh century.[†] At that time, the city and neighbouring country is said to have furnished troops to the number of 120,000 men; but after repeated engagements, the city was taken by storm, and given up to pillage. The present castle of Istakhr is doubtless that which is said to have been subsequently erected by the Arabian general Ziad, and in which Azzed ad Douleh constructed his famous reservoir. The *Koh Ramgerd* appears also to have had its fortress, called *Saied abad*, which was distant, according to Ebn Haukal, one *farsang* from that of Istakhr.[‡] Hamdallah, the Persian Geographer, represents Istakhr as extending from the borders of Khafreg (a village of that name) to the extremity of Ramgerd; a distance of fourteen (others make it twelve) *farsangs*. " It was ten farsangs in breadth; and in this space were comprehended buildings, and cultivated fields, and villages; also, three very strong castles, on the summits of three mountains; one, the castle of *Istakhr ;* the second, *Shekesteh* (broken);

---

* Morier, vol. ii. p. 85.

† See Ouseley, vol. ii. pp. 343, 347.

‡ Ouseley, vol. ii. p. 348. It could not be at that distance from the *kureh* (district) of Istakhr, as erroneously stated in the printed work, since it is said: " This castle, which is at Ramgerd, *in the kureh* of Istakhr, stands on a lofty mountain of difficult access, from the summit of which to the castle is about one *farsang.* The village of Saied-abad is mentioned by Sir R. K. Porter as occurring in his route from Sewund to Persepolis, not far from Hadji-abad.

the third, *Shangwan* (or *Sangwan*, called also *Sepidan*
and *Saknaun*) ; and these were called *Seh Gumbedan*,
or the Three Domes." *

The *Kúh e Nefisht*, by which is evidently meant
the steep and lofty rock overlooking the Takht, is
described by the same writer as being " in the *vicinity*
of Istakhr;" that is, of the castle so called. This rock
is now sometimes called the *Shah Kúh*, a title exactly
corresponding to the Βασιλικον ὁρος (royal mountain)
described by Diodorus, as distant from the palace eastward, 400 feet (4 *plethra*), and' as containing the
sepulchres of the kings, up to which the bodies were
drawn by some mechanical contrivance.† It is also
called *Kúh e Takht* and *Kúh Rahmet* (the mountain
of mercy), but never Istakhr. The modern town of
that name is said to have been small: in the tenth
century, it was equal in extent to " two-sixths of a
farsang," or about a mile, standing in the immediate
neighbourhood of the citadel which commanded it ;
and the Khorasan bridge was at the city gate. ‡ If,
therefore, the *Takht* was within the ancient city, it

* Ouseley, vol. ii. pp. 379, and 314, *note*.

† Ctesias relates, that Darius Hystaspes caused a tomb to be
constructed for himself on the double or two-topped mountain
(διττος ὁρος) ; but, when it was completed, the Chaldean sooth-
sayers warned him not to enter it. His father and mother, however, impelled by strong curiosity, went to the mountain, and
forty priests were employed to wind them up by means of ropes to
the entrance: while they yet hung between earth and sky, the
sudden appearance of some serpents on the rock so terrified the
priests, that they let go the ropes, and both were killed. Although
the circumstance appeared accidental, Darius put all the forty
priests to death. Whether this tomb be one of the excavations in
the steep rock at *Naksh-i-Rustum*, or the single sepulchre in the
Kúh-e-Takht, discovered by Niebuhr, Sir W. Ouseley professes
himself unable to determine. It turns upon the question, which
better answers to the epithet of the two-topped mountain.

‡ Ouseley, vol. ii. pp. 348, 9.

probably marks the southern extremity of Persepolis, as the fortress of Istakhr may be supposed to do its extent in the opposite direction; and all the intermediate plain may have been comprised within its original circuit. A complete survey of this celebrated plain is still a *desideratum*. The narrow pass by which Alexander entered it, has not been ascertained; * and after all the labours of Niebuhr and Chardin, Kæmpfer and Le Brun, Porter, Ouseley, and Morier, much yet remains to be investigated by future travellers and learned antiquaries, before the chorography and monumental remains of Persepolis can be considered as having received adequate illustration.

We must now suspend for a short time our description of the route to the northward, in order to accompany Sir William Ouseley in his journey to the borders of Kerman, in search of the supposed Passagarda, which some writers had placed at the modern town of Fassa.

FROM SHIRAZ TO DARABGERD.

THE road from Shiraz to Fassa runs from the Saadi gate, over a plain, on which are scattered several mud-walled villages, to the *rahdari* of *Pul-i-Fassa* (the Fassa bridge), at the foot of a small hill: here, the route to Ferouzabad turns off to the right. A broad and deep stream is crossed at a ford, and the road, which is generally flat and good, thence runs along the foot of the *Kûh Karabagh*, having, on the left, an extensive plain, which becomes in winter the *Derya-i-*

---

* Those *pylæ*, or straits, where the Persians resisted Alexander, Sir W. Ouseley is " inclined to place fifteen or sixteen miles from the *Takht*, or about half way between that ruined edifice and *Mâin* (*Mâyeen*), the chief town or district in the village of Ram-gerd,"—OUSELEY, ii. 330.

Nemek (the lake of salt). At certain seasons, the water of the lake approaches very near the steep, rugged rocks that project from the mountains, and form various indentations into the plain. About twenty miles from Shiraz, is seen an extraordinary insulated mountain, called, from its detached form, *Kúh Gurikhtah*, on which are said to be ancient ruins, " probably one of those castles once very numerous in Fars." About seven hours (24 miles) from Shiraz, Sir W. Ouseley halted at the caravanserai of Mahalú. The general direction of the day's route was S.E.   A few trees at the village of Vazirabad (seven miles from Shiraz), and two handsome *bann*-trees, about thirteen miles beyond, were the only trees seen throughout this tract. A few spots naturally verdant, yielding beautiful flowers and fragrant shrubs, alone diversified the sterility of its general aspect. The lake appeared from 20 to 25 miles long, and is said to be about 12 *far-sangs* in circumference ; but its extent varies with the season.

The second day's route was to Servistan, distant between seven and eight *farsangs* in an easterly direction.   At about three *farsangs*, the great arid rock above mentioned, bearing the name of *Kúh Gurikhtah*, rises abruptly from the bare plain, which here changes its name from *Kaffah-i-Mahalu* to *Kaffah-i-Servistan*. The latter place, though large and populous, is considered only as a *dhey* or village. It derives its name, apparently, from the cypresses for which it was once remarkable,* although but eight or ten are now to be seen ; but other trees abound here, and the gardens are proverbially good ; the place is not, however,

---

* *Serv* or *Sarv*, the cypress, and *stdn*, place or country. By a change of *v* into *b*, and of *r* into *l*, very common in Persia, it is vulgarly pronounced Selbistan.

deemed salubrious. Dreary and depopulated as is the whole tract between Servistan and Shiraz, (a few Eelauts were the only human beings seen after leaving Mahalu,) the botanist and mineralogist, Sir W. Ouseley says, might find abundant employment.

At five miles from Servistan, on the third day, Sir W. Ouseley crossed the deep bed of a river nearly dry, and, one mile further, a small running stream; the road then entered the hills, passing over a *kutel* or mountain road, uneven and stony, but prettily wooded with small trees, which led into a spacious plain, bounded, on the left, by the *Kùh Hharman.* Two ruined caravanserais were passed, and, at about seventeen or eighteen miles, the foundations of some buildings. A few miles further, the learned Traveller turned out of the road to the left, and proceeded, by a most rugged and difficult path, to visit a ruined fortress called the *Kalaa àtesh kadah* (Castle of the Fire-temple.) " The castle exhibits little more than stones in vast and shapeless masses: of the original masonry, some vestiges remain at the bottom, and some on the summit of the hill, where a wall is still visible, and a few towers appear on the almost perpendicular sides. A spring of admirable water fills a reservoir just below the castle." The fire-altar, which gives name to the castle, is found 200 or 300 yards from the fountain. It is a single upright stone between 10 and 11 feet high, and 3½ feet square at the bottom; not quite so broad at top. On the southern and western sides are traces of Pahlavi inscriptions, each within a circular tablet sunk about an inch into the stone. On the top, is cut a deep hollow, designed to receive the vessel containing the sacred fire. A rude low wall or fence of large stones incloses the altar, having a narrow entrance on the south.

The first view brought strongly to the Author's recollection, the Druidical remains he had seen in Wales
and Ireland ; and a few old trees seemed to represent
one of those sacred groves which were, in early ages,
attached to religious structures.

The *munzil* or halting-place, this night, was at
Tang-i-Kerm (or *Kerram*), a few miles from the
fire-temple, and reckoned eight *farsangs* from Servistan. This is a mud-walled village, about a mile in
length, with many flourishing gardens. The traveller
has now entered upon *Shebangarah*, considered in the
fourteenth century as an independent district. Over
much of the country through which the day's route
lay, small bushy trees were rather thickly scattered,
with fragrant shrubs and flowers, some of which seemed
equally rare and beautiful.*

From Kerm, the route, changing from an easterly
direction to nearly S.S.W., continued for some way
along the stony bed of a river, which conveys to Fassa,
during winter, a considerable body of water. A stream
from the fountain of the fire-temple, conducted between artificial banks at a level of many feet above the
river-bed, runs for several miles along the road. At
five miles, close to the road on the right, are some walls
and towers of a small castle, and a poor village, " all
built of mud, ruined, and deserted." At between ten
and eleven miles, the course of the road turning more
directly S., the author reached Fassa, distant from
Shiraz, according to his account, twenty-six *farsangs*,
or about one hundred miles.

" My examination of this town," says Sir William,

* Among these, Sir W. Ouseley mentions the *shebbu*, " a plant,
as its name imports, of nocturnal odour, which is said to be so
powerful that it causes a vertiginous affection resembling intoxication."

"was soon completed, for its narrow lakes are not numerous, and half the mud-built houses of which they are chiefly composed, seem untenanted and falling to ruins; the few buildings of brick are not in better condition; the people, generally, wear an aspect of poverty and misery; and on leaving Fassa, I might almost have used the words of Pietro della Valle, who says, that he found in it nothing worthy of remark but the palm or date-trees, which are not seen in more northern parts of the country, the oranges, and the double narcissuses. He duly celebrates, however, that majestic, beautiful, and most venerable cypress which I had admired at the distance of several miles. It has not, probably, increased since his time (nearly two centuries ago), either in height or bulk, for it was then very aged, and its trunk would fill the expanded arms of five men; neither does it exhibit many symptoms of decay, yet it is said to have been, for above a thousand years, the boast and ornament of Fassa.

The only ancient edifice is a large brick building, " perhaps three hundred years old, of which the upper story seemed originally designed as a habitation for the living; the lower part was a receptacle for the dead, the floor being checkered with many tombstones." Of the epitaphs, many were Arabic; but none were of an age that entitled them to notice. There is a spacious and handsome *madrasseh*, built not many years ago, but already in a neglected state; and an old mosque, which, like every other building in the place, is going rapidly to decay. Sir W. Ouseley explored several places in the neighbourhood, in the hope of discovering some vestiges of ancient monuments, but without success. Yet, Fassa, according to the native writers, once equalled Shiraz in magnitude, and was preferred to that city, on account of the superior purity of its air and water. In the tenth century, it was famous for its manufactory of hangings, rich embroidery, and cloth of gold. It is said to have been founded by Bahman, the father of Darab I.[*] Whoever was the founder, it is quite certain, that this place has no pretensions to be regarded as the Pasargadæ of Cyrus.

About two miles S.W. from Fassa, a broad and deep ditch incloses an area above a mile square, within which rises abruptly a vast mound, apparently artificial, which bears the popular name of the *Kalaa-i-Zohák* (or Dhehák). The tradition is, that " one of the most ancient kings, being desirous of erecting a castle here, caused the clay and sand which compose this heap, to be brought from Hindostan, as the foundations formed of the local soil had proved insecure." The view from the elevated summit of " this acropolis," to which our Author climbed by a difficult path, is uncommonly grand. At its foot runs a small stream. Some holes in the side, made, perhaps, by jackals or other beasts, are supposed to terminate in caverns, in which treasures of incalculable value are guarded by talismans and dragons. Vestiges of buildings, though not visible on the heap itself, are numerous in the plain below. A little beyond, and about a mile to the right of the road,[1] is the village of Dastah.

" At four miles from Fassa," Sir W. Ouseley continues, " we discerned, also on the right, and crowning the summit of a hill, an object which resembled, on a distant view, one of our British Druidical *crom-*

---

[*] Or, according to Tabrí's Chronicle, by Darab, " the father of the Darius whom Alexander conquered." Another tradition ascribes its foundation to Fasar, the son of Tahmuras Divebund: having been destroyed, it was repaired by Gushtasp, and, in later times, rebuilt by Atabeg Javeli. It is written also Basa and Passa,

lechs. It lay above a mile off our road,....and is called *Khaneh-i-Gabran*, the mansion of the fire-worshippers. It is a mass of stone, or rather of the hardest cement, in which stones of different kinds and colours are thickly incrusted; of an irregular oblong form, about 50 feet long, and 12 or 13 high, with a passage through it,....about 4 feet high, and smooth on the sides and ceiling, and in some places considerably polished." Art has evidently been employed, but no sculptures or inscriptions were discovered. For several hundred yards about this spot, numerous vestiges of stone and mortar buildings, with foundations of walls, are seen; and near the entrance of the outer inclosure is a deep well. The steep and rugged mountain on which this singular monument is found, is washed at its base by a clear rivulet.

At five miles from Fassa, the road passes the village of Sahraroud; at three miles further, it leaves that of Mohammedabad on the left, and runs to the foot of the *Kúh-e-nokreh* (silver mountain), where is a mine which formerly was worked.* Here there is a small brook; also the bed of a large river, which the route crosses further on, passing between two steep rocky mountains. It then enters upon an extensive plain, in some parts very highly cultivated, and several villages occur. At four *farsangs* (about 17 miles) from Fassa, the Author reached Zahedan, a village of about 300 houses, supplied with water by artificial conduits.

The next day's journey was a tedious ride of twelve hours to an inconsiderable village called Khusuieh; a

* This mine had probably been abandoned, like many others in Persia, because the produce was found inadequate to the labour of working, or, as a peasant expressed it, *deh kharje, nuh hasel;* the expense was ten, the profit nine.

computed distance of 10 *farsangs*,—Sir W. Ouséley says, not less than 40 miles. Of these, thirty-four presented such a scene of desolation as cannot easily be imagined ; for, after passing the mud hovels of Nasrabad, the Travellers saw neither habitation nor human being. The rugged road extended with a dreary sameness over long tracts of barren plain, or passed among stony hills, where it was often so narrow as scarcely to admit a loaded mule. There occurred neither river nor running stream, not above ten or eleven trees, and only one well of bad water.* "We had now entered," continues our Author, "the vast *sahra* or uncultivated plain of *Garápaigán*, bounded, on both sides, by lofty mountains, where, it is said, king Baharam Gour frequently indulged in his favourite pleasure of the chase. At 12 or 13 miles from Zahedan, our road lay among the tomb-stones of an *Iliat* cemetery : one exhibited á Persian epitaph, neatly and recently cut, and another, some rude characters. The Iliat tribes return with their flocks at certain seasons, to those spots which they had before occupied. A little beyond this cemetery, we passed the dry bed of a river ; at 20 miles, we rode through another river bed, very deep, but likewise without water. Six or seven miles further, we stopped at the *Cháh-e-kuch*, a well that gives its name to the plain. Here we filled with water two leather vessels (called *matarrah*) ; but these were exhausted before the end of our journey. Several of the party thought themselves fortunate in discovering among hollows at the

* Soon after leaving Zahedan, a road turns off on the right (southward) to Jahrum (written sometimes Gerom and Jaarown, and pronounced Jahroon), a town of Fars, said to have been founded by Bahman the son of Isfendyar, and which, in the tenth century, was famous for its silk stuffs. It had a strong castle called *Khursheh.* The climate is very hot.

foot of rocks, a stagnant puddle, of which they attempted to drink; but, the green surface being slightly stirred, the mud and water appeared so animated by insects, that we would not allow even the thirsty mules and horses to imbibe them. From this, we proceeded along the desert; then, for some miles, over a *kutel* or hilly country; and at length, saw the date-trees of *Khesuieh*, a mean village, where I was lodged in the mud-built castle. The best room had been prepared for my reception, its former tenants, five or six soldiers, having removed their carpets to the roof. These men were stationed here, that they might protect the inhabitants and travellers from robbers, who had lately begun to commit depredations in this district."

Khesuieh belongs to the territory of Darabgerd, from which it is distant five *farsangs*, or about 18 miles. At a mile and a half from the village is seen the *Kúh Múm-i-Ay* (Mummy Mountain), so called from the black bituminous matter which oozes from the rock, in a cavern near the village of Ayi, and which, on account of its supposed medicinal properties, the Persians deem more precious than gold.* A

---

* It is to be regretted, that the learned Traveller was unable to visit this cavern. A writer of the tenth century, describing the place, states, that numerous officers were stationed there to guard it. Once a year only, the door of the cavern was opened, and the *mum* which had distilled during the year, (a quantity equal in size to a pomegranate,) was taken out, and sealed up, to be deposited in the royal treasury. " The soil of Ayi," says Cazvini, "a village in Shebangareh, is most remarkable for this production; it has therefore been called after that place, *mum-i-Ayi*, or the wax of Ayi····it has the property of curing faintness, palsy, convulsions, epilepsy, and vertigo; it is also useful in heaviness of the tongue, inflammation of the throat, fractures of the limbs, splenetic affections, and palpitations." Some of this precious catholicon was brought by Mirza Abul Hassan, in 1809, as a present from the

very bad road over steep hills leads down into the
plain of Bizdoon, which is almost inclosed by mountains, and is shaded by date-trees.   A bridge of twelve
arches, near a village of that name, crosses a stream
which in winter must be considerable.   At eleven
miles is seen the mud-built castle and village of Juzjan,
and at fourteen miles, the *Kalaa-now-Darab*, or new
castle of Darab; both on the right: about these places
were many date-trees and extensive corn-fields.   Here,
Sir W. Ouseley was supplied, by a hospitable *Eelaut*
of a neighbouring camp, with milk and curds, and some
excellent cheese.*   When within three miles of Darab,
he turned off on the right, to visit the *Kalaa-i-De-
hiayeh*, the name given to an extensive piece of ground
inclosed within a deep and wide fosse and a rampart
of earth, in the midst of which rises a huge, rugged,
insulated rock, at least 20 feet high.   In the sides of
this extraordinary rock are several caves, some natural, and others probably artificial, two of them communicating by a door-way cut through the solid stone.
There are numerous remains of buildings about this
place, which deserve, Sir W. Ouseley says, a more
minute examination than he could bestow upon them.
But the greatest curiosity is an irregular cluster of

Shah to the Queen of England.   A man at Isfahan would not accept less than nine *tomauns* (about 8*l.*) from a gentleman in the
British ambassador's suite, for as much as could have been contained in a walnut-shell.

* This cheese was " pressed into balls not larger than an apple,
and white as snow," which became in a few days extremely hard.
One, which the Author kept for several months, when bruised and
diluted with water, formed a cooling and pleasant beverage, slightly
acid.   " Coagulated milk, thus indurated by compression and ex-
siccation," is said to last a considerable time; and Pliny, on the
authority of an old tradition, informs us, that Zoroaster lived
twenty years in desert places, on this cheese—" *Caseo ita temperato
ut venustatem non sentiret.*"

large and rude stones, on a rising ground in another
part of the inclosed area, which, from its appearance,
" a British antiquary might be almost authorized to
pronounce Druidical." Some of them are from 20 to
25 feet high. One, very tall, stands nearly in the
middle; another, towards the west, resembles a table
or altar, being flat at the top; and under two or three
are recesses or small caverns. The arrangement of these
stones, the learned Traveller thinks, may be partly,
but could scarcely be altogether natural or accidental.
According to the accounts of the natives, the citadel
of Darabgerd once stood in this spot, the city having
extended at that time thus far. Sir W. Ouseley
strongly recommends the site to the investigation of
future travellers. He left it by a path near some
walls and arches, still 20 feet high, the remains of an
ancient aqueduct; and passing on his left the little
village of Dehirayeh, proceeded by a pass between two
rocky hills, about a mile and a half from Darabgerd,
into the fine and rich plain on which the town stands.

Ferdousi, giving an account of the foundation of
this city, informs us, that " king Darab, having gone
forth one day to visit his horses pasturing in the low
grounds,* ascended a hill, whence he beheld a vast
and deep river, or body of water; and he desired that
expert mechanics should be brought from India and from
Greece, who were instructed so to direct the course of
this water, that a stream might flow through every
district. Those ingenious men having opened the
mounds or dikes, Darab commanded that a city should
be built; and when it was girded round with walls,
they named the place Darab-gird. The monarch then
kindled a fire on the summit of a mountain, to which

* The site of the city is said to have been previously called
Aspán Fargan, horse-pasture.

crowds of persons resorted, worshipping the flame *Aser*; and they procured the most skilful artists of every description, by whom the city was embellished." Cazvini states, that the city was perfectly circular, as if the plan had been delineated by a compass; and in the midst of it was once a well-fortified castle, with a very deep ditch; but this was in ruins in the fourteenth century. Sir W. Ouseley feels persuaded that this castle must be the *Kalaa-i-Dehayeh*, with its surrounding rampart and its broad ditch, once easily filled by means of the aqueduct; and the large rock in the centre of the inclosure, is what a native writer describes as a mountain in the midst of the city, which resembled a dome, or a building with a vaulted roof. " It was, perhaps, on this rock," he adds, " from which he could easily have beheld every part of the recently founded city, that the illustrious Darab terminated his labours by the solemn performance of a religious ceremony, and probably the establishment of a new fire-temple; though the circle of rude stones, situated likewise on rising ground, may indicate the vestiges of a consecrated structure." .

The modern town is reduced to a mere village: half the houses appeared deserted or in ruins, and the greater part of the area which it once covered, is now occupied with gardens and orange-groves.* The climate is very warm, and it was once, according to native writers, a very flourishing and delightful place, with the drawback of having the worst water in the province, and being subject to frequent visitations of

* Pietro Della Valle, who passed through this city nearly 200 years ago, mentions its numerous population, its date-trees, and the running stream that filled a small circular fish-pond in the bazar : " there is nothing else," he says, " in Darabghierd, to be seen or observed."

the plague. The only monuments of antiquity in its neighbourhood, are, the castle of Dehayeh, a *Naksh-i-Rustam*, and an excavation of a very remarkable character, called the *Caravanserai-i-Doob*, about four miles to the S.E. of the town, of which Sir W. Ouseley gives the following account.

" Having left the town, we proceeded about a mile in a south-eastern direction, to the decayed brick edifice with arched windows and niches, called *Kabr-i-Pashang* (the burial-place of Pashang), whom our guide was willing to believe the ancient hero of that name celebrated in the Shah Namah ; but it was evidently the monument of a Mussulman saint : close to it, on the very road, were numerous graves covered with well-cut stones, bearing Arabic and Persian epitaphs, which proved the cemetery to be at least from 400 to 500 years old. Near this spot were tombs of several *imám-zadehs*, now fallen to ruins. A little beyond those, was a heap of stones, on which lay one about two feet in length, simply ornamented with a plain, carved line : it probably marked a modern grave, and is worthy of notice only as being supposed the work of remote ages, and ascribed to some female personage whose history I was desirous of tracing ; for, throughout this part of the country, remains of conduits, bridges, and causeways, towers, caverns, sculptures, and almost every thing that wears the semblance of antiquity, are denominated *mál-i-dukhter* (work of the daughter), and are regarded as memorials of some unknown damsel or virgin. We saw on our left, a few miles distant, vestiges of the castle called *Kálaa-i-Rúma*,[*] and at three miles passed a deep well or pit. The person

---

[*] This site would appear, from its name, to invite the visit of future travellers, as tradition seemingly ascribes it to the Macedonian Greeks.

who constructed it, was probably commemorated in
an inscription rudely chiselled on a stone impending
over its mouth.   Still more barbarously executed
(perhaps by Iliáts) were some characters on the natural rock, not far from this well. We advanced about
a mile further by a most rugged path, and having
passed on the left an aqueduct, a mill, and some other
buildings, turned off towards the right. Our road
had been hitherto that which leads to *Deh-i-Kheir.*
We alighted soon after at the *Caravanserai-i-Doob.*

" It is a spacious chamber, hollowed with admirable
ingenuity and by means of prodigious labour, into the
very heart of the mountain. Its roof seems formed of
arches, supported on (thirty-six) square pillars, of
large but not ungraceful proportions; the roof, however, the pillars, the arches, and the walls, are all of
the solid rock. It receives a little light at the entrance, an ample and handsome door-way in the side
of the mountain, and from a square aperture in the
centre of the roof, where the rock is ten or eleven feet
thick. The chamber itself is a square of 70 feet, regularly divided into four parts by the rows of pillars
intersecting one another. Twenty-one or twenty-two
feet may be considered as its extreme height between
the arches.......Near the door were inscriptions carved
in the Arabic character, not very ancient (about A.D.
1305 or 1350). In the wall terminating the main
aisles on the left and right, and opposite the door,
were niches not unlike the fire-places in European
houses, and sculptured with some degree of elegance.
Inscriptions in the same character as those above
mentioned, served for ornaments, and filled the frames
or borders.......Having ascended the rock over the
chamber, I examined the opening through which it
partially receives both light and air : this is 10 feet

5 inches square. Near it lay a large stone that seemed, from its cubical form, to be what once filled the aperture."[*]

. To the right of this chamber, is another small square excavation, with an arched door-way in the face of the mountain; but Sir W. Ouseley had not leisure (owing to the impatience of his guides and the alarm of robbers) to ascertain whether it communicated with the grand excavation. To the left of this are three natural caves, and the mountain contains many others. He thinks it not improbable, that some of these may be connected with the first by secret passages. The inscriptions and pointed doorways are in the modern Saracenic style, and have no pretensions to high antiquity; but the excavation can scarcely have been the work of Mussulmans, or have been originally designed for the purpose which its modern name indicates. It may have been a place consecrated to Mithraic rites; and certainly deserves the attention of future travellers.

From this mountain, the learned Traveller crossed the country nearly in a straight line for about three miles, over fields and rocks, through streams and extensive groves of date-trees; and at length arrived at the sculptured rock, where, in the gigantic figure of the supposed Roustam, he recognized another monument of the glory or vanity of Shapoor. The sculptures, in bold relief, occupy a tablet about 20 feet high and 36 feet in length, cut in the rocky face of a steep mountain, over a basin of excellent water abounding with fish. Shapoor is on horseback; close to him is seen his usual emblem of victory, a dead body extended on the ground; before him is a crowd

---

* Ouseley, vol. ii. pp. 138—140.

of Romans, and he lays his left hand on the head of
their captive chief. A youth extends his arms towards
the neck of his horse, as if imploring mercy. The
Romans, all bare-headed, fill the right end of the tablet, and on the left are four ranks of Persian guards,
most of them wearing the pointed cap. No inscriptions were discoverable. Judging from the Author's
sketch, the sculpture is extremely rude, the work of a
very inferior artist, no regard being paid to either
proportion or perspective. A little beyond this place,
he came out on the Fassa road.

Darabgerd was the termination of Sir W. Ouseley's progress towards the south-eastern regions of
Persia. He returned to Shiraz by a different and
unusual route, which had nothing but its novelty to
recommend it. He proceeded two *farsangs* W.N.W.
through a fertile plain, covered with fine corn-fields
and date-trees, and watered by numerous water-courses
and conduits: he then passed a decayed village, and
keeping close to the hills on his right, halted at a
circular, vaulted edifice of brick, resembling in shape
a bee-hive, erected on a platform of stone work, and
called *Mal-i-Gabran* (a work of the Guebers). It is
situated on an eminence, near a delightful spring that
starts from some rocks among a variety of reeds,
rushes, and small trees, at the foot of steep and lofty
mountains rising almost perpendicularly above it: it
is called the *Chashmeh-i-gulabi* (rose-water fountain).
The building, which is doubtless ancient, had lately
served to shelter cattle. A fine stream issues from
the fountain. Further on is an Iliát cemetery, and
on the right is a large mountain of singular appearance, called the *Kúh-e-nemek* (hill of salt).* All the

* Cazvini speaks of a mountain in the territory of Darabgerd,
yielding salt of seven colours. This salt, another native writer

plain in this part glitters with particles of salt. The ruins of a castle are seen at the distance of about three miles, with some caverns. At about five *farsangs* (20 miles) from Darab, the Author reached the village of Madavan. Here, the thermometer, at three o'clock, stood at 78° in the shade, and rose to 123° in the sun. Myriads of flies of various descriptions infest the place; some resembling the common English sort, some of the dragon kind, exceedingly beautiful; others of a pale yellowish green, as large as bees; with a multiplicity of very formidable wasps and horse-flies (*sembur*), that give notice of their approach by an extraordinary hissing noise. Fly-flaps, neatly made of chip or straw, were lying in almost every window, both at this place and the three preceding stages.

The next day's stage was to Iretch (or Eredje), a distance of about five and twenty miles, by a very bad road. Passing two or three ruined or decayed villages, the Author came, at four miles, to a narrow pass between perpendicular banks of yellowish clay, 80 or 90 feet high. A little beyond this, is a second chasm in the mountain, still more narrow, between lofty rocks. A stony *kutel*-road leads down into the plain, in which, at ten miles, is the village of Derakan, a collection of mud-hovels inclosed within walls of the same material. This plain, called the *Sahra-i-Karabulagh* (plain of the black district), is said to be at some seasons covered with water. At between thirteen and fourteen miles is an extensive cemetery, and near it, remains of a well-built aqueduct. The road then changes from

says, " the people fashion into trays, and whatever else they wish, and send into distant regions. In all other countries, salt is produced from the bosom of the earth, or from the concretion of water, but here it appears in the form of entire mountains." Quicksilver (*simab*) is said to be found in the same place. See authorities in Ouseley, ii. 134, 155.

N.W. to a *N.E.* direction, descending into a vale between mountains and rocks of stupendous magnitude.
At length, the Author came to the narrow pass of
Tang-i-Iretch, four miles beyond which he arrived at
his *munsil* or halting-place.

Within thirty or forty years, this was a much more
considerable village, and it was once a town of some
importance. ·Its name is said to have been that of a
son of king Darab. Many walls and towers still appear on its fortified mountain, at an astonishing height
among the ledges of rock; and there is also a succession
of reservoirs, one below another, communicating by
sloping conduits of masonry, with an aqueduct extending above a mile along the plain : so far may be traced
the vestiges of the town, which is now reduced to a long
line of mud-built houses, shaded by many trees. There
is a *masjed*, now no longer used for religious purposes,
which must have been handsome. " This day," remarks Sir W. Ouseley, " afforded another lamentable
proof of the depopulation and decay which have latterly prevailed in Persia. During the course of at
least five and twenty miles, we saw not above six or
seven people of the country; and the two villages that
we saw, bespoke poverty and misery. Works, however, of considerable extent and utility, may be traced
in various parts both of the mountain and the plain.
We saw remains of arches and foundations of houses,
walls of excellent stone-work supporting banks of
earth, and fragments of aqueducts, all attributed to
that beneficent but unknown damsel."

On the third day, soon after passing a *gumbez*, or
circular tower, and some ruins, the road began to
wind among the hills in a direction N.N.W., the
rugged *kutel* in many places requiring not less circum-
spection than the worst passes between Bushehr and

Shiraz. At the end of about nine miles, it led out into the plain of Savonat. Proceeding about four miles further towards the W.N.W., the Author arrived at that village, after a journey of nearly fifteen miles.

Astahbonát, pronounced Savonát, though it ranks only as a *dhey* (village), seemed more populous, and offered a greater show of bustle and business, than either Fassa or Darab, which claim the rank of *shahr* (city). Linen (called *kerbas*) is manufactured here, and a great deal of earthenware of a superior description. The materials are procured from stones of the neighbouring mountains, some of which are reduced, after undergoing a process not described, to an impalpable white powder.* They glaze the clay with much neatness and very expeditiously; and the principal artist had succeeded in imitating fine porcelain so exactly, that Sir W. Ouseley found it difficult to distinguish his ware from the Chinese originals, both of the blue and white pattern, and painted in flowers and figures. This man was, however, very poor, and complained of being deterred from prosecuting this branch of his art, by the exorbitant price of some particular colours.

In the fourteenth century, Cazvini described Savonat as a town abounding in trees, enjoying a temperate climate, yielding fruit of every kind, and copiously watered by several streams. In its territory there was a strong castle, which, during a contest between

* Sir W. Ouseley suggests, that Pliny possibly alludes to the mountains near Savonat, in giving his account of the substance found in Carmania (Kerman), which furnished the murrhine vases or cups so highly esteemed among the ancients. (Nat. Hist. xxxvii. 2.) That the murrhine vases were but a kind of porcelain, is the opinion of many able antiquaries.

the Seljoukian princes and the people of Shebangareh, was destroyed by the Atabeg Javeli, but was afterwards rebuilt.* " Of this description," says Sir W. Ouseley, " I was able to ascertain the general accuracy. Some remains of the castle are still visible ; the gardens of Savonát yield grapes, apples, and a great variety of fruits ; the air was exceedingly pleasant, and comparatively cool, for, at one o'clock P.M., Fahrenheit's thermometer rose only to 70° in the shade. Indeed, the *Súr al Beldán* enumerates this place, with Idge, Istakhr, and others, among the towns belonging to the *Sard-sir*, or colder division of Pars. It appears accordingly, that the palm does not flourish here ; and Savonát is, I believe, several *farsangs* beyond that imaginary line which restricts, as many Persians have told me, the actual growth of dates to the *Garmsir*, or warm regions. There is a sufficiency of water, although it does not seem to flow in such quantities as when Hamdallah wrote, nor is it remarkable for salubrity. Savonát has probably suffered less than any other town in Pars, from that pernicious system of government which spreads desolation so widely throughout this province. To what fortunate circumstance it owes this partial exemption, I have not learned. Of its houses, five or six only seemed untenanted or in decay. Its population was numerous, and wore an air of industry and comfort. To this, without doubt, the manufactures (of linen and earthenware) contributed in a high degree ; and one of inferior note may be

---

* There is a large *masjed* in the town, ancient and wanting repair, but still frequented by a few dervishes, which was said to be a thousand years old ; and from several inscriptions on the walls in the Kufic character, this appeared to the Author no exaggetation.

added.. Here are made spoons (*kashuks*) of the box-tree (*shimshád*) and rose-tree or pear-tree (*gulabi*) wood; some with long and very slender handles, most ingeniously carved and ornamented with open work; the hollow part of considerable size, and rendered so thin and elastic, that the sides may be pressed together as if formed of paper.* Such are the spoons used by people of the highest rank: a coarser and cheaper sort is fashioned from the same materials, or wood of a similar grain." There are many trees of extraordinary bulk and age; but the glory of the place is a majestic *chinar* of ample foliage, 26 feet in circumference near its base, and perfectly straight to a considerable height. Although four hundred years old, according to the local tradition, it was sound and in the fullest bloom. A seat or bank had been constructed near its foot, insulated by a little trench, through which a stream of water perpetually flows.†

The next day's stage, from Savonat to Kheir, was performed in four hours; the distance being between fifteen and sixteen miles. For the first six, the road lies over the level plain; it then skirts the mountains on the right, in a direction W.N.W., the heights of the *Kúh Hharman* being within view on the left, though at a distance, probably, of more than 30 miles. At thirteen miles, the road bending more N.W., is seen the village and mud castle of Meimun, at the foot of a steep mountain, and near it, a small vaulted

---

* The hollow part floats on the surface of the sherbet, like the punch-ladles formerly common in England, the long handle resting on the edge of the vessel; and the Persians drink out of these spoons, holding them near the bowl, as goblets are never introduced at dinner.

† This description may serve to illustrate the beauty of the simile, Psal. 1. 3. "He shall be like a tree planted by the water-courses."

edifice called *Kadem-gah-e-Khezr*, " the footstep of Khezr :" it is probably the tomb of a Moslem saint. At length, proceeding in a direction N.N.E., the traveller comes in sight of the great salt lake of Bakhtegan; so denominated from a village of that name, now in ruins, to the east of Kheir.

Kheir (or Kheireh, pronounced Kheil) is a small village, and near it are two or three clusters of mean houses with mud walls, and a few trees. It is the last village in this direction before entering upon the inhospitable desert which extends to within ten miles of Gawakoon, distant fifty miles. At about half-way is the ruined caravanserai of *Khan-e-Kerd*. The road lies in a W.N.W. direction, close to well-wooded hills on the left: on the right is the lake, covering the plain, which is bounded by mountains, and varies from eight or ten to fifteen or sixteen miles in width. At six miles from Kheir, a warm spring, slightly brackish, gushes from a rock under the mountains on the left, and forms a small stream that runs into the lake. Near the caravanserai, a few huts were occupied by some Eelauts, who informed the travellers, that the place was nearly abandoned, from dread of the wild beasts which haunt the wooded mountains, and of the flies which, every summer, destroyed many mules and horses. Multitudes of wasps. and horseflies seemed to attest the latter part of the statement; and the rubbish of the half-finished caravanserai, harbours snakes, scorpions, and lizards of beautiful and extraordinary colours. *   Near a small mud - built

---

* " They ventured sometimes to approach very near me, peeping with a most inquisitive look; but they seemed equally timid and active; for, on the least motion of the head, even the twinkling of an eye, they vanished among the stones and shrubs."....
" The quick-eyed lizard," Lord Byron, with his usual felicity of expression, describes it.—OUSELEY, vol. ii. p. 176.

Imám-zadeh, a fresh stream flows towards the lake, full of the largest and ugliest frogs that our Traveller had seen, and noisy in proportion. 'Within a mile of the caravanserai, was a *rahdari,* with a solitary guard·! The plain, which is partially encrusted with salt, now expands ; and the lake is, probably, at some seasons, five or six *farsangs* broad.* At seventeen or eighteen miles from the *Khan-e-Kerd,* where the salt lake ends, and vegetation begins, the traveller enters the once populous district of Kurbal. In a cemetery near two ruined villages, Sir W. Ouseley found some tomb-stones neatly carved with Arabic and Persian epitaphs. Here, the Bendemir falls into the lake, and the remainder of the stage to Gawakoon, lies along the left bank of the stream.

Gawakoon is an inconsiderable village. Three miles and a half beyond, the Bundemir is crossed by a long bridge, (the *Pul-i-Gawakan,*) where it suddenly falls seventeen or eighteen feet.† The route then lies over a level plain, intersected by numerous drains, in a direction still W.N.W., to the village of Bundemir ; a stage of five *farsangs.* During nearly the whole journey from Kheir, a distance of between seventy and eighty miles, the road had traversed a level country, bounded on each side by ranges of lofty mountains.

* Its variable limits may in part explain the discordant accounts given of its extent. It is denominated the lake of Bakhtegan by the old eastern geographers, but is now generally called, from the principal town in its vicinity, the *Derya-i-Niriz.* Its extent, according to Ebn Haukal, is 20 *farsangs* in length: another writer, cited by Sir W. Ouseley, makes it 12 *farsangs* in length, 7 in breadth, and nearly 35 in circuit. "It extends to the confines of Shakel (or Sahek) in Kerman. Adjacent are tracts of soil impregnated with salt." It appears to have been unknown to the Greek and Roman geographers.

† Here must be the *Bund-i-Kassar,* by which the Lower Kurbal was watered. See p. 5 of this volume.

From Bundemir, Sir W. Ouseley crossed the plain of Merdasht to the *Takht-i-Jemsheed,* a distance of three hours; and thence returned, in about nine hours and a half, to Shiraz.[*]

We must now resume our route to the northward, which was suspended at Persepolis, and conduct the reader

FROM SHIRAZ TO ISFAHAN.

THE direct road to Isfahan, which is practicable only in summer, leaving on the right the plain of Istakhr, runs to Fute-abad, " a miserable village," three *farsangs* from the *Takht;* and thence, through Mayen to Yezdikhaust, where it unites with the winter road. It is the latter which we are now to follow.

At Hadji-abad, the territory of Merdasht or Istakhr terminates, and we enter upon the district of Hafreg, containing twenty-one villages.[†] A few miles further, near the village of Seidoun, the rocky range terminates towards the east, and the road, bending to the left, follows the course of the Sewund branch of the Kur,[‡]

[*] Ouseley, vol. ii. ch. 8 and 9.

[†] According to Mirza Joon, the territory of Merdasht begins at one *farsang* from the *Pul-i-Khan,* and comprises twenty villages fallen to ruin, and thirty still inhabited. One of these is Kenáreh, one mile S. of the Takht, containing nearly 200 families. Another is Mirkhasgoon, near which Sir W. Ouseley passed in his way from Bundemir to the Takht.—OUSELEY, vol. ii. pp. 408, 187. Mr. Morier mentions a village called *Rish-mey-Joon,* as the residence of the governor of Merdasht, whose district, he says, contained seventeen villages.—*Second Residence,* p. 82.

[‡] " The river, which, through all its wanderings, generally bore the name of Kur-aub, and near whose banks we had so long shaped our course, at the point where the vale of Sewan (Sewund) expands into a plain, divides into two branches; one flowing through the country at the back of the Persepolitan hills : the other fills a rocky channel in the valley of Hadjee-abad, retaining its own celebrated title till it is lost in that of the Bund-emir."—PORTER, vol.

to the village from which it takes its name. The valley of Sewund is surrounded with rugged hills, and, like the plain of Merdasht, is covered with the liquorice-plant, of which the camel is very fond. The village of Sewund, distant about three *farsangs* from the *Takht*, is situated on an eminence at the foot of an abrupt part of the mountain, at some distance from the river. During the excessive heats of summer, when water becomes scarce, the inhabitants remove into the valley, and live in tents of black hair-cloth, or rude booths covered with furze and branches of trees, on the banks of the stream.* Snipes, ducks, herons, and bitterns frequent this part of the valley.

The next stage is to Kemeen, not long ago a flourishing village, but ruined by the extortions of the late governor. It is pleasantly situated amidst gardens and vineyards. Within one *farsang* of it are vestiges of an old mud-built edifice called the Red Tower (*Gumbez-i-Surkh*) supposed to be one of the seven villas or hunting-seats erected by Bahram Gour. Nothing, however, remains to indicate either its importance, beauty, or antiquity. Immediately opposite to it is a deep cavern, with two or three interior caves, whence issues a particularly translucent spring. It is called the Cave of the Forty Daughters ; and innu-

i. p. 512. The Sewund branch, according to Morier and Ouseley, is generally called the *Rood-khonéh Sewund*, and also the Falfar (Palwar). See p. 5 of this volume, and Ouseley, vol. ii. p. 421. In his way to Hadjee-abad, Sir Robert K. Porter passed the village of *Saied-abad* (perhaps Seidoun), in which seems to be preserved the name of a castle on the *Koh Ramgerd*, one *farsang* from Istakhr. See p. 87.

* " On coming near the village, we saw him (the governor) extended under a shed fast asleep on the ground, with a spear stuck at his bolster-head, which now, as in the days of Saul, marks the spot where a man of consequence reposes. 1 Sam. xxvi. 7."—Morier, vol. ii. p. 116.

merable old lamps still left in the place, give support
to the tradition, that it was formerly inhabited by a
succession of holy persons. Sir Robert K. Porter states,
that he crossed no fewer than *forty* beautiful little
rivulets in the pleasant little vale of Kemeen, all
bearing their tribute to the broader stream, which
winds among the deep hollows of the hills, collecting
on one side numerous mountain streams, while it is
drained in almost the same proportion, on the other,
by channels of irrigation.*

From the plain or valley of Kemeen, which is about
a *farsang* in width, a narrow pass of two miles, running eastward between two abrupt chains of mountains, leads into the plain of Moorgh-aub. Then,
turning suddenly northward, the road runs in that
direction about 14 miles to the village of Moorgh-aub ;
distant from Persepolis, according to Sir R. K. Porter,
" forty-nine measured English miles." Within two
miles of the village, the traveller's attention is arrested
by some remarkable ruins on the right, which mark
the site of some considerable city. The learned world
are indebted to Mr. Morier for the first suggestion
that these are the ruins of

* Porter, vol. I. pp. 484, 510.—There are two roads from Sewund
to Kemeen. That which was taken by the British Envoy, made
the distance (according to Sir W. Ouseley) 17 miles. Mr. Morier
mentions a shorter road " through the *Teng Parou,* a pass so narrow that it will not admit of the passage of a loaded mule." Sir
Robert K. Porter, in travelling to Shiraz, passed through Kemine,
and halted at " a cluster of fortified houses," called *Buchun,* at the
southern side of the vale, 4 *farsangs* from Mourg-aub. The next
day, a stage of 4 *farsangs* brought him to *Sewan-pa-ine.* An hour
further up the valley, S. 45° E., is *Sewan-bala,* a village most
romantically seated among the rocky promontories. The former
must be the Sewund of Morier, and the Sivend of Ouseley.

PASARGADÆ.

" PROCEEDING over the ploughed fields," says this Traveller, " which nearly overspread the whole of this plain, I came to the bed of a river (lying N. and S.), and, on its banks, a village called *Meshed Omoun.* There is here a fort, and a few low houses, in which females only were left, as all the men had gone out to greet the Envoy. About a mile further are situated the collective ruins, called by the people of the country, *Mesjed Madré Sulieman,* the Tomb of the Mother of Solomon. The first object is a pillar erect, a plain shaft, without a capital, 10 feet 5 inches in circumference. Near it are three pilasters, the fronts of which are excavated in deep niches, and the sides inscribed with (cuneiform) characters. From the pieces of masonry around, the pilasters appear to have enclosed a hall, the interior of which was decorated with columns. But I resigned the hope of ascertaining the plan of its original form, when I saw two similar masses ; one at the distance of 150 yards, with a corresponding inscription ; and the intermediate space, and indeed the whole plain, strewed with the fragments of marbles.

" Having sketched these objects, I continued my way along the plain to the west, towards two buildings, which at a distance appeared scarcely worthy of notice, but, on a nearer inspection, proved full of interest. The first is a ruined building of Mohammedan construction, which is now turned into a caravanserai. The door was once arched, and on the architrave are the remains of a fine Arabic inscription. The other is a building of an extraordinary form. It rests upon a square base of large blocks of marble, which rise in seven layers pyramidically. It is in form a parallelogram : the lowest range of the foundation is 43 feet by 37 ; and the edifice itself, which crowns the summit, diminishes to 21 feet by 16 feet 5 inches. It is covered with a shelving roof, built of the same massy stone as its base and sides, which are all fixed together by clamps of iron. Through a fissure in the door, I could perceive nothing within but a small chamber blackened by smoke. Around it, besides a great profusion of broken marbles, are the shafts of fourteen columns, once perhaps a colonnade, but now arranged in the square wall of mud which surrounds the whole remains. To the present day, all the space within the enclosure is a place of burial, and is covered indeed with modern tomb-stones. On every part of the monument itself are carved inscriptions which attest the reverence of its visiters ; but there is no vestige of any of the characters of ancient Persia, or even of the older Arabic. The key is kept by women, and none but females are permitted to enter.....*If the position of the place had corresponded to the site of Passagardæ, as well as the form of this structure accords with the description of the tomb of Cyrus near that city, I should have been tempted to assign to the present building so illustrious an origin.* That tomb was raised in a grove; it was a small edifice covered with an arched roof of stone; and its entrance was so narrow, that the slenderest man could scarcely pass through : it rested on a quadrangular base of a single stone, and contained the celebrated inscription : ' O mortals, I am Cyrus, son of Cambyses, founder of the Persian monarchy, and sovereign of Asia : grudge me not therefore this monument.' That the plain around *Mesjed Madré Sulieman* was the site of a great city, is proved by the ruins with which it is strewed; and that this city was of the same general antiquity as Persepolis, may be inferred from the existence of a similar character in the inscriptions on the remains of both; though this particular edifice does not happen to display that internal evidence of a contemporaneous date. A grove would naturally have disappeared in modern Persia; the structures correspond in size; the triangular roof might be called arched, in an age when the true semi-circular arch was probably unknown;... and in the lapse of 2400 years, the absence of an inscription would not be a decisive evidence against its identity with the Tomb of Cyrus." [*]

In his Second Journey through Persia, the Author contrived to force the narrow door, and to gain an entrance into the tomb, unseen by his guides. " On the side facing the *kebleh*," he says, " the wall is sculptured with ornaments surrounding an Arabic inscription; and in a corner, we found a collection of dusty manuscripts, mostly transcripts of the Koran, besides a number of little offerings of tin lamps, &c., which are generally seen in the religious places of the Mussulmans. The body of the saint, we were told, is deposited within the roof of the building." [†]

This discovery of an Arabic inscription, supposing it to be coeval with the structure, would be fatal to the conjecture which assigns it a high antiquity. Mandelslo, who travelled in the seventeenth century, speaking of this sepulchre, which he describes as a little chapel of white marble upon a high square of free-stone work, adds : " Upon the wall of the chapel there are yet to be seen, in Arabian characters, these words, *Mader Sulieman.* The inhabitants say, that Solomon's mother was interred there; but the Car-

---

[*] Morier, vol. I. pp. 143—6.   [†] Ibid. vol. ii. p. 117.

melite Friars of Shiraz, with more likelihood of truth,
told me, that it was the sepulchre of Wallada, the mother of Soliman, the fourteenth khalif of the posterity
of Aly." This extraordinary piece of information
does not, however, appear to be sanctioned by any
native writer, and was probably a random conjecture.
All the various edifices which bear the strange title
of the temple, tomb, or throne of Solomon's mother,
cannot have been intended as monuments to the
memory of the khalif's mother; nor is there the
slightest reason to suppose that the old lady's body
was ever transported from Kufah or Damascus into
the heart of Persia. Two native writers cited by Sir
W. Ouseley, one of whom ranks high both as an
historical and a geographical authority, adopt the
vague popular tradition which ascribes this monument
to Bathsheba. The one referred to could scarcely have
been ignorant of its real founder, had either the annals
which he examined, or any inscriptions on the tomb or
the adjoining caravanserai, assigned it to a prince of the
Fatimite dynasty.* The other writer (Hafiz Abru),
having described the *Takht-i-Jemsheed*, adds: "There
is likewise another place in the district of Istakhr, on
the road to Aberkúh, called the *Meshehd-i-Mader-i-
Sulieman*, on whom be peace! Here also are stones of
considerable size, and sculptured in a wonderful manner; the work, as it is related, of those *jins* (genii)
who were subservient to Solomon, on whom be
peace!"

* Ouseley, vol. ii. pp. 432—8. Hamdallah Mastowfi, the writer
cited, does not appear, however, to have entered the tomb; since,
after citing from the *Fars Nameh* (a scarce work of the twelfth
century), the declaration that no person can enter or look into it,
from the apprehension of being punished with blindness, he adds:
" But I never discovered that any one had ventured to make the
experiment or ascertained the fact."

Both these writers speak of the tomb in question as being near the meadows of *Cálán*, but make no reference to the other ruins, or to the city of which they are the vestiges. That many of these are of high antiquity, is unquestionable ; and an inscription in the cuneiform character, copied by Sir Robert Ker Porter, which occurs on almost all the pillars at this place, seems to place it beyond doubt, that this is the actual site of the ancient Cyropolis or Pasargadæ. Professor Grottefund gives it the following translation : " *Dominus Cyrus rex orbis rector.*" If this translation may be depended upon, we may safely assume, that the *mesjed*, to whatsoever use it may subsequently have been appropriated, once contained, or covered, the remains of that great monarch, whom Mohammedan tradition has confounded with the Son of David,[*] and who is doubtless the true Jemsheed of the Persian legend.

Sir Robert K. Porter, who deserves great praise for his unwearied assiduity, devoted two days to the examination of these ruins ; and we are indebted to his pen and pencil for the most minute and accurate description of the tomb. " This interesting monument," he says, " stands on an eminence not far from the foot of the hills that bound the plain to the S.W. A wide area, marked outwardly by the broken shafts of twenty-four circular columns, surrounds the building. Each column is 3 feet 3 inches in diameter ; and they are distant from each other, 14 feet. Seventeen columns are still erect, but heaped round with rubbish, and barbarously connected with a wall of

* Sir Robert K. Porter suggests, that, possibly, " some palace or village, or even the grave of Mandane, the mother of Cyrus, might have distinguished this city ; and to the memory of her name may have succeeded the legend of the mother of Solomon. ,

mud. Within this area stands the tomb. The great base on which it rests, is composed of immense blocks of the most beautiful white marble, rising in steps: at the bottom of the lowest step, two sides of the base measure 40 feet; the other two sides, 44 feet.* A succession of gigantic steps completes, in a beautiful pyramidal shape, the pedestal of this royal tomb, majestic in its simplicity and vastness. At the base of the lowest step, a sort of skirting-stone runs round the foundation, almost even with the ground, and not striking very deep into it below; probably to what was the ancient level of the earth....The door opens into the north-western side of the tomb, the whole width of the side being 16 feet 10 inches, of which measurement the entrance occupies 2 feet 10 inches. The height of the door was exactly 4 feet. Four layers of stones composed the elevation of this superstructure: the first gave the sides of the entrance; the second served as its lintel; the third presented a simple projecting cornice; and what may be called the fourth, formed its pediment and sloping roof. Just over the door are two parallel ledges, which I should suppose held an inscription. When I entered, I found the thickness of the walls to consist of one solid single mass of stone, measuring 5 feet from the outside to within. The chamber is 7 feet wide, 10 long, and 8 in height. The floor is composed of two immense slabs, joined nearly in the middle of the chamber. Immediately opposite the door, both the floor and the wall are much injured; the marble surfaces are cruelly broken; and in the

---

* The steps are of irregular height: the first rises 5 feet 6 inches; the second, 3 feet 6 inches, receding 2 feet; the third, 3 feet 4 inches; the fourth, 1 foot 11 inches; the fifth and sixth, 1 foot 10 inches, and of the same breadth. Sir Robert's measurements slightly differ from those of Mr. Morier.

floor particularly, deep holes are left, which plainly
shew where large iron fastenings have been forcibly
torn away.   Doubtless,   their corresponding points
attached some other mass to this quarter of the building, similar depredation being marked in the marble
of the wall.   I searched every where for some trace
of a cuneiform inscription, but in vain.   The place
where such a one is most likely to have been, is on
the right of the entrance, where it has probably been
obliterated to make room for the present open scroll in
the Saracenic taste.   It is composed of a' narrow
border, thickly ornamented with flowers; and interwoven with this intricate line of work, there are
certainly Arabic characters, which, I do not doubt,
form the inscription that has been read *Mader-i-Su-
lieman*.   The lines containing this border, extend along
the whole of that side of the wall......Not a scratch of
any other kind, save the cruel dents from the hammers
of the barbarians, interrupts the even polish of the
other three sides.   The roof is flat, and nearly black ; so
are all the sides of the chamber, excepting that which
faces the door ; and that, with the floor, is perfectly
white.   Man has done all towards the mutilation of
this monument, which, from the simplicity of its form
and the solidity of its fabric, seemed calculated to
withstand the accidents of nature till the last shock."

According to Arrian, who wrote from the testimony of one who had visited the spot, the tomb of
Cyrus was within the royal paradise of Pasargadæ.
The basis of the tomb was of a quadrangular shape ;
above, was a small edifice of stone with an arched
roof; within was the golden coffin of Cyrus, over
which was a canopy with pillars of gold, and the
whole was hung round with purple hangings and
Babylonian carpets.   In the same inclosure was a

small house built for the magi, to whose care the
tomb had been originally entrusted by Cambyses, the
son of Cyrus, and the charge was transmitted from
fathers to sons.* The holes in the floor and at the
upper end of the chamber, are just in the positions,
Sir R. K. Porter says, to admit the iron fastenings of
the golden coffin. Had it been cased in a stone sarcophagus, he remarks, doubtless that would have remained; and the absence of any coffin makes against
the supposition that it has been used as a burial-
place for any moslem. With regard to its situation,
the paradises of the ancient kings of Persia, like those
of the Sefi monarchs at Isfahan, were spacious gardens, or rather parks, adjoining their palaces; and
the fertile and well-watered plain amply warrants the
supposition, that this monument was once surrounded
with a grove and garden. In what is now called the
Caravanserai, distant about 200 yards to the northward, he supposes that we may recognise the house of
the attendant magi, the guardians of the sepulchre.
The Saracenic porch and inscription shew that it has

---

* Arrian, b. vi. c. 29. (Rooke's Transl. ii. 122.) There is some
obscurity in the account. The golden coffin is stated to have lain
upon a bed: if that was the case, it could not have been fastened
to the floor in the manner supposed. A canopy is perhaps intended. Cyrus is represented to have been interred in his royal
robes of Babylonian workmanship, a chain round his neck, with
bracelets, ear-rings, and a sword, all of gold, adorned with precious
stones. A costly table was also placed in the tomb. When Alexander came, all was gone except the bed and coffin. The
latter had been stripped of its cover, and the body cast out; the
robbers had also endeavoured to break it to pieces, but were forced
to leave it behind. Aristobulus was directed by Alexander to re-
store the monument; to replace in the coffin the parts of the royal
body which still remained; to provide a fresh cover for the coffin,
and new ornaments to the bed; and to have the entrance into the
little edifice walled up with stone, and the royal signet applied.
The latter part of the commission would seem not to have been
executed.

been applied to the use indicated by its present appellation, in times much later than its origin; but on examining the lower part of the building, the same style of architecture is discernible as that of the tomb. It is a quadrangle of about 60 or 80 feet. A great gate appears to have opened into it from the S. E. A range of small dark chambers, even with the ground, run along the four sides of the square, each having its door, scarcely 4 feet high, opening into the quadrangle.[*]

At the distance of about a mile N. E. of the Caravanserai, is found an immense mound or terrace, from which rises a square marble pillar 15 feet high. The elevation is a parallelogram 150 feet by 81, and is divided by two rows of pedestals of irregular dimensions, all of the dark rock of the country, except the third in the range to the N. E.: this is of white marble, and being larger and higher than the rest, has, perhaps, sustained a shaft or statue. There appear to have been two entrances, facing the N. E. and S. W. At about 6 feet from the N. E. front, rises the square column, which appears perfectly distinct from all the others; it is formed of a single block, and, on examining it, Sir Robert was delighted at discovering a bas-relief occupying nearly the whole of the side fronting the N. W., and surmounted with the same inscription in the arrow-head character that is found on the other marbles. The sculpture consists of a full-length figure, in profile, clad in a long, close-fitting robe, trimmed with a border of roses and a waving fringe, beautifully carved. The face is much broken, but shews a short bushy beard, curled with the greatest

---

[*] Sir W. Ouseley supposes the Caravanserai to be not above 600 years old, but adds: " I suspect that the more ancient ruins have contributed materials towards its construction."

regularity: on the head is a close cap or helmet, coming down almost to the neck, and from it issues a very singular ornament, doubtless of an emblematical import.* From the shoulders issue four large spreading wings; two extend upwards above the head; the others, opening downward, nearly touch the feet. The chiselling of the feathers is exquisite. The figure, from head to foot, measures 7 feet, and stands upon a pedestal 2 feet high and 5 feet wide. It faces the terrace; the hand is uplifted and open, as if in the act of benediction; and this writer supposes it to represent the tutelary genius of the country, wings being the peculiar symbol of ministering spirits.†

Half a mile to the N.W. of this elevation is a low mound, to which the inhabitants of the plain have given the name of the Court of the *Deevs.* It bears evident marks of having formerly been ascended by steps. From the centre rises a perfectly round column, between 30 and 40 feet high, and measuring 10 feet in circumference: it is composed of four blocks of polished marble, the lower one comprising half the height of the whole. As no fragment of a capital is discernible, it has probably been higher. The base is totally buried in the surrounding rubbish. A spacious marble platform supports the column, the square area of which is marked by four pillars, distant from each other 108 feet. Those that denote the N.W. face of the building, are not much dilapidated, but

* Sir Robert calls it a horned mitre, and the lower part of the ornament has certainly the appearance of branching horns, supporting some sort of crown. A very similar head-dress occurs on some of the bas-reliefs in the great temple at Philæ.

† The figure strongly reminded Sir Robert of the descriptions of the cherubim and seraphim in the Old Testament, more especially, Exod. xxv. 18—20; 1 Kings vi. 23—9; and Isa. vi. 1, 2.

the ruinous state of the place alone shewed where the
opposite ones had been, by baring their foundations.
The most northern of the pair in the best preservation,
is composed of three stones surmounted with a sort of
cornice, the whole being 15 feet in height. The three
stones are all concave on the side facing the N.E.: on
the contrary side, is an inscription near the top, corresponding exactly to that found on various parts of
these ruins. The other column is much broken,
there being only two blocks remaining: its inscription
faces the other, looking N.E. A third mass of
marble, in a yet more mutilated state, stands 30 feet
in front of these, dividing exactly the middle of the
face of the square: its inscription is on the N.W. side.
Sir R. K. Porter searched in vain for the trace of a
wall that might have connected the corner pillars.
" Hence," he says, " I conjecture the place to have
been completely open to the air; and, from the lofti-
ness of the centre column, it seems hardly possible for
it to have had a roof. In viewing the plain from the
elevation of this mound, it appeared one rich velvet
of vegetation, without the interruption of the smallest
unproductive spot, rendered barren by the fallen
rubbish of any decayed stone buildings. I mention
this as an extraordinary peculiarity, that, among so
many fine ruins, there should be no trace of minor
ones between."

Rather more than a quarter of a mile further N.W.,
rises a solitary square pillar, consisting of two stones,
12 and 8 feet high, surmounted with some broken
work like a ledge. The faces of the column are nearly
4 feet wide. In the western face, the stones are
hollowed into deep niches; the other three sides are
beautifully smooth, and on that to the north is a short
inscription of four lines in the arrow-head character,

clear and sharp, and perfectly uninjured. Due north
of this, at the distance of a quarter of a mile, is a
square tower-like building, supposed· to be an ancient
fire-temple. It is built of immense blocks of marble ;
but the extent of the edifice does not seem proportioned to the magnitude of the component parts, each
face measuring not more than 9 feet in width, and its
height appeared· under 50 feet, there being fourteen
layers of stones, each measuring 3½ feet. · Something
like a door marks the north-west front, and the remains of a projecting cornice finishes the top. It bears
a general resemblance to the fire-temple at' Nakshi
Roustam ; only the latter is higher and narrower, but
the blocks are of the same width.*

At the distance of a quarter of a mile N.E. of this
structure, and not far from the road to Mourgaub, is
what appears to have been the grandest elevation : to
this, the natives have given the name of the *Takht-
i-Sulieman*, which we might almost venture to
translate, the seat of Cyrus. What now remains, is
an elevated terrace or platform of hewn stones, raised·
nearly to a level with the summit of a rocky hill
against which it is built. The materials are of white
marble, put together with exquisite nicety, the blocks
being carefully " clamped " to each other on their
horizontal surface, and beautifully chiselled. The
great front, looking N.W., measures about 300 feet
in length, and 38 feet 6 inches in height, being formed
of fourteen layers of blocks 2 feet 9 inches thick, but
varying in length and breadth. The sides of the plat-

* This is the building which Sir W. Ouseley's rustic guides
called *Zindan-i-Sulieman* (Solomon's Prison), and which, he says,
" was once exactly like the square edifice at Nakshi Roustam."
Mr. Morier also remarked its exact correspondence, " in dimensions, structure, and ornament," to that fire-temple. See p. 81,

form, from the front to where they touch the hill, measure 298 feet. At the distance of 72 feet from the front, they form a deep recess. This casing has been filled up at the top, so as to form a level area, with pieces of the native rock, a dark limestone. The marble must have been brought from a distance; and on each block, Sir R. K. Porter remarked a peculiar figure, near one of the corners, which he supposes to have been intended to guide the mason in placing them.* This platform, as well as all the other buildings, has suffered much from the rapacity of depredators, who have torn away the masonry to obtain the iron by which it was bound. Wherever this was effected, large holes are left, which the present inhabitants, attribute to the footsteps of *deevs*. The top of the platform is strewed with fragments of rock from the hill, and is very much sunk in the centre. This Traveller was unable to discover any marble fragments or any traces of either columns or other superstructure. From its position among the heights, and its accessibility on all sides, the idea of its having been a place of strength, he says, is untenable; and on no point of the adjacent cliffs are there any vestiges of fortification. "The hill unquestionably commands the entrance to the plain of Mourgaub, but the strong natural barriers which the mountains present to the south and the north, rendered additional walls unnecessary.†......

* Mr. Morier says: "The stones are cut into regular squares, with an *alto-relief* upon each; and at the section of the lines which connect the stones, are holes, cut at regular intervals, the purposes of which we could not divine. They might, however, lead to the conjecture, that these walls, like those at Ecbatana, were ornamented with plates of metal."—MORIER, vol. ii. p. 119.

† The author supposes this to be nevertheless the spot which Pliny calls the Castle of Pasargadæ, and which was occupied by the magi. But the tomb of Cyrus was *within* that castle. (Plin. vi. 26.)

Why may we not consider this immense platform as the spot on which the altar, priests, and royal party stood, during the ceremonies of their religious convocation ? " *

Sir W. Ouseley thinks, that " the terrace may have supported a wooden fabric, or a pavilion, capable of containing the king sitting in state upon his throne. From such a situation, the monarch would be conspicuous to multitudes of vassals and troops assembled on the subjacent plain, to behold his splendour during the *Nouroos* or other ancient festivals." Had the terrace been intended to support any permanent fabric, there would, probably, be found traces of some reservoir or aqueduct to supply the palace or fort with water, as at Persepolis. When it is considered, that Cyrus was a warrior, accustomed to live in camps ; that it is still the custom in this country, to desert, during the heats of summer, the walled town for the tented plain ; and that the throne of the present Shah is not unfrequently set up in a moveable pavilion ; it will appear, we think, no improbable supposition, that the original design of both the *Takht-i-Jemsheed* and the *Takht-i-Sulieman*, was merely to serve as a stage or platform for the pavilion which inclosed the royal throne. The halls of *Chehel-Minar* were the work of after-times. At Mourghaub, no palace appears to have risen upon the spot consecrated by the recollections of the illustrious monarch who here held his state ; no sculpture commemorates the scene. The reason is obvious. Pasargadæ does not appear ever to have been a royal residence. In these plains, Cyrus

He may be right, however, in supposing that Pasargadæ was a holy city consecrated to the colleges of the magi, rather than a capital, or the seat of empire.

* Porter, i. pp. 485—508.

encamped, and here he founded a city; but the Persian capital was Persepolis, and the royal residence of his successors was transferred according to the season, at Persepolis, Susa, Babylon, and Ecbatana. There they had their palaces, as the Pharaohs of Egypt had theirs at Memphis, Sais, or Taphaanes; but of those structures, no more trace remains, than was left by the summer pavilion on the shifting, sandy plain. The tomb and the pyramid remain, the durable land-marks of history, and the speaking moral of the scene.*

Mourghaub † is described by Mr. Morier as a large and pleasant village, with a fort and many inclosed gardens: near it are springs of fine water which irrigate the whole plain. The surrounding hills were covered with vines, and the village itself had an appearance of renovation, surprising to a traveller accustomed to the aspect of ruin and decay which characterises Persian scenery. Its walls had been repaired, and new houses here and there rose conspicuous. The district had, for nearly 600 years, been in the possession of a family of Arabian origin, whose chief, Aga Khan, still maintained himself in his

---

* With regard to the identity of Mourg-aub and Pasagadæ, Sir Robert K. Porter remarks, that the latter was in the vicinity of the Kúr or Cyrus; that, according to Pliny, it was to the east of Persepolis, and Mourg-aub is much to the N.E. of the plain of Merdasht; that, *after* Alexander had taken possession of the capital, the city of Cyrus fell into his hands; yet, in his subsequent march to Ecbatana, in pursuit of Darius, he passed through Pasargadæ, which must therefore have been northward of Persepolis. These circumstances, taken in connexion with the inscriptions, seem to be decisive of the true situation of the city of Cyrus.

† *Margh*, Sir W. Ouseley informs us, denotes in Persian, the verdant herbage with which the plain is covered; hence, *margh-zar* signifies pasture-land. This word, pronounced *moorgh* and compounded with *ab*, water, gives the name of the village. But the plain itself bore, in the thirteenth century, the name of Cálás. Mourghaub is also the name of a river and district in Khorasan.

government. To this circumstance, and to the superiority of the Arab character over the Persian, this Traveller is disposed to attribute the comparative prosperity of the district. In the neighbourhood of Moorgaub are lead mines ; and the son of the Aga informed Mr. Morier, that a *maun* (7½ lbs.) of the ore was worth 20 *abassees* (about 8*s*). Mourgaub is about five miles from the ruins. Several other villages are scattered round the plain, which, when Sir R. K. Porter travelled, was " in the most fruitful cultivation." *

A very bad road, with three rough *kutels* or mountain passes, leads from Moorgaub to Ghazioon, a distance of about twenty miles. At twelve or thirteen miles, the route crosses the river *Beni Arus.* Near Ghazioon are remains of another mud-built " Red Tower," ascribed to Bahram Gour.† Ghazioon is in the *boolook* of Kongouri, which contains thirteen villages. The temperature here is sensibly cooler, and indicates a much more elevated region. A mountain called the *Koh Kasr Yakoub,* is to be seen from the village, on which are said to be many ruins, but Mr. Morier supposes them to be only Mohammedan. Another mountain, called the *Koh Khourgoon* from a village of that name, rises above all the rest, its summit being composed of a number of small conical hills.

The next day's stage (following Sir G. Ouseley's route) is to Deloonazer, situated also in the cold region, distant fifteen miles N.W. Not quite half way is the village of Kishlook, watered by a little

* On his way, this Traveller started a serpent 5 feet long, its head extremely small, the thickest part of the body about the diameter of a gun-barrel ; the colour of the belly, a pale yellow ; the back, black, with bright green stripes. He saw, also, several tortoises.

† His yellow villa (*Kiushk-i-Zard*) is seen in the neighbourhood of Asepás ; and his Green Tower is between Shiraz and Zargoon. See p. 3.

brook of good water, and surrounded with some culti-vated spots; * and at no great distance, an extensive burying ground, with three lofty domed tombs, indi-cates that a considerable town once stood in this neighbourhood. Near Deloonazer is a stone gateway, which the peasants declared to be thousands of years old; but Sir W. Ouseley believes it to be part of a modern edifice.

The plain in which this village stands, is of great extent. On leaving it, the route led next day through a succession of mountain dells, each with its stream, terminating in a rugged and formidable defile called *Teng-Asseri*, which opens into the plain of Ekleed. For the last three hours of the stage, the road lies between immense mountains of granite and marble; and after the constantly sterile appearance of this tract, the contrast is most striking which is presented by the rich landscape that Ekleed affords. From a thick wood of walnut, plane, willow, poplar, pinaster, and various fruit-trees, rise, in very picturesque forms, the towers of four different forts. On entering the town, Mr. Morier says, " we were as much surprised as delighted to observe trees of great size spreading their branches into the most beautiful forms, and giving shade to delicious spots, watered by clear rivu-lets that flow in all directions. The principal stream takes its rise at about a mile to the S.W. of the inha-bited part of the wood, and issues in a considerable

* From Ghazloon to Kishlook, the road lies through a long, narrow hollow in the plain, which extends nearly to Deloonazer; it affords good arable and pasture land; the surrounding plain is arid and sandy. Mr. Morier noticed here several curious birds, particularly one which abounds throughout the northern provinces, called in Turkish *bokara-kara*, in Persian *siah-sineh*, both meaning black-breast. They fly in flocks, and are good eating. See the description in Morier, ii. p. 121.

volume at once from under a rock overshadowed with trees. It is full of fish, and its existence is attributed to a miracle worked by their prophet. The whole spot, fishes and all, are regarded as sacred; for, without it, indeed, Ekleed would be a desert. This place, as well as Ghazioun and Deloonazer, are under the government of the same Arabian family that rules Moorgaub."[*] The distance from the last *munzél* was twenty-eight miles.

Ekleed (pronounced Keleel) contains a mosque, a caravanserai, and public baths, and is ranked by the native geographers among the chief towns of Fars, being the head town of a district comprehending ten or eleven dependent territories. Of these, the principal is Surmeh, once a flourishing town, but now reduced to a collection of huts within a square mud fort, surrounded by ruins indicating its original extent. Its name is remarkable as being the same as that of the *collyrium* used for tinging the eye-lids; but, whether the *surmeh* is found in the neighbourhood, we are not informed. To the northward of the fort are remains of an old castle, surrounded with a ditch, and containing a number of vaulted chambers and subterranean inlets. It is ascribed to King Bahram, but Mr. Morier believes it to be of later date.[†]

[*] Morier, vol. ii. p. 122. The spring is named *Chushmch-i-Peighamber*, Prophet's Fountain.

[†] Morier, vol. i. p. 150. The Author passed through this place in his first journey. From Moorghaub, he proceeded over the hills nine miles, to the caravanserai of *Khoneh Kergaun*, near which is a bridge over a river running west; and thence, sixteen miles further, to the caravanserai of *Deibeed;* performing the twenty-five miles in seven hours and a half. The country is bleak, naked, and arid; and in winter, the snows have sometimes impeded the progress of travellers for forty days together. Near Deibeed (*Deyh-i-bíd*, the village of willows), is an artificial mound, covered with foundations of what was once, probably, its castle.

The next day's stage was to Abadah, distant five *farsangs* (eighteen miles and a half). This must once have been a considerable place, as the plain, for several miles in its vicinity, is covered with walls, vestiges of gardens, and ruins of mud-built houses. The present population is all enclosed within a square fort. It is surrounded with gardens, from which some good fruit is sent to Shiraz; but water is scarce, the irrigation being carried on by *kanauts*.* From this place to Shurgestoon, the next stage, a distance of twenty miles and a half, the road continues good, running over a plain, bounded on each side by barren, insulated mountains, which rise abruptly in the most extraordinary forms. The little fort, mosque, and caravanserai of Shurgestoon (Shoolghestán) are seen six miles before they are reached. The plain is of gravel lightly mixed with earth, producing nothing but thistles and soap-wort: near the village, which is supplied with water by *kanauts*, there are some signs of cultivation. The road continues over the same gravelly soil till within two miles of Yezdikhaust, the

(See Ouseley, vol. ii. p. 443, *note*). The next day, Mr. Morier travelled fourteen miles to the caravanserai of *Khoneh Khorreh*. From this place, it is a stage of six *farsangs* (N. 40° W.) or five hours forty minutes, to Surmeh; a fine hard road leading to it along the right extremity of a plain. The next day, the road and bearing being similar, this Traveller, in four hours, reached Abadah. In this depopulated region, the immediate cause of devastation is said to have been, the long wars between the Zund and the Kujur families, of which it was the scene.

* Abadah is watered by the Kour, or, as Sir W. Ouseley says it is there called, the Pulvar. About a mile to the westward is Kooshkat, which Sir Robert K. Porter made his halting place instead of Abadah. He describes it as " an extensive village with a small fortress in the centre, round which the low flat-roofed houses cluster within an outward line of embattled walls. Gardens surround it, and umbrageous trees; and an abundant supply of delicious water flows through every street."

next stage; distance nearly 21 miles. The mouh-
tains gradually dwindle to hills, seeming to form a
termination to this long plain, by throwing themselves
in lessening forms across it. They continue barren,
brown, and inhospitable, without a shrub to enliven
their rugged masses. The situation of Yezdikhaust
is very singular, and its appearance is thus described
by Mr. Morier.

" We could perceive the town of Yezdikhaust a
long time before we reached it, and supposed, therefore, that it was situated at the foot of the eastern
hills, on the same plain as that on which we were
travelling. Our surprise was of course excited, to find
ourselves on a sudden stopped by a precipice in our
route. From its brow, we overlooked a small plain
beautifully watered by a variety of streams, and par-
celled out in every direction into cultivated fields and
gardens. The country which we had crossed, was
unbroken by the labours of the ploughman : here, his
industry was displayed, and richly rewarded. We
had seen scarcely one scanty rill : here, water mean-
dered in profusion. And though this little spot was
now stripped of its verdure, and chilled by the gloom
of winter, the contrast between cultivation and a
desert was still striking and cheerful. This valley is
like a large trench excavated in the plain. It is five
miles long from E. to W., and about 300 yards broad
in the line where we crossed, but the breadth is un-
equal. At the eastern extremity, on the brink of the
precipice, hangs the town of Yezdikhaust. Its situation is most fantastical ; and its mean and ill-defined
houses appear at first sight to belong to the rocks on
which they rise, and which, in varied and extravagant
masses, surround the valley. The substance of the
rock is soft. Beneath it is a caravanserai, an elegant

building, erected nearly 200 years ago by a pious queen of the Sefi race. It is still in good repair. On the verge of the precipice is a small mosque built by the same queen, and, around it, a burial place. To the east,[*] over a rude draw-bridge, is the entrance to the town, which, without the use of cannon, seems almost impregnable. It is there an isolated rock, connected with the others around only by this bridge."[†]

The rock upon which the town is built, is a conglomerate, consisting of rounded pebbles of quartz, serpentine, and limestone, united by a calcareous cement. The surrounding soil seems impregnated with iron. At the foot of the rock are an immense number of subterranean chambers excavated in the side of the cliff.[‡] The valley or ravine which it overlooks, has all the appearance, Mr. Fraser says, of having once been the bed of a mighty river. He estimates its depth at 150 feet, and its breadth at 200

---

[*] "The approach is inaccessible, except by a draw-bridge at the *north-west* side, which is thrown over a deep ditch, and allows communication between the place and the valley. The rock on which it stands, is perpendicular on all its faces, presenting a very grand object, surmounted with this embattled town."—PORTER, vol. i. p. 456.

[†] Morier, vol. i. p. 153.

[‡] Alexander, p. 144. Colonel Johnson says: "There are caverns in the rocks, 60 feet below the houses of the fort, inhabited by many families; among them are several shops. Along the rocky sides of the valley, to the distance of half a mile from the fortified village, there are similar caverns: they were doubtless originally intended for burial-places. The rocks here are all amygdaloidal, and composed of stones and gravel indurated into one mass of various colours, blue, red, yellow, and white: some of the more compact parts are of a bluish tint, and apparently limestone; they are traversed by ramifications of a milk-white substance, of nearly the same degree of hardness. Tombstones are made of this substance, which, if polished, would appear like marble."—JOHNSON, p. 92.

yards. "I learned," he adds, " that the road to Yezd lies for three days in the same hollow, running eastward ; and that it can be traced for a great way further in the same direction across the salt desert. A ravine thus cut in the alluvial soil of a great valley, certainly suggests the agency of water ; yet, at present, although a petty rill does run in a smaller hollow in its bottom, it is so far from being equal to a work like this, or even to overflow its banks in the time of floods, that the cultivation of the village is entirely in the bottom of the great ravine. I was informed of a tradition which exists in the country, that a great river, navigable for boats, once did occupy this ravine, taking its rise in the Buktiaree mountains, and running eastward till it joins the lesser Jeyhoon. Like all traditional stories of the sort, it is connected with miraculous agency : in this case, Solomon and the *deevs* are pressed into the service. It is, however, of some interest, for appearances strongly support the idea, that this was once the channel of a river." [*]

Yezdikhaust (Yezid Khaust) is situated in lat. 31° 31' 4" N., long. 52° 17' 24" E. It may be considered as the frontier town of Fars, although the actual boundary between Fars and Irak is some miles further northward.[‡] Before the Affghan conquest, it was a

---

[*] Fraser's Khorasan, p. 117. How, in a course not exceeding 70 or 80 miles at most, the supposed river could have attained a size navigable for boats, which no other Persian river can boast of, the Writer admits to be a difficulty; but the subject merits attention.

[†] Most travellers have represented this ravine as the boundary or " valley of division;" but Hamdallah, the Persian Geographer, describes Yezdikhaust as belonging to the *Sardsir* (cold region) of Fars; and the Isfahan government begins at Muksood-beggee, 24 miles further N., the boundary line being nearly intermediate.— See OUSELEY, vol. ii. pp. 451, 2.

place of some consequence, but it has never recovered from the effects of the devastation spread by those barbarians. The houses are generally of three stories, with small staircases and galleries. There is here an ancient church, in which is preserved a round piece of marble resembling the sun, which had been an emblem worshipped by the Sabians. In the extensive burial-grounds in the vicinity of the town, are many sepulchres on which are sculptured a lion and a sword, denoting them to be the graves of *puhilwans* or heroes. The bread of Yezdikhaust has obtained a proverbial celebrity among the most excellent productions of Persia. It is a common saying: " *Shiráb e Shiraz; noon e Yezdekhást; zan e Yezd:*" wine of Shiraz; bread of Yezdikhaust; women of Yezd.*

The summer road from Shiraz to Yezdikhaust was followed by Sir Robert Ker Porter in returning to Isfahan; it is described also by Mr. Fraser and Lieut. Alexander. The first stage, as has already been mentioned, is to the village of Futeabad; a distance of 5 *farsangs*. The next stage, between 6 and 7 *farsangs*, leads to Mayan, a considerable town. The road, at first, lies W.N.W., and, at six miles, enters a narrow valley running W. for two miles, at the end of which the Bundemir is crossed by a noble stone bridge of

* Ouseley, vol. ii. p. 450. Alexander, p. 145. A horrible tragedy was acted at Yezdikhaust in 1779. Zuckee Khan, who seized the government on the death of Kurreem Khan, (see vol. i. p. 214,) entered this place in his march to Isfahan, and demanded a large sum of money of the magistrates. On their declaring their inability to comply with his demand, he ordered twenty of the principal inhabitants to be thrown down the precipice. One of the wretched victims survived, and was living in 1818. (Porter, vol. ii. pp. 26—30.) On his proceeding to issue further orders of a similarly atrocious nature, his own body-guard, disgusted at his cruelty, despatched him with their daggers.

several arches. Near the western extremity of this valley, rises a very lofty, insulated mountain, flat-topped, and precipitous on every side, which the natives called *Kala Gul-aub*, the fortress of rose-water.* The road, turning northward, then winds along the foot of beautiful hills, below which are extensive rice-grounds; and after crossing two streams, conducts to Mayen, which is romantically situated in a " circus of rocky steeps." †

The name of this town, according to Chardin, sig-nifies fish, and has been given to it on account of the abundance of fish which is found in its waters at cer-tain seasons. " It is," he says, " a very delicious place. There are rivulets of the clearest and sweetest water in the world, and flowing in such quantity, that the place is at it were inundated during seven or eight months; and its territory is more than two leagues in extent. It is full of gardens which bear the most excellent fruit, especially grapes and pomegranates, of which the inhabitants have sometimes given me some as large as the head of an infant. I have not any where seen finer pomegranates. They are later at Mayen, as well as all the other fruits, by three months, than at Isfahan, and four months later than at

---

* " I had first seen it," says Sir Robert K. Porter, " from the ruins of Persepolis, rearing its scarred head pre-eminent in rugged wildness, among the varied and less savage aspects of the hills which form a natural bulwark behind those beautiful remains." This is, perhaps, the castle of Shekesteh. See p. 87. Lieutenant Alexander, however, says: " We passed a good bridge, near the ancient and impregnable fort of *Istakhr*."

† " It is 15 leagues from Mayn to Shiraz by the ordinary route, the first eight of which are through the plains of Persepolis. You enter upon them on going out of Mayn, and, at the end of three leagues, pass the river Araxes, after having crossed another large river, which they call *Chabaroum*, and another smaller stream, which is without name."—CHARDIN, tom. iii. p. 98.

Kashan. In the neighbourhood of this town, some
Persian authors maintain, was the country and habitation of Job, where he endured that sharp temptation
which has become one of the most remarkable ex-
amples of patience. The notion does not appear to
me absurd. The country affords abundance of sheep,
horses, oxen, and asses, in which chiefly consisted his
great wealth, and which are not found, at least to an
equal degree, in the other places which have been
taken for the land of Uz." * We do not imagine that
Job was ever in Persia, any more than King Solomon; but certain it appears, that Mayen is a highly
favoured spot; far superior, Lieut. Alexander says,
to the usual character of Persian towns; well watered,
well shaded, and surrounded with gardens abounding
with fruit. The thermometer at noon, on the 29th
of July, rose to only 80°.

The next day's stage leads N.W., through another
narrow valley, bounded by craggy mountains, to
Imâm Zadeh Ismael; a village which takes its name
from the tomb of a saint. The road is extremely bad,
over rough, loose stones; but the valley is adorned
with groves of wild almond, hawthorn, and mulberry-
trees, intermixed with large bushes bearing a flower
resembling lavender. The village has an unusually
comfortable and flourishing aspect; the southern face

---

* Chardin, *tom.* iii, p. 97. We have thought it worth while to
copy the above passage for the sake of the Author's description of
the country; but, as to his notion which makes the Persepolitan
plains to be the land of Uz, his reasoning is worthy of his authorities. Uz has been placed in Trachonitis, near Damascus; in
Cœlo Syria; in Moab; on the Jabbok; on the Orontes; and about
the sources of the Tigris. See CALMET'S Dict. *Uz*. It is clear,
however, from Lam. iv. 21, that it was in Idumæa or Arabia
Petræa; and it may be inferred from Jer. xxv. 20—23, that it bordered on Egypt and Philistia.

of the mountain behind it, is clothed with the vine, and every little sheltered spot has been cultivated, although the only water is from wells. "We were surprised," says Sir R. K. Porter, " at finding the women not only walking about in freedom, but completely unveiled, and mixing promiscuously, in discourse or occupation, with the male inhabitants; neither did they retreat on our near approach. Their features are regular, with dark complexions and large fine eyes ; and their figures are good, with a general appearance of cleanliness, a grace not very common among the lower classes of Persia. The chief cause of such humble affluence and manifest content lies in the sacred village being exempt from tribute of any kind ; and the prince-governor of Shiraz pays a yearly sum of forty *tomauns* towards the repair and decoration of the Imaum's tomb." The exemption from taxation which this village enjoys, is in virtue of its being the residence of ten families of *saieds* or descendants from the prophet. They are not even obliged to furnish the *soorsaut;* that is, provisions and lodging for travellers attended by a *mehmandar*, which all the places on the line of route are bound to do. It is not easy to account for the *Frankish* manners which seem to prevail here : holy cities have generally a bad moral character.

From this place, the route lies along the valley for three miles, and then, taking a direction due N., ascends for two hours a very steep and rugged *kootul*, at the top of which is a *rahdari*. The descent is not less steep and perilous. It leads through a glen and gently sloping plain, into the extensive vale of Oojan, the favourite hunting-field of Baharam Gour. The village of Oojan, distant four *farsangs* from the last *munzil*, is now deserted and in ruins. A caravanserai is the only accommodation which remains. The villagers, Mr. Fraser informs us, were so oppressed by the exactions of Government and by the demands for *soorsaut*, that, a few years ago, they removed further up the valley, to a small hillock, which they fortified.* The plain affords excellent grazing, and the prince-governor occasionally sends here his brood mares: it was now spotted with the black tents of the Eelauts. Near the deserted village, a narrow stream is crossed by a bridge of nine arches, and the road runs along the eastern side of the vale, three *farsangs*, to Aspas.

This is now a collection of wretched huts straggling round the foot of an artificial mound crowned with the ruins of an old fortress. During the reign of the Sefi monarchs, it was a flourishing manufacturing town and military station. Shah Ismail colonized it with Christian families from Georgia, and Shah Abbas placed a strong garrison here, which, with the government of the surrounding district, he entrusted to the chivalric Sir Anthony Sherley. The place is remarkable on another account. Here is the fatal pool or spring in which Baharam Gour was engulfed. Two serjeants, who accompanied the last mission of Sir John Malcolm, lost their lives in the same place. " The pool," Lieut. Alexander says, " seems to be of considerable depth, but there is only a small part free from sedges and flags." The whole plain abounds in springs, some hid under marshy ground, and others opening into pools or streams ; but

* Fraser, p. 113. The oppressions occasioned by the abuse of the custom of *soorsaut*, which has originated in ancient hospitality, have led to the total abandonment of many villages in the line of its operation, and whole districts have gone gradually to decay. Hence, neither the state of the country nor the manners of the natives, can be fairly estimated by the appearance of things on the great routes.

It is supposed, that all their sources communicate at a great depth. Antelopes and mountain-goats may be seen scouring the plain in herds; partridges and various species of water-fowl are numerous; also, a beautiful bird, between the bustard and the pheasant in size, covered with a brilliant silvery plumage, the wings tipped with jet black; it is called the *hoborrah.**

From Aspas to the caravanserai of *Kiosk-i-zurd* (yellow palace),† the next stage, is five *farsangs.* The route leads over the mountain above Aspas, by a rocky narrow pass, in a general direction of N. 45° E. At the end of two hours, it opens into a fine upland pasture tract, stretching away far to the S.E., where it is said to join the vast arid plain of Deloonaser. For twenty miles, Sir R. K. Porter says, neither village nor hut appeared; they met no human being; saw no animal of any kind; and neither the chirp of a bird nor the hum of an insect, broke the silence of this dreary region. The next stage, to *Deh-i-Girdoo* (village of walnuts), leads through a succession of glens between low, rocky hills, over nearly the highest ground in this part of the empire; distance seven *farsangs* (twenty-eight miles). The road, for several *farsangs* more, winds through rocky defiles; and there is a formidable pass, called *Kootel Nakshi Khanah,* defended by a *rahdari.*‡ At length, at the end of seven *farsangs* (thirty miles), or eight hours, the traveller arrives at Yezdikhaust.

---

* Porter, vol. ii. p. 13, 19. Alexander, p. 143.

† Sir R. K. Porter writes it *Koosh Kizar;* Mr. Frazer, *Khoosh-keezurd.* It takes its name from one of Baharam Gour's hunting-seats, which was near the village.

‡ *Rah-dar* means, literally, keeper of the road (or pass).— FRASER, p. 116. These are, properly, police-stations or guard-houses.

After passing these heights, a change is very observable, Mr. Fraser says, in the scanty and now dry vegetation of the valleys. The liquorice-plant, which covers the plain of Merdasht, the tamarisk (*gez*), found near the water-courses, and the thorny plants which sprinkle the mountains in the same district, now give way to various aromatic herbs, among which a species of very fragrant rue is most abundant. A peculiar sort of thistle, and various papilionaceous plants, some dwarfish black-thorn, and a few smaller herbs, are found not only on the plains, but even on the rocky and splintered sides of the hills. The most interesting production is the *oshauk*, the plant yielding the gum-ammoniac, which grows in great abundance on the plains of Yezdikhaust. It resembles fennel or hemlock, growing to the height of from three to six feet, with a rich dark-green leaf.* This plain, which extends all the way to Koomishah, presents a melancholy picture of the general declension of the national prosperity. Ruins of large villages

---

* The best description of this curious plant, which, according to Mr. Fraser, is of the *pentandria* class, is to be found in Col. Johnson's "Journey from India to England," p. 93. Some of the stems, he says, are of a dark colour, "like sugar-cane," and others of a light green, tinged with lake near the joints. It bears leaves only on the joints near the ground, and they diminish in size at every joint. The fifth joint has a long single branch of flowers, proceeding out of a long sheath or spathe. Towards the latter end of June the lower leaves turn yellow, and the plant becomes ripe; but, in the month of May, while the plant is soft, an insect of the beetle kind begins to puncture the stem in every direction. As the stem shrinks and dries, a milky juice exudes from these punctures, and flowing down, indurates near the joints, "like wax on a candlestick," whence it is gathered by the natives about the latter end of July. The quantity collected from each plant is somewhat less than a pound. It is, probably, the same plant that abounds in some parts of Arabia, called by the natives *oshour*.—See MOD. TRAV., *Arabia*, p. 175.

with the skeletons of caravanserais, are thickly scattered about, " telling of better times ;" and the whole plain is dotted over with the small mounds which indicate the course of *kanauts*, once the source of fertility and wealth, now all choked up and dry.[*] At seven hours (24 miles) from Yezdikhaust, is the ruinous village of Muksoodbeggee, remarkable only for its large pigeon-house,—a round tower 50 feet high. [†] " Nearly intermediate between these places," says Sir W. Ouseley, " were the remains of a considerable town, called Aminabad, situate on the line now supposed to divide the province of Fars, or *Persis*, from *Irak Ajemi*, Parthia or Media. And here began the jurisdiction of the *Amin-ad-douleh*, or chief of the Isfahan government. We saw a few people in the mud-built castle, and some wretched families that seemed to occupy half-ruined hovels near the *Rebát*, or Caravanserai *Mader-i-Shah ;* so denominated from its founder, the mother of Shah Abbas." [‡]

Koomishah (written Ghomesha, Comicha, Komesha,

[*] Fraser, p. 118.

[†] " Persians never eat pigeons: they are kept in these immense dove-cots for the sake of their dung, which is used in the melon-grounds. All the way to Isfahan from hence, and round that city, pigeon-towers are to be seen in every direction ; but most of them are now tenantless."—ALEXANDER, p. 146. " Another use of the dung in older times," Sir R. K. Porter says, " was to extract saltpetre for the purpose of making gunpowder." ii. 451. The dung of pigeons is the only manure used in Egypt.—See MOD. TRAV., *Egypt*, vol. ii. p. 2.

[‡] Ouseley, ii. 451. Col. Johnson was agreeably surprised (in 1817) to find, that very great progress had been made in rebuilding this village on a very judicious plan. Only seven years before, it was a flourishing town. The new buildings had been erected within the three last years by the patriotic governor of Isfahan. " Five miles to the westward is the fine town of Isferjoon, which, as it abounds in water, and has superior advantages of security, has become populous."—JOHNSON, p. 94, 5.

Komaishah, Kumsheh, by different travellers), a stage of four *farsangs* (15¾ miles) from Muksoodbeggee, once bore the rank of a city, and is still a large and flourishing place. Sir R. K. Porter describes it (in 1818) as extensive but deserted, and tumbling to pieces in every direction, its walls and towers dilapidated; and after passing through its lofty gate, he traversed a long line of bazars without meeting an individual. It presented the same appearance to Mr. Fraser three years after.* It was ruined by the Affghans; and when, more recently, it was beginning to recover some degree of prosperity, the rapacity of the governor, Kaussim Khan, plunged the people again into misery. Since then, however, the government has been transferred to the hands of the *Sudr Ameen;* and when Lieut. Alexander passed through in 1824, the walls and bastions were in excellent order, and the surrounding country was in high cultivation.

The next stage is to Mayar (Mahyar), a distance of five *farsangs* (19 miles or six hours); throughout which, says Sir W. Ouseley, " we did not see any wells, streams, houses,† trees, or human creatures.

---

* " It is difficult to conceive anything more complete than the desolation which now reigns there: we were led through narrow lanes of ruined and fallen houses and long-deserted bazars that seemed endless; all of mud, it is true, but which once must have sheltered numerous inhabitants. Our conductors seemed to take a pride in parading these relics of departed prosperity before us, for we thought they would never have brought us to the spot still occupied by human beings."—FRASER, p. 118. Sir R. K. Porter states, that the whole way from the tomb of Shah Reza to Koomishah, " a tract four miles in extent," was a continuation of devastated habitations. The tomb, however, is only a mile and a quarter N.N.E. of the town.

† Sir R. K. Porter mentions, however, the extensive village of Isfa on one side of the road, and, at two *farsangs* from Mayar, a walled mill.

The plain was studded with many insulated rocks or small mountains, of conical or pyramidal shapes." At Mayar, the limestone rock disappears, and the hills are composed of red sandstone. Sir R. K. Porter describes it as a considerable village in a well cultivated valley, three or four miles in width, bounded by sterile mountains of the wildest forms. The country around looked cheerful from its planted fields and gardens, but the ruined villages seen at every turn, destroyed every pleasurable feeling. Chardin describes the plains between Mayar and Koomishah as the most fertile that can be seen; " covered, from the middle of March to the middle of November, with flowers, flocks, corn, fruit, vegetables, and other good things of the earth." * From this state of fertility and beauty, they would seem miserably to have declined.

A disagreeable stage of nearly 24 miles, leads over the mountains to the village of Isfahanek. A dangerous *kootul* intervenes, called the Pass of *Oortchini;* but the worst parts may be avoided by a little circuit, making the stage about 25 miles. † Isfahanek (little Isfahan) was, in Chardin's time, a mile in extent. A little beyond it, is passed an inconsiderable round fort, but with a very broad and deep wet ditch, which Lieut. Alexander calls Old Isfahanek. " Inconsiderable as it seems," he adds, " this place was defended successfully against the Affghans, and more recently held out for several months against the whole Persian army," under Hussein Koolee Khan, the brother of the present Shah, who made a feeble effort to dispute the throne. From Isfahanek, it is reckoned three *farsangs* (eight miles) over a range of hills, to

<hr>

* Chardin, iii. 91.   † Ouseley, ii. 456.

H. Adlard, sc.

ISPAHAN.

London, Published by J. Duncan, Paternoster Row, April 1827.

the capital of Irak, which, during the brilliant reign of Shah Abbas, who transferred thither the seat of empire from Cazvin, ranked as the metropolis of the empire.*

ISFAHAN.

" Nothing can exceed," we are told, " in beauty and fertility, the country in the vicinity of Isfahan; and the first appearance of that city" (approaching it from the S.) "is very imposing. All that is noble meets the eye; the groves, avenues, and spreading orchards with which it abounds, concealing the ruins of this once famed capital. A nearer view, however, dispels the illusion; but still, much remains of wealth, if not of splendour." † " The approach to the southern side of the city," Sir R. K. Porter says, " is infinitely more magnificent than the entrance on the north. Among the first objects that struck our eyes in the present view, were the numerous noble bridges, each carrying its long level line of thickly-ranged arches to porch-like structures, some fallen into stately ruin, others nearly entire, but all exhibiting splendid memorials of the Sefi race. These bridges, once the scene of many a glorious cavalcade, were still, though deserted, unimpaired. All spoke of the gorgeous, populous past......We entered the southern gate of the town, and immediately came out into one of those umbrageous avenues of trees, which render the interior of Isfahan in this quarter a very paradise. It terminated at the great bazar of Shah

* Sir W. Ouseley estimates the whole distance from Shiraz to Isfahan, by way of Moorghaub, at 247 miles. By the summer route to Yezdikhaust, Hamdallah makes it 70 *farsangs*, equal to about 210 miles; viz. 44 *farsangs* to Yezdikhaust, and 26 thence to Isfahan.—Ouseley, ii. 457.

† Sketches of Persia, vol. I. p. 250.

Abbas, the whole of which enormous length of building is vaulted above to exclude heat, yet admit air and light. Hundreds of shops, without inhabitants, filled the sides of this epitome of a deserted mercantile world, and having traversed their labyrinths for an extent of nearly two miles, we entered the *Maidan Shah*, another spacious theatre of departed grandeur. The present solitude of so magnificent a place was rendered more impressive by the distant echoing of our horses' footsteps, as we passed through its immense quadrangle to the palace that was to be our temporary abode." *

The city presented a very different spectacle when Mr. Morier entered it, in 1809, in the suite of the British envoy, Sir Harford Jones; and we shall avail ourselves of his picturesque description of the scene.

" At about four miles from Isfahan, we were met by an advanced party of the inhabitants. As we approached the city, the crowd increased to numbers which baffled our calculation or guess. Although the stick was administered with an unsparing hand, it was impossible to keep the road free for our passage. People of all descriptions were collected, on mules, on horses, on asses; besides an immense number on foot. First came the merchants of the city, in number about three hundred, all in their separate classes. Then followed a deputation from the Armenian clergy, composed of the bishop and chief dignitaries in their sacerdotal robes. They carried silken banners, on which was painted the Passion of our Saviour. The bishop, a reverend old man with a white beard, presented the Evangelists bound in crimson velvet to the Envoy, and then proceeded with his attendant priests, chanting their church service.

* Porter, vol. ii. p. 37.

" When we came into the plain, the city of Isfahan
rose upon the view, and its extent is so great east and
west, that my sight could not reach its bounds. The
crowd now was intensely great, and at intervals impeded our progress. Slowly, however, we were approaching the city, and yet the governor had not
appeared. The Envoy intimated, that he would receive no *istakball* (deputation), unless the governor
headed it. Two of the chief men of the place met
us, as we arrived at the entrance of a fine, spacious,
road, between two lofty walls. This was the beginning of the Isfahan gardens, yet the walls of the city
itself were still a mile from us. We turned to the
left through a narrow porch, which led to a piece of
ground planted on one side by lofty *chenar*-trees, and
bounded on the other by the beautiful river Zaiande-
rood. At the extremity of this spot, was a tent.
We were told that it had been prepared by the governor for the Envoy, and that he was himself there in
waiting. The Envoy stopped his horse, and declared
that, unless he was met by the governor on horseback,
he would take no notice of him, but proceed to his
own tents, and march straight forward to Teheran.
This produced the desired effect. The governor
came forth, and met us a few paces from his tent, and
we then proceeded towards it, and alighted. The
place where the tent was pitched, was called Sa-
atabad ; a pavilion had been built there by Shah
Thamas. The tent itself rested on three poles ; its
sides were of open-worked chintz, and its floor was
strewed with carpets, on which were laid out fruits
and sweetmeats in great profusion. Chairs of an old
fashion, like those in the sculptures at Persepolis,
were prepared for us, and we were not put to the
inconvenience of pulling off our boots. We were

then served with *kaleoons,* and afterwards with sweetmeats.

" When this ceremony was over, we proceeded along the banks of the Zaiande-rood, on the opposite side of which were rows of firs and ancient pinasters. We saw three bridges of singular yet beautiful construction. That over which we crossed, was composed of thirty-three lower arches, above each of which were ranged three smaller ones. There is a covered way for foot-passengers: the surface of the bridge is paved, and is of one level throughout the whole extent. After we had crossed it, we proceeded through a gate into the *Chahar Bagh,* which is a very spacious piece of ground, having two rows of *chenar-* trees in the middle, and two other rows on each side. The garden is divided into parterres, and copiously watered by the canals which run from one side of it to the other, and which, at regular intervals, are collected into basins, square or octagonal. This fine alley is divided into terraces, from which the water falls in cascades. Of the *chenar*-trees which line the walks, most can be traced to the time of Shah Abbas ; and when any have fallen, others have been immediately planted. On each side of the *Chahar Bagh,* are the eight gardens which the Persians call *Hasht-behesht.* They are laid out into regular walks of the *chenar*-tree, are richly watered, and have each a pleasure-house. We were conducted to occupy the best— that, at least, which was in better repair than the others. The rest are in a state of decay, and corroborate, only by the remains of the beautifully painted walls and gilded pannels, those lively and luxuriant descriptions of their former splendour which travellers have given." *

* Formal as the plan of these pleasure-grounds may seem, the

"On the right of the *Maidan*," continues Mr. Morier, " and nearly in the centre of the *Chahar Bagh*, is a college called *Medressé Shah Sultan Hossein*. Its entrance is handsome. A lofty portico, enriched with fantastically twisted pillars, and intermixed with the beautiful marble of Tabriz, leads through a pair of brazen gates, finished with silver, and their whole surface highly carved and embossed with flowers and verses from the Koran. The gates lead to an elevated semi-dome, which opens at once into the square of the college. The right side of this court is occupied by the mosque, which is still a beautiful building, covered with a cupola, and faced with two minarets. But the cupola is falling into decay; the lackered tiles on its exterior surface are all peeling off; and the stairs of the minarets are entirely destroyed. The interior of the dome is richly spread with variegated tiles, on which are invocations to the prophet, and verses of the Koran, in the fullest profusion. I ascended the dome, from which I had but a partial survey of the surrounding country; and that which I did see, was scarcely any thing more than a series of ruined houses and palaces. The other sides of the square are occupied, one by a lofty and beautiful portico, and the remaining two by rooms for the students, twelve in each front, arranged in two stories. These

effect of so many avenues and brilliant rills, Sir R. K. Porter says, is amazingly grand. Through various openings in the wood, the *hesht behesht*, or eight paradises, " appeared glittering, at the bottom of the green aisles, and among the foliage, like . so many gay pavilions raised by enchantment; but, when we drew nearer, the spell dissolved. We found gorgeous structures, indeed, but of too heavy and discordant a taste. A close inspection reminded me of a cumbrous style of building much in vogue about a hundred and fifty years ago, in Holland and England; a monstrous union of the Grecian with the Saracenic taste."

apartments are little square cells, spread with carpets, and appeared to me admirably calculated for study. Indeed, the quiet and retirement of this college, the beauty and serenity of the climate, and the shrubbery and water in the courts, would have combined to constitute it in my eyes a sanctuary for learning and a nursery for the learned, if it had been in any other country.

" The palaces of the king are inclosed in a fort of lofty walls, which have probably a circumference of three miles. The palace of the *Chehel Sitoon* (forty pillars)* is situated in the middle of an immense square, which is intersected by various canals, and planted in different directions with the beautiful *chenar*-tree. In front is an extensive square basin of water, from the further extremity of which the palace appears beautiful beyond either the power of language or of the pencil correctly to delineate. The first saloon is open towards the garden, and is supported by eighteen pillars, all inlaid with mirrors, and (as the glass is in much greater proportion than the wood) appearing, indeed, at a distance, to be formed of glass only. Each pillar has a marble base, which is carved into the figures of four lions, placed in such attitudes, that the shaft seems to rest on their united backs. The walls which form its termination behind, are also covered with mirrors, placed in such a variety of symmetrical positions, that the mass of the structure appears to be of glass, and, when new, must have

* " We visited the Cheyl Sittoon, or Forty Pillars, which we found to be a most superb palace. It is supported by *twenty* pillars, which, by reflection in the tank, appear as forty, and hence the name is derived. The audience hall is 120 feet long, by 60 broad, and 50 feet in height." JOHNSON's *Journey*, p. 107. Mr. Morier, however, says, there are only eighteen pillars in the façade; and forty is more probably used indefinitely, as in other instances.

glittered with most magnificent splendour. The ceiling is painted in gold flowers, still fresh and brilliant. Large curtains are suspended on the outside, which are occasionally lowered to lessen the heat of the sun.

" From this saloon, an arched recess (in the same manner studded with glass, and embellished here and there with portraits of favourites) leads into an extensive and princely hall. Here, the ceiling is arranged in a variety of domes and figures, and is painted and gilded with a taste and elegance worthy of the first and most civilised of nations. Its finely proportioned walls are embellished with six large paintings, which, though designed without the smallest knowledge of perspective, though the figures are in general ill-proportioned and in awkward attitudes, are yet enlivened by a spirit and character so truly illustrative of the manners and habits of the nations which are represented, that I should have thought them an invaluable addition to my collection if I could have found time to make copies of them. The colours retain their original freshness.*

" Adjoining to the *Chehel Sitoon* is the harem " (called *Amaroot Noo*, the new palace) " erected by Mahomed Hossein Khan (the Nizam ad Douleh), and presented by him to his present majesty. From the garden of the *Chehel Sitoon*, an intricate passage leads under an octagonal tower into this new palace, and opens into an oblong square laid out in flower-beds,

---

* Four of the pictures represent royal entertainments given to different ambassadors during the reigns of Shah Abbas, Abbas II., and Tamasp. The other two are battle pieces. One of these represents a famous exploit of Shah Ismail, who, in the great battle with Soliman, Emperor of the Turks, cut an aga in two before the Sultan. The other represents the victory of Nadir Shah over the Sultan of Delhi. In the banqueting scenes is displayed the most licentious revelry.

straight walks, and basins of water, and surrounded
with chambers for women of inferior rank. On the left
side of this court, a door opens into a species of green-
house called the *Narangistoun*, in which are only
young orange-trees. From this, there is but one step
into the principal court, one whole side of which is
occupied by the king's apartments. The front room
is adorned with two portraits of his majesty; there
are other pictures, of which the most remarkable represent Timour, Jenghiz Khan, and Jemsheed. The
walls are very richly painted with bouquets of flowers,
birds, and other animals. The arch which occupies
the side facing the great window, is a beautiful composition of glass and painting. The ceiling is highly
ornamented ; gilded flowers and bright looking-glasses
glisten on every side, and give great liveliness to the
whole. Behind this is another room, equally well
painted : the upper windows are most artfully constructed of plaster, which is pierced into small holes,
in figures and flowers resembling lace-work, and admitting a pleasing light. In this room also are portraits, one of which is called the *Shah Zadeh Freng*
(European prince) : he is represented in our dress of
the sixteenth century, in which all the portraits of the
Europeans appear, and which is sufficiently explained
by the recollection that Shah Abbas had Dutch
painters in his pay. The other rooms in this department are similarly decorated and gilded : in some
hang portraits of the king, to which the natives, as
they approach, all make an inclination of the head.
Under the great room are summer apartments excavated in the ground : they are all lined and paved
with marble slabs, and water is introduced by cascades,
which fall from the ground floor, and refresh the
whole range. A passage leads to the bath, which,

though small, is elegant. The domes are supported by columns, *taken from the Armenian church at Julfa.*

" From this court, a passage leads into several others for the attendants; and then into two rooms built by Ashraff, one of the Affghan kings. The latter are, indeed, by no means equal to those which I have already described. They have massive glasses and gildings, and coarse paintings of fruits and flowers, without any representation of the human figure. On the whole, however, we found throughout the palace, much sameness, both in the arrangement of the rooms, and in the distribution of the grounds. In the love of water and running streams, a Persian taste is fully gratified at Ispahan, through which the Zaiande-rood affords, for all their ornamental purposes, an unceasing supply.

" From the interior of the palaces, we ascended the *Ali Capi* gate, which forms the entrance. This gate, once the scene of the magnificence of the Sefi family, the threshold of which was ever revered as sacred, is now deserted; and only now and then, a solitary individual is seen to pass negligently through. The remains of that splendour so minutely and accurately described by Chardin, are still to be traced; the fine marbles remain, and the grandeur and elevation of the dome are still undemolished. A ragged porter opened a small door to the right, by which we ascended to the pavilion where Shah Abbas was wont to witness the games of the *Maidan* and the exercises of his troops. This also is sinking rapidly into decay, and retains nothing to attest the beauties which travellers describe, except the shafts of the wooden columns, some pieces of glass, and some decayed paintings. From this, we ascended by a winding staircase, still further, to the very summit. Here, as this is the highest building in the city, we enjoyed a most extensive view, and could form a tolerably just idea of its whole extent. Houses, or ruins of houses, are spread all over the plain, and reach even to the surrounding mountains. From this point I took a panoramic view of the whole. There is no difference in the colours of the buildings; they are universally of a light yellow, and, were it not for an abundant intermixture of trees, which, in spring and summer, enliven the scene, the view would be too unvaried. The trees are mostly the *chenar;* but there are, besides, the Lombardy poplar, the willow, and an elm of very thick, rich foliage and a formal shape. The domes of the mosques are a field of green or sometimes blue-lackered tiles, with ornaments in yellow, blue, and red; the inscriptions are in the same colours. They are crowned with a golden ball and a crescent. The mountains which bound the plain eastward, are the most distant; and those to the west are the most strongly marked: all are dark, without any verdure. The general appearance of the soil in the town is light, nearly of the same colour as the houses.

" All the cannon, which, in Chardin's day, were inclosed in a balustrade before the palace, are removed, and not a vestige remains even of the balustrade itself. The *Maidan Shah,* the great public place,* no longer presents the busy scene which it must have displayed in the better times of this kingdom. Of all the trees which surrounded it, there is not one standing. The canals are void of water; the houses which surrounded

* According to Chardin, the great *Maidan* measures 440 paces by 160. Olivier says, about 700 by 230, which agrees with Della Valle. Kæmpfer says 660 by 212; Le Brun, 710 by 210; Sir R. K. Porter, 2600 *feet* by 700.

thé *Maidan* are no longer inhabited, and the very doors are all blocked up, so that there are only dead arches to be seen all round. The great market, which once spread the whole area with tents, is now confined to one corner near the *Nókara Khanéh.* All the rest is quite empty; scarcely a person is seen to pass along. I saw no traces of the pavilion of the clock, which, in the time of Chardin, so much amused the people by the mechanism of its puppets. The *Mesjid Shah,* or Royal Mosque, is still a noble building, if I might judge from its outside. We did not go further than the iron chain which is thrown across the entrance of its great gate leading into the *Maidan.* The Mezjid of Lootf Aly is exteriorly in good repair. The great bazar is entered under the *Nókara Khanéh* by a handsome gate, the paintings on which still exist, but the large clock, the place of which is still seen, is no longer in existence; nor is there any trace of that which was once on the summit. The other side of the gate opens into the fine bazars, formerly called the *Kaiseree,* now the *Bazar Shah.*

" In the bazars, the confluence of people is certainly great ; but, as every one in the course of the day has some business in this spot, the rest of the city is comparatively deserted. The north and east divisions are the best inhabited....Considering the state of ruin in which, perhaps, half of Ispahan is at present, we cannot place its actual population at more than 400,000 souls ; a calculation which is supported by the accounts of the houses or families, of which there are 80,000."*

* Morier, vol. i. pp. 161—171. Lieutenant Alexander says: " The present population of Isfahan is 250,000 ;" but he does not give his authority. Sir W. Ouseley doubts whether, in 1811, 200,000 could be found resident in the city; and Mr. Morier himself, in his Second Journey, brings it down to 60,600 ! ;

Isfahan (written *Asp-han*, *Spahan*, and *Sepahan* by the native historians) has been supposed to represent the *Aspadana* of Ptolemy, although he places that city in Persis. Ebn Haukal describes it in the tenth century, as consisting of two towns; one called *Yehudiah*; the other, *Medinah* (the city) or *Shahr báneh*. According to another authority cited by Sir W. Ouseley, the ancient town was denominated *Jei*, and is said to have been founded by Iscander (Alexander).* The quarter *Yehudiah* (Judea) is stated to have received its name from a colony of Jews whom Bakhtnasser (Nebuchadnezzar) led away captive from Jerusalem.† Originally, says Hamdallah Cazvini, there were four distinct villages, *Karran*, *Der-i-kôshk*, *Jubareh*, and *Der-i-desht*,‡ which, when Kai Kobad made this place his capital, were gradually united so as to form a considerable city. One district, the *Shahristan*, called also *Shahr-i-now* (the new town), was founded, he adds, by Secander, and rebuilt by Firouz, the Sassanian monarch. In the tenth century

* *Jei*, in Pahlavi, signifies pure or excellent.

† " When Bakhtnasser led away captive from Jerusalem the most ingenious artists, they arrived at the spot where Isfahan now stands; and finding that in all the qualities of air and water it resembled their holy city, they chose it for their residence, and established themselves there."—MS. cited in Ouseley, iii. p. 6. An Arabian prophecy is cited by Hamdallah, which intimates, that Dejal, or Antichrist, should come from the Yehudiah of Isfahan.—Ib. p. 9.

‡ In Chardin's time, Isfahan consisted of two principal districts, *Deri-desht* and *Jubareh—tome* iii. p. 6. These denominations, Sir W. Ouseley says, yet remain; and that of Yehoodeea still distinguishes the Jews' quarter. The extensive ruins of Shahristan, " once famous for being the residence of the nobles of Ispahan," are found to the eastward of the city. Kherron (Karran ?) is enumerated by Chardin among the suburbs, its name signifying Deaf men, according to a silly legend. *Derikushk* is perhaps " the village of the palace."

of the Christian era, Ruk'n ad Douleh Hassan surrounded the whole with a rampart 21,000 paces in
circumference.* Such is the substance of the very
meagre and doubtful information furnished by the
Mohammedan writers. It is evident that they were
ignorant of the meaning of the name, some maintaining that Ispahan was a son of Yafet, and others, that
the word implies " the city of horsemen."

. Isfahan was in its glory in the reign of Shah Abbas,
who built the *Chehel Sitoun*, the *Char Bagh*, the
principal bridge over the Zeindehrood, and several
other public edifices. The city is said to have contained at that time from sixty-five to seventy thousand families.† No fewer than 1500 villages, according to Chardin, were situated on the adjacent plains
within a space of ten leagues. " Of these villages,"
Sir W. Ouseley says, " several have totally disappeared,
or exist only in a state of absolute decay; many, however, still flourish, and continue to supply Ispahan
most abundantly with the produce of their fields and
gardens." The decline of the city dates from the
Affghan invasion, in the beginning of the eighteenth
century, when it sustained a ruinous siege of eight
months, during which the adjacent country was laid

* Chardin allowed a circuit of 20,000 paces to the mud walls, as
they stood in the seventeenth century.

† Chardin says: " The city of Ispahan, including the suburbs,
is one of the largest in the world, and is not less than 12 leagues or
24 miles in circuit. The Persians say, to exalt its greatness, *Sefa-
hon nispe gehon,* Isfahan is half the world····Many persons carry
the number of the inhabitants to 1,100,000 souls. Those who place
it the lowest, affirm that it amounts to 600,000. The accounts
given me were very various on that point, but they agreed sufficiently as to the number of edifices, which they made amount to
38,240; namely, 29,469 within the city, and 8780 without····After
all, I believe Isfahan to be as populous as London, the most populous city in Europe."—CHARDIN, iii. p. 3.

waste by the barbarous policy of the enemy. The
162 mosques comprehended within the city walls in
Chardin's time, are now reduced to sixty, of which
only forty were in repair in 1810; the colleges (*madrassehs*) are stated still to amount to 84; the baths,
to between 80 and 100.* The city has been greatly
improved, within the past twenty years, under the
able administration of the *Ameen ad douleh*, who has
erected several new edifices, repaired others, re-colo-
nized several of the deserted villages, and materially
increased the trade and revenue. But foreign merchants no longer throng its bazars, where the black
Persian cap now universally prevails; and the removal
of the seat of government to Tehraun, is a circumstance
which must greatly affect the prosperity of the city,
as well as its political consequence.

The suburb of Julfa has suffered particularly. It
was the first part of the city that was taken and sacked
by the Affghans. It lies on the southern side of the
Zeindehrood, and is now connected with the town
only by long tracts of ruins. " Its ten thousand inhabitants," says Sir R. K. Porter, " have diminished
to three hundred wretched families, dwindling, every
year, both in respectability and numbers.† Its thirteen churches are reduced to two, ‡ and those are

* Ouseley, vol. iii. p. 34. Chardin's account makes there to
have been within the walls, in 1674, 162 mosques, 48 colleges, 1802
caravanserais, 273 baths, and 12 cemeteries.—*Tome* iii. p. 82.

† According to Kæmpfer, Julfa contained, in 1685, no fewer than
30,000 souls; and in the time of Shah Abbas, it is said to have
comprised 3400 houses or families. Sir W. Ouseley supposed that
there might be from 350 to 400 families in 1811." A recent census,
however, states the Armenians of Julfa at 12,500 souls. See p. 232
of vol. l.

‡ This would seem to be a mistake. Sir W. Ouseley understood,
that, of thirteen churches, *seven* still exist. Mr. Morier says,
twelve. Mr. Martyn attended service in the principal Armenian

dark, dirty, and dismal; the mean and even ragged decorations of their altars, according too well with the general air of squalid misery which prevails over the whole district of this now expiring colony." Mr. Morier, however, speaks of the principal church as a fine building, handsomely ornamented inside; " and, what is esteemed a great privilege in Mohammedan countries, enjoys the use of a bell." Lieut. Alexander describes the cathedral as very lofty, its walls adorned with pictures of our Saviour and the apostles, and the saints. The archbishop, " a grave and mild-looking personage about forty-five years of age," joined with his fellow-priests in speaking with much bitterness of some Armenian renegades, who had, a few days before, turned Mussulmans from worldly motives. The Armenians of Persia are now, in fact, a contemned and degraded race, their character having suffered a deterioration corresponding to the decline of their fortunes. Sir R. K. Porter describes them as addicted to fraud in their dealings, to gluttony and drunkenness in their habits; and so low are they sunk, that they do not scruple, he says, to sell their daughters into dishonourable concubinage.* There is a convent here of Armenian nuns,—" a company of ignorant old women," by whom Sir W. Ouseley was treated with

church in 1812, at which were present two out of the four bishops, and other ecclesiastics, but only three persons in the body of the place. He adds: " Most of the Armenians at Julfa, which is now reduced to 500 houses, attended at their respective parish churches, of which there are *twelve*, served by twenty priests. Julfa had formerly twenty bishops, and about one hundred clergy, with twenty-four churches. All the Armenians can read, and have the New Testament."—MARTYN's *Journal.* Lieut. Alexander speaks of a very ponderous bible in the cathedral, which the Armenians perform long pilgrimages to visit.

* " The children which spring from these temporary unions, are numerous throughout the country, and in a lamentable state."

a favourite cordial, made of arrack saturated with
spices. Whether this was reserved for visiters, does
not appear. The nuns are dressed from head to foot
in a coarse dark-blue cloth, with a leathern belt and
naked feet.

The Romish Christians, who were once numerous
at Julfa, were reduced, in 1811, to about eighteen individuals. Padre Yusuf, the last of the missionaries
of the Propaganda, was the only remaining monk; and
he is since dead. His church, belonging to the order
of the Dominicans, (of which four or five monks used
generally to reside at Isfahan,) was in good repair
and good order, clean, and better ornamented than
could have been expected ; but his circumstances, and
those of his flock, were so necessitous that they scarcely
knew how to live. Formerly, the Carmelites and
the Jesuits had each their church and monastery at
Julfa, while the Augustins and Capuchins had theirs
within the city itself; but these have long ceased to
exist.* In the extinction of these missions, there
is nothing to regret. They were adapted to retard,
rather than to advance the progress of Christianity in
Persia, by identifying it, in the minds of the natives,
with an idolatrous worship.

To the south of the city is a desolate tract called
the *Hexâr-dereh* (thousand valleys), which is said to
extend 100 miles from E. to W., and is, in different
parts, from 15 to 20 in breadth. It is mostly composed
of a slaty soil, and derives its name from the multiplicity of flat and hollow intervals between the barren,
insulated mountains which are scattered over the territory of Isfahan. This was the scene, according to
Persian legends, of the combats between Roustam and

* Morier, ii. 147. See also Martyn's Journal.

a terrible dragon, to whose poisonous exhalations the barrenness of the soil is ascribed. A mountain to the S.W. of the city takes the name of *Takht-i-Rustam*, from some inconsiderable ruins on its eastern summit, which are said to have been once the throne or palace of that redoubted personage.* "But neither did those remains," says Sir W. Ouseley, "nor the consecration of this rock by the visit of Solomon and his queen,† so strongly interest my curiosity, as the neighbouring mountain on the left, called *Kuh-e-Sofah*, rendered, by a more probable tradition, almost classic ground; for it is said, that, from a place of security contrived on its steep and lofty side, the unfortunate Darius beheld his troops defeated with prodigious slaughter by the Macedonians under Alexander. Its name is derived from an edifice occupying a terrace on the northern side, facing the city: this terrace forms a seat or resting-place, which may be expressed by the adopted Arabic word Sofa; and the villa erected there, about 150 years ago, by Shah Suleiman, is sometimes styled his *takht* or throne. Le Brun describes it as containing several handsome apartments, shaded by trees of various kinds, and refreshed by a fall of water. Some changes and considerable decay have been occasioned by the lapse of a century. When seen from the *Kabristan-i-Pulad* (Pulad's cemetery) near the gate of the Saadetábád gardens, the edifice seems to fill up a small natural chasm of the mountain, about half way up its side. One tradition indicates this to be the station of Darius; and it is

* These ruins have been delineated by Le Brun.

† King Solomon is said to have transported the fair Balkeiss, queen of Sheba, to this spot, as the only means of recovering her from a dangerous malady. The Jewish monarch has perhaps been confounded with Shah Suleiman.

sufficiently high to command a very extensive prospect.
But other reports exalt the monarch to a more elevated region, and place him where the remains of
walls are seen immediately over the summer-house.....
An English artillery-man succeeded in ascending to
that second stage; he found there only some remains
of masonry on a small flat terrace, but he could perceive that the approach had once been rendered more
easy by a path, now scarcely passable, which seemed
to encircle the mountain in a direction nearly horizontal, exhibiting at some angles the vestiges of a
parapet, and of towers on the most prominent parts.
We could also discern from our lower situation, that
even the very summit had once been decorated or
fortified with some building, assigned to Darius by a
third account. This likewise relates, that Shah Suleiman's villa occupied a spot formerly reckoned sacred,
as the residence of a dervish, whose cell was in a dark,
natural cavity behind an edifice on the left: here,
it is said, a fountain of limpid water issued from the
rock, overshadowed by majestic planes and cypresses,
which, during a succession of 900 years, were held in
superstitious veneration. Of those ancient trees, I
sought in vain some relic......With the original trees,
the place has lost its sacred character; and during the
last century, the villa has been a scene of the most
profane merriment and of the grossest debauchery.
No longer frequented by its royal owners, it is stripped
of its splendid furniture; the doors have been removed; its roof has partly disappeared; and it occasionally serves the profligates of Isfahan as a retreat,
where, with their effeminate dancing and singing
boys, they enjoy the forbidden delights of wine, and
indulge in excesses the most criminal." *

* Ouseley, vol. iii. pp. 41—44.

An extensive view of the city is obtained from a small round tower on an elevation to the southward, called *Mil Shatir*. A Kufic inscription round the cupola attests the antiquity of the fabric, which is sepulchral; and the legend to which its name refers, makes it to be the tomb of a royal *shatir*, or footman, who ran from Shiraz to this spot, and died there. *

The easterly environs of Isfahan are neither so flourishing nor so populous as those to the westward; but, at the village of Sheheristan, in the former direction, are remains of a handsome mausoleum with a high minaret, and extensive ruins; also, a bridge over the Zeindehroud. That river, which has its rise in the Baktyari mountains, about 80 or 90 miles W. of Isfahan, flows through the territories of Char-Mehal and Linjan, to the point where it is crossed by the *Pul-i-Chehar-bagh* (or the Julfa bridge); it then passes close by the palaces of *Haft-dest* and *Saadetá-bád*, and, near the gate of *Khaju*, is crossed by another handsome double bridge, called the *Pul-i-Khaju*; thence, it flows eastward to the *Pul-i-Shahristan*; and after watering, by means of *bunds*, the districts of

---

* The popular story is, that a certain king of Persia promised his daughter] in marriage to any one who would run before his horse all the way from Shiraz to Isfahan. One of his *shatirs* had so nearly acccomplished his task as to have reached this eminence, when the king dropped his whip. The *shatir*, aware that to stoop would be certain death, owing to the ligatures with which he was girded for the task, contrived to take up the whip with his foot, and carried it to the monarch. This trick having failed, the king dropped his ring. The *shatir* saw that his fate was decided, and exclaimed, " O king, you have broken your word;" he then stooped, picked up the ring, and expired.— MORIER, ii. 137. Chardin says, however, that the tower received its name, because all who aspired to the office of *shatir* to the king, were to run from the gate of the palace to this tower, a distance of a league and a half, twelve times and back, between sunrise and sunset.

Berahan, Rudesht, and Varzeneh, " settles on the earth." *

To the westward of the city, there is a considerable village called Guladoon (*Kalehdân*), celebrated for its quinces, but still more famed for its shaking towers. These are two minarets which flank an arched building, the tomb of an *imam-zadeh*. " The miracle was exhibited to us," says Mr. Morier, " by sending boys to the summit of each pillar, who, applying all their force to shake them, made not only the pillars, but the roof of the building below, tremble as sensibly as if they were agitated by an earthquake. We supposed that it proceeded from some defect in the architecture,

---

* Ouseley, vol. iii. pp. 10—18. The name of this river is of doubtful orthography, and its meaning varies accordingly, serving the natives to play upon. *Zinderhud*, we are told, implies the living stream ; *Zalandcrud*, the stream that gives life or fertilizes ; *Zarinrud*, or *Zarinehrud*, as it is sometimes written, means golden stream ; and one meaning of *Zendeh* is great. Various accounts are also given of its source. One authority places it at a spot called Tebakan or Betakan ; another at Melkan ; a third, at the fountain of Janan ; a fourth, at the *Char-chasmeh* (four fountains), about 80 or 90 miles W. of Isfahan ; a fifth writer places the source in the mountains of Shamkheh, in the Baktyari country ; and a sixth, Hamdallah, traces it to the *Kuh Zordeh* (*Koh-i-zerd*) or Yellow Mountain, in Looristan, and to the territory of *Jui-sarv* (cypress stream), flowing thence through the district of Rudibar. Mr. Kinneir, adopting this statement, adds, that an aqueduct may yet be seen there, near its source, by which Shah Abbas attempted to unite its waters with those of the Karoon. The *balouk* of Linjan is one of the most fertile in Persia ; and is covered with villages. It extends about 70 miles E. and W., and 40 in breadth. Among its numerous villages is one called *Peerbakeran*, about 16 miles W. of Isfahan, which is a place of great resort to the Jews, on account of its containing the tomb of Sarah, a celebrated Jewish matron.—KINNEIR, pp. 109, 10. Hamdallah states, that the Zeindehroud, after a course of 80 *farsangs*, is dissipated or absorbed at *Ravid Sestein*, in the land of Gawkhani ; but that some say, it there sinks into the ground, and, after a subterraneous course of 60 *farsangs*, re-appears in Kerman, and reaches the sea.—OUSELEY, iii. 14.

but the Persians were more inclined to attribute it to the saint below."

About two miles from the shaking pillars is a triangular hill, distinctly seen from afar, called the *Atesh Gah* (place of fire). It is composed of several *strata* of rock; and upon its summit are some old buildings, composed of sun-dried brick with layers of reed, which the natives ascribe to the Guebres. This mode of building is undoubtedly ancient, and is the same that prevailed in Babylonia. From this hill, an extensive prospect is enjoyed of the richly-cultivated country on the winding banks of the Zeindehroud. In this part of the environs are numerous pigeon-towers, upon which more care appears to have been bestowed, Mr. Morier says, than upon the generality of the dwellings, for they are painted and ornamented, and have a picturesque appearance. The dung is used almost exclusively for the rearing of melons; and the revenue of a pigeon-house is about 100 *tomauns* per annum; sometimes more.* The pigeons are of a cindery blue. " It is remarkable," says Mr. Morier, " that neither here nor in the south of Persia, have I ever seen a white pigeon, which, Herodotus remarks, was a bird held in aversion by the ancient Persians," —probably as an evil omen.

Isfahan is situated in lat. 32° 39' 34" N., long. 51° 44' 37" E.† It enjoys the reputation of a very salu-

---

* The great value of this dung, Mr. Morier remarks, may, probably, throw light upon 2 Kings vi. 25; a passage which has been misunderstood; and the extraordinary flights which may be seen to alight upon one of these buildings, struck him as affording a good illustration of the simile which occurs in Isa. lx. 8. " Their great numbers and the compactness of their mass, literally looked like a cloud at a distance, and obscure the sun in their passage."—Morier, vol. ii. pp. 139—41.

† Fraser, p. 136 of Appendix. Cazvini makes the latitude 32° 25', which is adopted by Kinneir, who makes the long. 51° 50'.

brious climate, but bilious fevers and aguish complaints are very prevalent on the approach of autumn; and these sometimes assume the character of a virulent epidemic, carrying off great numbers of the inhabitants.   The British mission of 1812, arrived in that city in July: the nights were then found pleasantly cool, but the heat, very early in the morning, was considerable.   During the first fortnight of August, the thermometer, at noon, frequently rose to 98° or 100°.   On the 15th of that month, a violent thunderstorm occurred, (a rare phenomenon in this dry climate,) after which the thermometer sank to 71°, and continued till the end of the month below 89°. This change had been foretold by the natives, whose prognostications concerning the weather, Sir W. Ouseley says, seldom prove fallacious.   About the 1st of September, the nocturnal warmth returned, and the thermometer rose in the day to 96°.   Great sickness now began to be prevalent.   "The excellence of the air of Isfahan," says Mr. Morier, "is a favourite topic with every Persian; but, to our cost, we found it much the contrary, for scarcely one of us escaped without a fever or ague, or, at least, head-ache and bilious symptoms.   Our distress commenced with the death of our coachman; our treasurer, an old Armenian, was next attacked with a fever, and brought to the brink of the grave.   Almost all the palanquin-bearers, and many of the Indian body-guard, fell ill. The English artillery-men were more or less laid up; and the natives themselves were not more exempt than we......Although they asserted that they never before experienced such a changeableness in the climate and consequent sickliness, yet, upon closer investigation, we found that it is often the case at the commencement of autumn.   They hold fruit to be unwholesome at that period ; but such is their love for it, that they eat it, particularly melons, to excess, to which their sickness may be in a great measure attributed."*

Mr. Fraser was at Isfahan in November. The air was then raw and cold, but occasionally very dry. Heavy clouds threatened snow, which fell on all the mountain tops around. The thermometer, at sunrise, varied from 28° to 40°: in the day-time, it rose to 50° and 56°. Hoar frost was common ; and once, the ice that covered the pools, remained the whole day. Sir R. K. Porter, in May, found the mornings extremely pleasant, and the days not less so; the thermometer in the shade seldom rising above 75°; but the evenings were oppressively close, followed by nights extremely cold and sharp. No dew fell; and on the 31st of May, no fruit was ripe; but both cherries and plums were eaten as a delicacy in their crude state.†

The population of Isfahan are characterised by the Author of Sketches of Persia, as an active, industrious people. " They are considered as the best manufacturers and the worst soldiers in Persia. But, whatever may be their deportment in the field of battle, they are remarkable for the boldness of their language in the field of argument, and have great confidence in their ready wit and talent for repartee....At Isfahan, almost every man above the very lowest order, can read and write; and artisans and shopkeepers are

---

* Morier, vol. ii. pp. 152, 3. Ouseley, vol. iii. pp. 23, 39. On the first of October, the weather became cool at night and morning. At this time, daily deaths became numerous in the city, many of the young and vigorous falling victims to the illness of a few hours The trees now began to shed their leaves.

† Fraser, p. 139. Porter, vol. i. p 441.

often as familiar as those of the higher ranks with the works of their favourite poets. The love of such learning seems, in some of the youth of this city, to degenerate into a disease. These *Talib-ool-ilm* (seekers of science), as the students are called, may be seen in crowds round the gates or within the walls of its college, reciting stanzas, or discussing obscure dogmas or doctrines in their works on philosophy or religion; and they often become, from such habits, unfitted for every other pursuit in life. The merchants of Persia form a distinct class. I had now seen those of Abusheher, Shiraz, and Isfahan, and found their general character nearly the same. So long as they have no concern with state affairs, and accept of no employment from government, they enjoy considerable security. The plunder of a merchant, without some pretext, would shake all confidence, and be fatal to that commerce from which a great proportion of the public revenue is derived; the most tyrannical monarchs, therefore, have seldom committed so impolitic an act of injustice. But this class have suffered so severely in the late revolutions of the country, that they continue to act with great caution. They are not only very circumspect in their dealings, but, like wary diplomatists, every merchant has a cipher, known only to himself and his correspondents. By this means, they receive and convey that intelligence which is essential to give safety to their speculations. Some few make a display of their wealth; but in general, their habits are not merely frugal, but penurious. This disposition often increases with age, to a degree that would hardly be credited, if we had not similar instances in our own country." *

---

* Sketches of Persia, vol. i. pp. 253—7.

The Isfahanians, if not brave soldiers, have the reputation of being great braggarts; and for many centuries, their civic broils have been a frequent source of tumult and even bloodshed. They are divided into two parties or factions, like the "blues" and "greens" formerly at Constantinople, and the Nicolotti and Castellani at Venice. A slight difference of religious opinion is said to have been the origin of this animosity; but Chardin represents it as a strong hereditary jealousy, amounting to antipathy, between the inhabitants of the two quarters of the city,—the *Joubareh Neamet Olahi* on the east, and the *Deridesht Heideri* on the west.* Both parties, however, unite in looking down upon the inhabitants of all other places, as their inferiors; and they have long entertained a peculiar jealousy of the Shirazians, which might be attributed to the preference given to Shiraz by Kurreem Khan, were it not of much longer standing. It is, indeed, reciprocal.†

The manufactures of Isfahan consist of brocades, satins, and silks; calicoes, chintzes, and other cotton goods, manufactured from the plant that grows in the neighbourhood; ‡ paper and paper boxes, pen-cases (*kalmdoons*), and book-covers, beautifully ornamented; also, sword-blades, glass, and earthenware, but not in large quantities. There is no regular bazar for books,

---

* Chardin, *tome* iii. p. 6. Neamet Olahi and Heider are said to be the names of two princes or provosts, who formerly divided the whole Persian nation into two parties.

† See vol. i. p. 364; and Ouseley, vol. iii. p. 55, *note*.

‡ The principal cotton-manufacture is the *kadek*, a strong and excellent cloth resembling nankeen, which is worn by people of all ranks, from the Shah to the peasant, and is exported to Russia, where it is used as the undress of the soldiery. The *kerbas* is another cotton cloth, of which the shirts and drawers of the lower orders are made.

but manuscripts are procured by the *delals* or brokers ; and pictures very neatly executed in water-colours, and some in oil on canvass, are daily offered for sale in the bazars. Some of these are of a very licentious description.

The houses of Isfahan are only one story in height, but are composed of so many compartments, that the meanest of them occupy a considerable area. They are built of earth or brick, and their uniformity in height and colour produces a dull appearance. The entrances are generally mean and low : a poor man's door is scarcely three feet in height, a precaution intended to prevent a horseman from entering. A great man's habitation is known by his lofty gate ; but the rich merchants have purposely mean entrances to their houses, while the interior is often ornamented with great luxury.* To a stranger, the bazars are the most amusing place of resort : there, he finds a continual concourse of people of all descriptions, especially on Friday, the Mohammedan sabbath. On that day, too, the women may be seen in parties, going to the cemeteries on the skirts of the city, to mourn over the graves of their deceased relatives. Among the public buildings, in addition to those already described, may be enumerated, the octagonal pavilion called the *Kuláh i Frangki* (Frank's hat), or the *Nemek-dan* (salt-cellar), near the *Kabrestan i Pulad* ; the *Ayneh Kheneh* (palace of mirrors),—a royal palace built on the plan of the *Chehel-Sitoon*, but on a smaller scale ;

* " In Turkey," remarks Mr. Morier, " the vanity of some people is such, that when the building is in itself a small one, they will build a gate to it large enough for a palace ; but they generally finish by paying dear for their ostentation. ' *He that exalteth his gate, seeketh destruction*,' said the wise king (Prov. xvii. 19)."— MORIER, vol. ii. p. 136.

numerous mosques ; and the once celebrated citadel, called the castle of Tabarrak, the ruined walls of which are now mouldering into heaps of clay, but the thickness and height of some towers and bastions not yet fallen, and the depth of its ample ditch, indicate its former strength and extent. For further' details respecting the palaces and pavilions, the gardens and *maidans*, the gates, mosques, colleges, baths, caravan-serais, and bridges of this noble capital in the days of its magnificence, we must refer such of our readers as are not already satiated, to the faithful pages of honest Chardin.*

FROM ISFAHAN TO TEHRAUN.

FOLLOWING the route described by Mr. Morier and Sir W. Ouseley, the first stage from Isfahan in the direction of Tehraun, is to Gaz (or Gez), about 16 miles from the city. The road lies over the level plain, which is of a soft and crumbling soil, strongly impregnated with salt, and in parts rendered muddy and swampy by the streams which intersect it. Dikes cut from the Zeindehroud irrigate the whole plain, which is covered with ruins. Near Gez, which is a considerable village, are extensive plantations of melon, cotton, and the castor-plant. Its caravanserai, though falling into decay, is still handsome, a monument of the magnificence of the Sefi monarchs. Seven miles beyond, on the next stage, is a ruined caravanserai of the same style; and nearly opposite to it is a well,

* The following prices of different articles at Isfahan are given by Colonel Johnson :—Rice sells at 3½ rupees per *maund;* candles, 13½ ; soft sugar, 1 rupee per lb.; mutton, 2½ rupees per *maund;* milk, 1 rupee for seven quarts; eggs, 40 for 1 rupee; chopped straw, ¼ rupee per *maund;* barley, 1 rupee per *maund;* wood, one day's fuel, ½ rupee.

to which a path descends, fifty yards in length, excavated on an angle of 45°. It is a spring of fine water, full of small fish. Six miles further, there is a very handsome caravanserai on the right of the road, which, with its baths and reservoirs on the left, was erected by the mother of Shah Abbas. It is built of brick on a foundation of fine blue stone, and is still in good preservation. The front is ornamented with an open brick-work and some neat mosaic, and the portico leading into the square court, is · crowned with a superb dome. Behind, are vaulted stables. The *hummum* is ruined, but the reservoir is still in good repair. From this place, it is five miles, completing a stage of 18 miles,* to Mourcheh Kourd. The road passes over a part of the plain on which Nadir Shah gained his decisive victory over Ashraff, the Affghan monarch.+ The soil is hard, in some places argillaceous ; and the whole tract of country traversed in this stage, is poor and depopulated.

At Mourcheh-kourd,‡ there is a mud-built castle, with about 200 houses. A handsome caravanserai is seen at the distance of 12 miles N. 15° W., which takes its name from Aga Kemal, an officer of the harem under one of the Sefi princes. The road to it lies over a flat and dreary waste, destitute of houses, trees, or even shrubs. For the next eight miles it crosses a barren undulating tract to a second caravanserai, called *Aakemal* (Aga Kemal) *bálá* (the upper), to distinguish it from the former, *Aakemal páiun* (the

---

* Sir W. Ouseley makes the distance 21½ miles ; and his distances are generally greater than Mr. Morier's calculation.

† Fought near Mourcheh-Kourd on Nov. 12 and 13, 1729. See vol. i. p. 199.

‡ Mr. Fraser places Moorchacoor in lat. 33° 5′ 25″ ; long. 51° 32′ 30″.

lower). Around it is seen a little cultivation, with a few poplars : all the rest is desert. About four miles to the left, is the small territory of Jushghán (Joshoogán), comprising the three villages of Bendai, Khosroabad, and Vazvoon, which are famed for their manufactory of carpets. They are situated under a red hill at the extremity of the plain westward. Beyond the first range of serrated heights are seen the snowy summits of a loftier chain. The road now becomes very bad and stony, leading over bleak hills, and through one narrow mountain pass, which will not admit two horses abreast. At the end of 12 miles, the traveller reaches the pleasant valley of Kuhrood (mountain river), extending towards the N.E.†

 Sir W. Ouseley makes the distance from *Murcheh Khurt* to *Aka Kemal paiun*, 15½ miles ; thence, to *Aka Kemal bdld*, 13 miles ; and to *Kuhrud*, 15 miles ; 43 miles instead of 32.

† From *Aka Kemal bdld*, there is another road to Kuhrood, which diverges to the eastward, through the village of *Sow*, distant from Murcheh Khurt, 25½ miles. This was taken by Col. Johnson in 1817. "The road continued along the plain, which is nearly level, and about eight miles in breadth, extending N.N.E. and S.S.W. There was an almost imperceptible ascent the whole way. Not a blade of grass was to be seen, the only vegetation consisting of a few lacteous shrubs, from 10 to 16 inches in height, thinly scattered over the soil. On the hills and mountains, not a tree or shrub was visible, nor were there any villages, either inhabited or deserted, to be seen throughout the valley····During this march, we certainly met no more than five or six persons travelling on the road, and the whole tract may be termed a desert····The caravanserai of So is a good one, and commands a tolerable supply of articles of food, but we found no grass. The mules, however, for the first time these many days past, were turned out to pasture on weeds in the neighbouring wild. In the evening, we observed at least twenty individuals, men, women, and children, employed in digging and eating their roots. Some were collecting and storing them in cloths for domestic use. It is hardly possible to conceive a state of society more cheerless, more hopeless, more wretched than this."—JOHNSON, p. 129—31. The distance to Kuhrud is 15 miles.

" This place," says Sir W. Ouseley, " is justly celebrated as one of the pleasantest in Persia, and comprehends two villages ; Kuhrud giving the general denomination, though comprising but 150 families, while the other, Juinan, is said to contain above 200. These are abundantly supplied with water by a beautiful stream, which accompanied us during the last half hour from the place where the roads of Sow and Aga Kemal unite. The houses, situate on the steep sides of a hill, almost seem to stand one upon another. Below is the caravanserai, and near it, on a rising ground, the remains of an old castle. Between various eminences the valley appears, richly cultivated and finely diversified with gardens yielding most admirable fruit. We thought the walnuts and apples particularly excellent."

The approach to this valley is highly picturesque. On descending from the narrow pass, a change is observable in the stony soil, and for the first time, a grey granite is perceived projecting in masses from the hills, which have hitherto been all of limestone or sandstone. " On viewing the ranges of mountains," says Colonel Johnson, " it was easy to distinguish the different substances that composed them. The most elevated of these was granite ; the body of the mountain was of a greenish neutral tint, with dark and reddish rocks, projecting frequently in strong light and shade ; next below them was a range of acuminated and precipitous mountains of limestone of a lighter colour ; the nearer and lower range was more even in its surface, which was of a reddish brown, but covered in many places with weeds ; its strongest feature, particularly along the bases of the hills and near the central stream, consisted in the masses of granite abruptly projecting from the declivity. The moun-

tains, nearly joining at their bases, render the appearance of this valley extremely romantic; and this effect
is increased by the rather uncommon view of extensive plantations of noble fruit-trees, of chinars and
poplars, which are seen along the whole bottom, and
to the distance of half a mile up the narrow vales
between the hills. These, checkered by patches of
corn-fields on irrigated terraces, and enlivened by the
presence of a large village on the acclivity of a hill,
protected by a fortification, constitute a landscape of
no ordinary interest. The caravanserai afforded
wretched accommodation, being ruinous and filthy.
The orchards were in 'a most thriving state, and were
all watered by streamlets. The houses of the village
appeared to be better built, and to be intermixed with
fewer ruins, than in other instances, but the fort was
totally neglected and suffered to fall to decay.

" In this sheltered spot, and in other mountainous
parts of Persia, landscapes might be selected, which,
if faithfully painted, would represent at once the characteristics of the four seasons in Europe. Thus, the
highest mountain, covered with snow, would exhibit
winter; the next range of rather lower mountains,
covered with light evergreens, would indicate the
nascent verdure of spring; the inferior range of calcareous and sandstone mountains, with their naked
and precipitous surfaces imbued with the glaring
colours of ochre, red, and yellow, and divested of all
vegetation, would seem as if parched by the sultry
heats of summer; while the nearer ground, diversified
by orchards abounding in ripe fruit, and by fields of
grain ready for the sickle, would announce the presence
of autumn. All this variety do the mountains of
Persia present in the month of May....The soil of this
place is sandy; the rocks are of granite, sandstone,

and limestone of different colours ; and in the valleys, there are strata of amygdaloid containing a great proportion of limestone."[*]

On leaving Kuhrood, the road for three or four miles winds picturesquely along the wooded hills to the left of the valley ; till, at about five miles, the traveller comes to an immense *bund* or dike of masonry, between 30 and 40 feet high, extending between two precipitous hills, and forming a large lake or reservoir. At the bottom is an arched outlet, through which escapes a moderate stream. The winding pass between the stream and the hills is, at night, particularly dangerous, the rocks being slippery, and the road in many places being formed only of planks covered with earth. The streamlet from the *bund* runs near, and frequently crosses the road, for seven miles, when it takes a N.E. direction towards the extensive plains of Kashan.[+] At the end of the pass, where the mountains on the right terminate, are the ruins of a mud-built village called *Guebr-abad* (the town of the Guebres) ; and within about three quarters of a mile of these ruins, is a fine caravanserai on an eminence, with a tank in front, of the time of Shah Abbas. At eight miles, the road passes over the crown of a hill, from which is seen the plain of Kashan, bounded by a distant range of mountains, of which Demawend forms the most conspicuous point, rising abruptly, in a very symmetrical cone, from a

* Colonel Johnson's Journey, pp. 132, 3. Chardin supposes that the valley of Kuhrood was the scene of Darius's last moments.

+ The river of Kuhrood, which chiefly contributes to supply this reservoir, " flows from the mountain of Khoonsar, to the N.E. of Isfahan ; and having passed through the territories of Jerbadekan, Louristan, and Koum, its waters, in the spring season, are lost subterraneously after a course of 35 *farsangs*."—HAMDALLAH in OUSELEY, vol. iii. p. 81.

long, unbroken chain. Its distance, in a direct line, cannot be less than 150 miles.* The whole road to Kashan is visible, and the city itself, with the long line of gardens behind it. Westward, the hills are backed by granite mountains, but no hills are to be seen on the right or N.E., at a shorter distance than 30 miles. Between three and four miles to the left of the road, at the foot of the hills, is a small shooting-seat belonging to his present majesty, called *Bagh-e-Fin*. The Shah, on his annual excursions from Tehraun to Isfahan, generally spends a few days at this " delightful residence," which affords a cool retreat amid these arid plains, being surrounded with well-watered orchards and gardens. Various mountain-streams from the left cross the road, all flowing towards Kashan. At 25 miles (8 *farsangs*) from Kuhrood, the traveller reaches the walls of that city. The glare of the light sandy soil renders this tract of country in summer extremely scorching,—more so, Col. Johnson says, than any that he remembered to have traversed in India.

Kashan (or, as it is pronounced, Kaushoon) is en-compassed with a wall and towers of brick and mud : in some parts, the wall is double, with a *fausse-braye*. It extends two miles E. and W., and one and a half N. and S. A long, covered bazar extends from the north gate to the centre of the town. Col. Johnson observed here, a larger proportion of buildings in good repair, and fewer ruins, than in the other towns on his route ; and to Sir W. Ouseley, the city appeared much larger, as well as more populous and lively, than Shiraz. Kashan is famed for the excellence of its weavers, and for its various manufactures of silk and

---

* Colonel Johnson says, 180 miles.

cotton stuffs, velvets and shawls, and above all, for its copper ware, generally tinned or whitened so as to resemble silver.*   It is celebrated also for its delicious fruits, especially apricots and melons, pears, figs, and grapes ; and to the warmth of its climate, from which these derive their flavour, may probably be attributed its abounding with black scorpions of a most venomous kind and enormous size, together with crowds of flies and mosquitoes. " Although the mornings and nights were cool," says Sir W. Ouseley, " the thermometer rose, between two and three o'clock on the 27th and 28th of October, to 72°. † Indeed, without the vaulted chambers and cellars (or those subterranean recesses called *sardábah*), attached to almost every house, people could scarcely endure the heats of summer in this place." The popular notion is, that the scorpions do not sting foreigners. On this point, the learned Traveller adds, " I can give but a negative testimony. None of our party suffered from these creatures ; yet, it was acknowledged by many of the inhabitants, that five and twenty or thirty persons had, within the last year, perished by their envenomed stings ; to avoid which, bedsteads raised from the floor on high feet were, as I heard, generally used."‡

* " At present, as in former times, its silk brocades are celebrated all over Persia. A particularly rich shawl is also made here, and is in as great request. The worms which produce the raw material, are carefully bred by the inhabitants of the neighbouring villages. Upon the whole, we may look upon Kashan as one of the most thriving places in this quarter of the empire."—PORTER, vol. i. p. 388.

† Sir Robert K. Porter found it only 82° in May, and the heat by no means oppressive.

‡ Ouseley, vol. iii. p. 91.—A similar notion prevailed in ancient times. Pliny relates, on the authority of Aristotle, that the scorpions on Mount Latmus, in Caria, while fatal to the natives, were harmless to strangers.—Nat. Hist. lib. viii. p. 59. The bruised

Kashan is situated in lat. 33° 54′ 32″ N.; long. 51° 17′ E.* According to information furnished by a native, it contains 30 mosques, 12 baths, and 10 madrassehs, has six gates, and is one *farsang* in circumference. The present city is said to have been founded by Zobeidah, the queen of Haroun al Rashid; but Sir W. Ouseley concludes, that she only enlarged and embellished the town, which is mentioned in connexion with Koom, as furnishing its contingent to the Persian army at the fatal battle of Kadesiah, in the year 636, and subsequently at that of Nuhavend.† Its name, *Kai-ashian,* the king's dwelling, favours the tradition, that, in very early times, a Persian monarch took refuge among the mountains of Kashan; and it is enumerated, with Nishapoor and Mekran, among the cities of which the foundation has been ascribed to Tahmuras.‡ In the *Char Bagh* (four gardens) of this city, are many old cypresses and firs, planted in the reign of Shah Abbas: the trunks of some of the firs measure from 20 to 24 inches in diameter.

There is another road from Isfahan to Kashan by way of Nathunz, which, though not so near, is more pleasant. The road lies over the plain to Sheherabad, distant 13½ miles. The country continues level and barren for the next 18 miles, but then descends a range of low hills into a small valley, and winds at the foot of the hills, till near the village of Serdahen, where those on the right stretch away E. The stage from Sheherabad, is 32¼ miles. The next stage is

---

scorpion, or its oil, is believed to be a cure for its sting; and Madame de Sévigné mentions the same popular belief as prevailing in Provence.

* Porter. In lat. 34° 0′ 33″ according to Morier.

† See vol. I. p. 124.   ‡ Ouseley, iii. 89—94; 569.

18 miles, to Nathunz. The road, after leading along the foot of small hills, with high mountains on both sides, ascends gradually to higher ground, and at length issues through defiles of low hills into a beautiful valley, represented by Mr. Kinneir as one of the most delightful spots that can be imagined.

" Natunz " (Nethenz, Nuthunz,) says this Writer, " 63 miles from Isfahan, and 43 from Kashan, is situate in a valley surrounded with high and rugged mountains, from which flow innumerable rivulets. The whole of this valley, about eight miles in length, is a continued garden of fruit-trees, in which the houses of the inhabitants are interspersed and hid from view. Natunz is famed for the salubrity of its climate, its pears, peaches, and pretty women. The walnut-trees grow to a size and luxuriance beyond what I have ever witnessed in any other country; and extensive groves of white and red mulberry-trees are cultivated for the sake of a worm which produces a silk not inferior to that of Ghilaun. This is the chief town of four *balouks*. It has a fort in the centre of the valley, an excellent warm bath, and an old mosque with a very handsome minaret, said to have been built 800 years ago." * " Nothing could be more singular and beautiful," the Author of the Sketches says, " than the commanding view obtained from one of the turrets of the citadel. The valley, inclosed by mountains, is itself a succession of eminences and small hills. The fruitful gardens, which occupied every spot where there were no houses, extended eight miles. Seldom above one, and never more than two of these gardens, were upon the same level: they either appeared in a circle, converging towards the

* Kinneir, p. 115.

common centre of an eminence that rose above the others, or were seen sloping in flights along the hills that bordered on the mountains. Rows of lofty syca- mores and spreading walnuts marked the lines of the streets and the divisions of the gardens: the latter were fenced round with thick mulberry hedges, the leaves of which, the Hâkim informed us, fed innu- merable silk-worms, producing the finest of the silk manufactured at Kashan and Isfahan. The sun was shining bright as we gazed upon this enchanting scene, and its beauty was greatly increased by nume- rous clear streams, which, pouring from the neigh- bouring hills, either flowed or were conducted among the gardens and orchards, where they appeared lost, till seen glittering through those parts where the foliage was lighter or wholly removed." *

On leaving this picturesque spot, an uneven, stony country succeeds, and the road runs among the hills, with mountain ranges on each side, to Hanjun, situ- ated in a ravine near a running stream: distance, 12 miles. For seven miles more, to a caravanserai, the same hilly, stony country continues; the road then leads for seven miles over a plain, the mountains on the left stretching away to the N.W.; hills again succeed, and at 19½ miles, is Khourumdusht. The next stage, 11½ miles, leads across the plain to Kashan. Total distance from Isfahan, 107 miles. †

A flat and good road leads from Kashan northward, to the mud-walled town and fine caravanserai of Nus- serabad, distant between 10 and 11 miles. At eight miles, the flourishing village of Ali-abad is seen on the right. Another stage of 10 miles leads over a flat

* Sketches of Persia, vol. I. pp. 275, 6.
† Kinneir, pp. 371—3.

and sandy waste *to the* caravanserai of Semsin (or Sinsin), built by the patriotic *Ameen ad douleh*, or lord high treasurer, so often referred to. The village is in ruins, but a few inhabitants occupy small fortified inclosures at about a mile's distance. The next stage is *Pasengan* (*Passaungoon*), distant about six hours and a half, or 24 miles. At four miles are the ruins of a considerable village, *Deh-i-nar*, destroyed by the Turkomans ; and at eleven miles, the caravanserai and village of *Ab-i-shoor* (salt water, so called from a brackish stream). The road, varying from N. by W. to N.W., is at first hilly, and then lies over arid, stony, and sandy plains, along the base of the southern range of mountains, distant from three to five miles. A thin scattering of weeds is the only vegetation, and a naked desert extends on the right as far as the eye can see. In fact, the road from Kashan to Koom winds, for the most part, along the edge of the Great Salt Desert. Demawend is in sight throughout the stage, rising far above the horizon towards the N.E. At sun-rise, Col. Johnson says, it appeared as near to their observation, as hills would appear in India at only 40 miles' distance. " The white colour of its snow-clad surface was not then perceptible, on account, probably, of the vapour which at that hour overspread the plain, and its shadowed side being pre-sented." Several deserted villages and inclosures were seen from the caravanserai ; one of considerable extent, about two miles N.E.

Another stage, of 12 miles,* over a level and good road, leads to Koom. At five miles are the picturesque

* Col. Johnson makes the stage from Semsin to Passangoun, 24 miles and a half, and thence to Koom, 12. Sir W. Ouseley makes the former 21¾, and the latter 16¾. Mr. Morier, in his First Jour-ney, makes the whole distance only 25 miles.

ruins of a village called Laungrad (or Lankerood), with a rapid stream. During most of the way, the gilded cupola of the tomb of Fatima is in sight, appearing at sun-rise like a globe of fire. On approaching the city, the remains of habitations, gardens, and tombs, become so numerous as to evince that this district has formerly been very populous. Among the sepulchral ruins are several tombs of *imám-zadehs*, distinguished by their tiled cupolas; and the gateway and two minarets of a mosque are standing, of very antique construction. Many of the domes have the conical arch. On the pinnacles of the highest buildings, the storks build their nests, which are so large, that sparrows find room to construct theirs in the cavities and irregular projections on the perpendicular sides of the stork's habitation. This bird is held in high veneration by the Persians, and has obtained the epithet hadjee.

Koom, Mr. Morier informs us, is remarkable for three things; " its numerous priests, its gilded cupola, and its ruins. The greater part of its inhabitants are *seyeds*, descendants of Ali, who form a powerful body in Persia. The mausoleum at Koom is one of the most celebrated sanctuaries throughout Persia, and thither the Persians frequently take shelter in distress. It is very seldom that they are forced out; but, in cases of great criminality, they are starved into a surrender.* The king frequently visits the tomb of Fatimeh, and makes costly offerings there.

* " In general, the tombs of all the *imám-zadehs* (descendants of imams) are looked upon as sanctuaries; yet, some are accounted more sacred than others. Without this almost single impediment in the way of a Persian king's power, his subjects would be totally at his mercy." This is a sanctuary " even for murderers;" but murder is not held the greatest crime in Persia. Here, the nephew of the unfortunate Hajji Ibrahim took refuge, and was clandestinely supplied with food for several days, by some compassionate

By such acts he has acquired among the priesthood a great reputation, which, when at Koom, he keeps up by going about on foot; an act of great humility in Persian estimation. * During the few days that we were at Koom, we saw great numbers of women riding on asses, escorted by men on foot, arriving in bodies of ten or fifteen at a time, from the neighbouring villages, to make the *ziaret* (*hiaret*, from *har*, to journey), as it is called, or to worship at the tomb of the saint. This is one of the few recreations of the peasantry of Persia; and they recur to it, perhaps, more in the spirit of pleasure than in that of devotion. As soon as they approached the mausoleum, the men chanted a dirge, which at a distance had a very solemn effect."†

Besides the shrine of *Fatimeh-úl-Masoomah* (Fatima the Immaculate), this city contains the relics of numerous beatified persons; and within the golden mosque are the tombs of two monarchs of the Suffavean dynasty, Sefi I. and Abbas II. "Upwards of two hundred ruinous places were shewn to me," says Sir R. K. Porter, "as once dedicated to the imaumzadis, the sons of the saints. There are also the remains of above forty mosques, with tombs innumerable." A Mohammedan writer, cited by Sir W. Ouseley, makes the number of saintly persons buried here, amount to 444. Koom is mentioned in the *Shah Nameh* as an ancient city, and its foundation is tra-

women, who came to him on pretence of making their devotions at the shrine of the saint. Meanwhile, the intercession of a powerful friend obtained his pardon.

* When a great man goes abroad in Persia, it is always on horseback, surrounded by attendants on foot, bearing his pipe, shoes, cloak, saddle-cloth, &c. This gives great force to Eccl. x. 7.

† Morier, vol. ii. p. 166.

ditionally assigned to Kai Kobad. D'Anville supposes it to be the *Choana* of Ptolemy. D'Herbelot cites an account of its origin from an oriental writer, which would assign it no higher antiquity than the ninth century of our era. The surrounding district is said to have composed a small sovereignty under Abdal-rahman, an Arabian prince, in which were included seven towns. This prince was overthrown by his enemies, and his country ruined; and the inhabitants of the seven towns built the city of Koom in the year 203 of the Hejira, dividing it into seven departments, each bearing the name of one of the ruined towns. This story sounds like a mere legend, and is at variance with the more credible accounts of other writers.* Hamdallah, the Persian Geographer, enumerates it, with Isfahan, Hamadan, and Rai, among the four chief cities of Irak-Ajem. In point of sanctity, it ranks next to Kerbela and Mushed; but the hostile

* Chardin gives a very different version of the story. After mentioning the tradition which assigns its foundation to Tahmurs, and makes it to have equalled Babylon in extent, he adds: "Other Persian historians refer its origin to the first century of Mohammedism, and relate that, in the time of Mohammed, there were seven large villages, and that, in A.H. 83, Abdallah Saydan, Khalif, having come into this country with an army, he *joined* these seven villages to one another by new buildings, and inclosing them with a wall, made one city of them, which at length grew to be twice as large as Constantinople. Mousa, son of this Abdallah, came from Basrá to Koom, and brought thither the dogmas of Ali, which they call the religion of the Sheahs, or Imamism. It has always been professed here, even to martyrdom, and the people tolerate no other. Timour Leng, who was quite of a contrary belief, entirely destroyed this city. It was gradually rebuilt in part, but has only begun to flourish again since king Sefi was buried there. ...In the year 1634, the waters destroyed a thousand houses; and only three years ago, a similar accident had nearly destroyed the whole place. Two thousand houses and all the ancient buildings were overthrown. It is surnamed *Dar-el-mouweholdin*, the dwelling of the pious."—CHARDIN, *tom.* iii. p. 213.

Sounies have never respected its walls, and in 1722, it was completely destroyed by the barbarous Affghans. Part of it has since been rebuilt, but it has still the appearance of a vast ruin: " at least two thirds of the buildings," Sir W. Ouseley says, " seemed to have been untenanted for the last fifty or a hundred years." The present Shah made a vow, before he ascended the throne, that in case of his accession, he would repair this city, and exempt its inhabitants from tribute. A very beautiful college near the great mosque has been built in fulfilment of the royal vow. Mr. Morier tells us, that his majesty also covered the cupola of the tomb itself with gold plates, instead of the lackered ones which he removed, and that he is *said* to expend 100,000 *tomauns* annually in the decoration of these monuments.* The latter part of the statement does not very well accord with the Shah's notorious economy; and the credit of at least part of this munificence belongs to the *Madre Shah*, to whom, some years ago, the King gave the city of Koom as an estate. The gilded coating of the dome, Mr. Fraser says, was given by the mother of his present majesty; but the brass plates are so thinly gilt, that the whole value of the precious metal employed, does not, he says, exceed 2000 *tomauns*.†

Chardin has given a very minute and curious description of this celebrated sanctuary as it appeared

---

* Morier, vol. i. p. 180.

† See Fraser, p. 143. Sketches of Persia, ii. 33. Ouseley, iii. 99—106. Kinneir, p. 116. Porter, i. 376. Johnson, p. 146. The latter Traveller states, but without giving his authority, that the original structure was erected over the sepulchre of Fatima by Buggy Baigum, daughter of Timour Shah. Chardin says, that the tomb of this Fatima has been thrice rebuilt. Her father brought her to Koom, on account of the persecution raised against his family by the khalifs of Bagdad.

in the seventeenth century; but the only European
of modern days, who is known to have penetrated
into its forbidden precincts, is the adventurous traveller last cited. Having ascertained that not even a
bribe could procure permission for an infidel to visit
this holy shrine, he determined to risk the attempt in
the character of a moslem. At dusk, assuming the
Persian dress, and attended by his Indian moonshee,
a *seyed*, to whom the shrine was familiar, he succeeded
in entering unobserved. We give the sequel, and the
description of the place, in Mr. Fraser's words.

" We passed through a mean gateway into a small
court, around which are cells, or chambers, for the
use of the *khadums*, or servants of the shrine. From
thence, a more respectable gateway, ornamented with
blue tiles, led to a larger court, around which were
lodgings of a neater and better description, for the
higher ministers. In this is a long tank of water for
performing ablutions, with a paved pathway up each
side; and the whole is laid out like a garden, with
trees and walks. From this, a communication leads
to the court in which the mosque is situated, and
which is smaller than the preceding, but very neatly
kept: here, also, is a tank for ablution. Having deposited our slippers without, we entered. It was the
hour of evening prayer, and the place was rather full;
but we walked round, and saw every thing remarkable. The gates leading to the mosque are adorned
with blue and white lackered tiles; and the front of
the mosque, which, as usual, comprehends three archways, is faced with tiles in mosaic work of various
colours and patterns. The inside of the centre compartment, under which is the tomb, is similarly
adorned, as is also its floor, on which a rich carpet is
spread. The interior of the dome is divided into

compartments of arch-work, lessening as they rise; a common and often an elegant mode of finishing these parts of a building in Persia. The tomb itself is inclosed in a sandal-wood box, about 12 feet long by 8 broad, and 7 or 8 high. A green canopy is spread above it, and it is surrounded with a silver grate of massy cross-bars, placed there by the mother of the present King. Within this is suspended the sword of the great Abbas, which my view was too cursory to remark. Two side compartments are fitted up with strips of carpet, merely as places of prayer. The tomb, with its covering, is as old as the time of Fatima's death; but the dome and mosque are the work of the present King, built upon the ruins of a smaller building erected and richly endowed by Shah Abbas. All the race of Suffavean kings added to its riches; and previously to the present era, they were great. Although the revenues of religious institutions have neither been meliorated nor entirely respected during the late reigns, this shrine still enjoys a good income. There are several villages attached to it, and a considerable sum is derived from the presents of pilgrims who resort to it, amounting, it is said, to 4 or 5000 *tomauns.* Eight or nine *khadums* attached to the shrine receive payment; and there are also a number of *moollahs,* who depend for subsistence on the money they obtain for educating pupils.

" After a rapid glance at the place and its contents, I sat down with the *seyed,* as if accompanying him at prayers; and while thus employed, I observed first one, and then another of the *moollahs* come and look at me. Then came others, holding lighted candles (for it was dark), who, after gazing awhile, spoke to the *seyed;* and I could easily see that there was much altercation between them, of which I was the subject. Some retired as if satisfied, but others continued to remonstrate, and were joined by fresh parties, till the agitation increased so much, that I began to fear something serious would happen; when the *mehmander* came in, and caused a diversion, under favour of which I left the place with my conductor. The *seyed* told me, that he had quieted the *moollahs* by an assurance, that I was a person very much inclined towards the Mohammedan creed; but probably the tale was not credited by those who had caused the altercation I witnessed. I should add, that their demeanour, though evidently hostile to me, was grave, decent, and far from uncivil.

" Koom is indeed, as Morier describes it, a wretched mass of ruins. The population is stated to consist of 2000 houses, or 10,000 souls; a great exaggeration, if we may judge by appearances.* The chief part of it consists of those attached to the various shrines in the place; but sanctity does not seem to thrive here so well as in India, or even in other parts of Persia, although the intolerance it too often assumes, is not wanting. Indeed, the place has been remarked for its inhospitality and impertinence, particularly to Christian travellers: the very children are taught to lisp abuse. While I was attempting a sketch of the place from the top of the caravanserai, certain young urchins, encouraged by their mothers, insulted us in the grossest language, until they saw us bestow charity on some beggars who came by; when their tone was changed, and they began to beg also, adding their

---

* " The families resident at Koom do not amount to 2000, as a native of the place acknowledged, nor even to 1700, in the estimation of a well-informed traveller....Of twenty handsome mosques once crowded by the pious Kúmites, two or three only have been saved from ruin."—OUSELEY, iii. 104.

prayers for our welfare ; but, finding this ineffectual, they resumed their violent abuse, until silenced by the interference of the *mehmander*." *

When Chardin visited this city a century and a half ago, it was said to contain 15,000 houses. It was surrounded with a ditch, and a wall flanked with half-ruined towers. There were two beautiful quays, the whole length of the city, on the banks of the river, and large gardens on the other side. He mentions, also, a very handsome bridge and fine bazars. " It is," he says, " an agreeable place, except for the heat, which is excessive. In summer, the stream which flows by, is but a rivulet ; but, on the melting of the snows, it becomes so swelled by the mountain torrents as sometimes not only to fill its channel, which is as large as that of the Seine at Paris, but to overflow the town. It is commonly called the river of Koom, but its real name is *Joubadgan*. + There is not a place in Persia where the sun is more powerful in summer. The people," he adds, " are very tractable and civil." ‡

Koom was formerly a place of some trade in fruit, (chiefly pomegranates,) silk, soap, sword-blades, and white earthenware. Every manufacture has now disappeared ; the bazars hardly contain more than forty shops ; and the only employment of the inhabitants, is cultivating a little corn and rice. The

* Fraser, pp. 140—2.

† Col. Johnson found its bed dry (in May), the waters being dammed up to the westward, and diverted into numerous channels for irrigation.

‡ Chardin, i. 213. Sir R. K. Porter found the heat intense. Its proximity to the great salt desert, the rocky mountains which inclose it to the southward, and the sandy plain in which it stands, sufficiently account for the insupportable heat of the summers.

sanctity of the city still, however, induces many de-
votees to order their bodies to be transmitted hither for
sepulture ; and Sir R. K. Porter passed a train of
mules, one or two of which were loaded with a couple
of coffins, consigned to the muleteer for this purpose.
The inhabitants of the holy city, not excepting the
moollahs, lie under the suspicion of entertaining au
heretical fondness for spirituous liquors, which they
profess to use as a remedy against the stings of scorpions. A scandal of the same import is whispered
against the true believers of Kashan.* This city is
situated in latitude 34° 45′ N., long. 50° 29′ E.

At Koom, the road to Tehraun separates from that
to Tabriz, the former bending towards the N.E. At a
distance of about two *farsangs* and a half, bearing N.
46° W., is seen distinctly from Koom, the *Nemek Koh*
(the mountain of salt), rising abruptly from the
middle of the plain, which Persian superstition has
invested with mysterious celebrity. It has received
the appellations of *Gaiten Gelmez*, Turkish words im-
plying that " those who go, never return ; " and
Koh Tellsm, the mountain of the talisman, because it
was long believed that the attempt to reach the
summit would prove fatal. Latterly, however, Mr.
Morier says, this notion has been exploded, and the
plain has been traversed in all directions. " It
should seem that it consists of a tract almost entirely
composed of nitre, which crumbles so easily under foot,
particularly after rains, that it is dangerous to walk
over it. Perhaps it resembles the *Hamman Meskou-
teen*, in Barbary, and the *Solfatara* near Naples." †

The first days' stage towards Tehraun, after
leaving the cultivated tract, leads over a flat, barren,

* Ouseley, iii. 104. † Morier, ii. 167.

gravelly plain, bearing no grass or vegetation, except the usual weeds, and strongly impregnated with salt and nitre. At twelve miles, (Sir W. Ouseley makes it nearly fifteen,) is a bridge of eleven arches, over the *Rood-khoneh Konsar*, a salt stream, 30 yards in width, abounding with fish.* It comes from the westward, and has its rise in the vicinity of Sava, collecting its waters from the barren hills to the north. The bridge is said to have been erected by the barber of Shah Abbas, to save others from a danger which he narrowly escaped, of being drowned in fording this river; and it is called *Púl-i-delák* (pronounced *pooli dellauk*), the Barber's Bridge. Near it is a small caravanserai. The banks of the stream are covered with barberry-trees and other shrubs, and very long reeds beautifully feathered at top. Several tortoises were seen, and some birds of the teal and wild-duck species. The copse is said to be haunted by wolves and lions.

For six miles from *Pooli-dellauk*, the road passes over heights and among hills. It then, for three hours, traverses a salt marsh called *Derya-e-Kebeer* (or *Kiveer*), a part of the great salt desert which stretches into Khorasan. It is said to extend one hundred and fifty miles E. and W., and to be in some places upwards of thirty-five miles in breadth.† The soil is a mixture of salt and clay; and here and there, are hollows of considerable magnitude, white with salt.

* Mr. Morier represents it as " so brackish as to be *almost* salt ;" notwithstanding which the cattle drank of it, and the Persians say that they thrive on it as well as on fresh; a fact mentioned by ancient writers. See Morier, ii. 167.

† The desert, in this part, extends westward to a range of hills distant 20 miles ; and eastward, Col. Johnson was informed, it reaches Mausila, distant 40 miles. Its breadth here is about 11 miles.

After rain or snow, it becomes a dangerous morass, where travellers frequently lose their way, or perish in the swamps. At twenty-one miles, is the small caravanserai of *Haooz-i-Sultaun* (Sultan's Reservoir). The change in the appearance of the ground, from a crust of white clay and salt, to a stony plain, indicates to the traveller that he has passed the morass; but soon after leaving the caravanserai, he enters upon a sort of pass, ten miles in length, through deep ravines and dreary wastes, which has received the portentous name of the *Melek al Moat Dereh*, "the Valley of the Angel of Death." The broken country, Mr. Morier says, forms in this part a labyrinth of little hills and intricate nooks, very perplexing to travellers. The road, however, when Col. Johnson journeyed, was "thoroughly good,"* crossing very often the beds of brackish mountain torrents, at that time nearly dry. The dreariness of the scenery has probably led to an exaggerated idea of the ruggedness and danger of the route. The natives believe, that this dismal region is one of the favourite abodes of the angel of death, who here holds his court, surrounded by *ghools,*—demons who can at pleasure assume the human form, but more commonly appear in hideous shapes with horns and talons: they entice travellers by their cries or songs, and then tear them to pieces, and devour them. Their number is be-

---

* This Traveller states, that "the land bears evident marks of the action of fire." The soap-wort is the most common shrub all over the face of the country, but no use is made of it. The appellation given to this dreary region, forcibly recalls the Prophet's description of the Arabian desert, Jer. xi. 6.] ["A land of deserts and of pits, a land of drought and of the shadow of death, a land that no man passed through, and where no man dwells." It may also illustrate Psalm xxiii. 4., MORIER, i. 183, ii. 168.

lieved, however, to have wonderfully decreased of late years.*

On emerging from this fearful tract, the road traverses a more level desert, crossing repeatedly a winding saline stream, called *Rood-khaneh-i-Carege*, flowing towards the Great Desert. Near it is passed the caravanserai and village of Zeeoun; and half a mile further, is the new caravanserai and village of *Kenar-e-gherd*. The distance from *Havoz-i-Sultaun*, is rather more than twenty-four miles, about seven hours. Here, the eye is refreshed with the sight of gardens and cultivated fields, with a few trees; there are also remains of walls and old tombs. On the north side of the caravanserai runs a fine rivulet, called *Kundleh-rood*, from a village about twelve *farsangs* westward. The next stage leads for two miles over a plain of gentle ascent, crossing numerous channels of irrigation. The road then ascends a steep hill, from which is obtained the first view of the plain and city of Tehraun. At eleven miles is the village of Cahrizek; at sixteen miles, a road branches off to Rhey; and at twenty-two miles (6 *farsangs*), the traveller arrives at the gate of the present capital.†

TEHRAUN.

The distant view of Tehraun is very imposing. It is situated near the foot of Mount Elborz; a part of the great range which stretches from Europe to the utmost limits of Asia, and which would appear high,

* See, for further accounts of the pranks of these *ghools*,— *Sketches of Persia*, vol. ii. p. 77, *et seq.*

† Sir W. Ouseley found the whole distance from Isfahan to Tehraun, 242 miles, " according to actual measurement made with the wheel or perambulator." Mr. Kinneir makes it 80 miles from Koom.

ENTRY OF THE KING OF PERSIA INTO TEHERAN.

were it not for the snowy peak of Demawend, rising above the clouds, and dwarfing every other mountain. To the right are seen the extensive ruins of the once proud city of Rhey or Rhages, scattered at the foot of the nearer mountains; and westward is seen a plain enriched with cultivation and enlivened by villages, forming a pleasing contrast to the rugged and stupendous rocks which skirt it on the north and south.*

The city, which stands in lat. 35° 40′ N., long. 51° 22′ 50″ E.,† is about four miles (8000 yards) in circumference, surrounded with a strong mud wall, flanked by numerous towers, and a noble dry ditch, with a *glacis* between it and the wall. There are, according to Sir R. K. Porter, four gates, very plain in their architecture; that to the S. leading to Isfahan, that to the N.W. leading to Tabriz, and the other two looking towards the hills in the corresponding directions. The only building of consequence within the city, is the *Areg* (ark or citadel), which con-

---

[* Mr. Morier speaks in very different terms of the beauty of this plain, from Mr. Kinneir. "Nothing can be so little attractive as the immediate environs of Teheran. Each of the *five* gates" (Sir R. K. Porter speaks of only four—Sir W. Ouseley says six) leads out to what the Persians call the *Sahara,* and what we term the desert; a designation not ill applied to the plain of Teheran, for, although it is in some places partially cultivated, yet, as there are neither hedges, dikes, nor railings to mark the limits of cultivation, the whole has the appearance of a waste. A tree is a scarce object, which is a curious circumstance, when it is known, that the region of Teheran is separated only by a ridge of mountains from one of the most wooded countries in the world, the province of Mazanderan. The roots of the Albors, which form the northern boundary, are more embellished with villages, trees, and rural scenery, than any of the other vicinities of the city."— Morier, vol. ii. p. 190.

† According to Fraser. The latitude agrees with that given by Mr. Kinneir. Sir R. K. Porter states it to be in lat. 35° 37′, and the longitude given by Kinneir is 50° 52′.

tains the royal palace. This is strongly fortified with a lofty wall flanked with towers, a *fausse-braye* and a deep dry ditch. The *Arag* comprises, besides the *Divan Khaneh-i-Shah*, or royal residence, quarters for the guards, and many extensive ranges of apart- ments. Among these, Sir W. Ouseley mentions the *Defter-Khaneh* (record-chamber), the *Sanduk-Kha- neh* (chest-house or treasury), the *Emáret-i-Khur- shed* (palace of the sun), a handsome building in which Futeh Ali Shah sometimes receives ambassadors ; also, private chambers, of which one is distinguished as the *emáret-i-servistan* (palace of the cypress-grove), and another is called the *gulistan* or bed of roses. Here too is the royal harem. The *Areg* contains, moreover, ten baths and two or three gardens, with reservoirs of different dimensions.

The town itself appeared to Mr. Morier about the size of Shiraz, but with fewer public edifices ; and, as it is built of sun-dried bricks, the whole has " a mud- like appearance." The *Mesjed Shah*, the principal mosque, was not finished in 1809 ; and there were then only six others, small and insignificant, with three or four *madressehs*, and, according to report, 150 caravanserais, and as many *hummums* or baths. Sir W. Ouseley, in 1811, was informed that the baths and caravanserais then amounted to twice that num- ber, and the mosques and colleges to between thirty and forty. The different bazars exhibited many well furnished shops ; but some of the streets would have disgraced, by the state of their pavement, the meanest town ; and the holes of the *kanauts* sometimes occa- sion accidents. Every morning, at the *Derwazeh Shah Abdulazem* (gate leading to the village of Shah Abdulazem) was held, about sunrise, a market of horses, mules, asses, and camels, and various goods exhibited in temporary booths; a custom, apparently, of high antiquity.

" Half a century ago," remarks Sir R. K. Porter, " the present metropolis of Persia would hardly have been considered as a town of sufficient importance to be styled the capital of a province. It started at once into the first consequence under the auspices of Aga Mahomed Khan, uncle to the present Shah, who was the first Persian sovereign that made Teheran a royal residence. Its vicinity to that monarch's paternal country, Astarabad, which has been styled the Garden of the East, and is entirely inhabited by the Cadjar people, the royal tribe of the king, was one cause of the distinction bestowed on this once humble village. It likewise lies in a central situation, between the provinces to the north-west, which border on Georgia, and those to the east, which are subject to incursions from the Turcomans and their restless allies of Afghanistan. Indeed, for a position of general *surveillance*, the Persian monarch could hardly have chosen a better situation than that of Teheran ;* though a pleasanter might have been presented by almost any one of the former capitals of the empire. The numerous spring torrents, which pour from the adjacent

* " There are many reasons which might 'have induced the late king to fix upon Tehraun as the capital of his dominions. It is a most centrical situation, and one from which the Persian empire can perhaps be defended better than from any other; the country in its neighbourhood being fertile and productive; and so many wandering tribes have settled around, that it is ascertained, his majesty can, on any emergency, assemble from those encamped between Casween and *Firoze Koh* (in Mazanderan), a body of 25,000 horse in the short space of five days....But there is another reason : it is not far from Astrabad, his native city, and from Mazanderan and Dahestan, countries possessed by the Kajer tribe, on whose power and affection to his person, his authority was, in a great measure, founded."—KINNEIR, p. 119.

heights, at the beginning of the warm weather, saturate the low ground about the town, sink into its vaults, and send up such vapours and dampness as to render it very unhealthy during that season of the year. The unpleasantness of the place, however, lies wholly in this unwholesomeness; for its aspect is far from disagreeable. The very humidity of the soil produces early verdure, and clothes the gardens with more abundant shade. Then, immediately behind the town, the high ranges of Elborz stretch eastward; and over their picturesque heads in almost a direct line northward, rises the towering peak of Demawend. The wide plain" (approaching the city from Tabriz) " affords an open and a noble view to the north-west; while the faintly discerned range of hills, skirting the horizon to the south, which divide the fertile land from the salt desert, hardly bound the eye in that quarter.

" Teheran, though modern as a capital, and comparatively obscure as a town, has, nevertheless, had some note of its existence, so far back as the fourteenth century.* A Persian writer of that period, mentions

* " At about the same distance from Rhages at which the present city of Teheran may be placed from the remains of Rey, appears the town of *Tahora* in the Theodosian Tables; a sufficient presumption that Teheran itself had an original and independent existence, and did not rise only from the ruins of the greater metropolis. Its continuance as a contemporary city cannot now be distinctly traced; it may indeed have borne a different name in Eastern geography, as it is the Teheran or *Cherijar* (Shahr-zur) of Tavernier. It re-appears, however, under its present name, in the journey of the Castilian ambassadors to Timour, at a period when the greatness of Rey was still very considerable. At the end of two centuries, Pietro Della Valle revisited it: he calls it the city of planes. The soil is, probably, particularly adapted to this tree; for Olivier mentions one in the neighhbourhood, that measured, round an excrescence at the root, 70 feet. It is the *Tyroan* of Herbert's Travels. Its name occurs, with scarcely a line of com-

It as ' a large village, with productive gardens, in the
vicinity of the city of Rey; its inhabitants having
their dwellings underground, for two reasons : to
avoid the excessive heats of summer, and the attacks
of their hostile neighbours, from the Roudbar mountains.'   Nearly three centuries after this, in the year
1637, the secretary of the Holstein ambassadors mentions Teheran as ' one of the *towns* which enjoyed the
privilege of maintaining no soldiers.'   The cold, I am
told, is severe in the winter months.   The weather,
towards the spring, I found to be delightful; but early
in June, the heat becomes so intolerable, that the city
is almost totally abandoned.   The court retires to the
more temperate plains of Sultaneah or Oujan, and
the people either to tents or villages among the hills.
Nearer to the base of the mountains, and a little on
the ascent, the earth is free from any degree of noxious moisture; the water is good, and the air perfectly salubrious.   Hence, we cannot but lament, that
the founder of the new capital had not sages about
him, of sufficient wisdom to advise his planting the
royal pavilion there, rather than in this summer
swamp.   The proximity of the commanding heights,
as formerly they might have been called, since the
introduction of modern art in defence and attack, need
never have been an objection in a military view; at
least, they would be none under the present reign, the
Prince-governor of Azerbijan having brought the
knowledge of European tactics to a practice which
never before had been thought of in this country.

ment, in a route' given by Hanway....It had been so much destroyed by the Affghans, (when, after the battle of Salmanabad,
they invested it, in the hope of seizing Shah Thamas, who had
retired thither,) that Aga Mahomed may be considered as almost its
second founder."—MORIER, i. 400.   See also Ouseley, iii. 117.

" On entering Teheran from the Casvin gate, and after proceeding two or three hundred yards into the town, a large open space presents itself, full of wide and deep excavations, or rather pits, sunk in the earth. Within the shaft of these well-like places, and round its steep sides, are numerous apertures, leading to subterraneous apartments ; some, the sojourn of poor houseless beings, who otherwise would have no shelter; others, a temporary stabling for beasts of burden. In these gloomy recesses, we doubtless find the village of Teheran, as it was described in the fourteenth century, by the Persian writer before cited. I could not learn with any degree of precision the population of the town, but I should suppose, from my own observations, that, during his majesty's winter and spring residence there, it may amount to between sixty and seventy thousand souls. Of course, I do not calculate in this number, the extraordinary influx from the provinces to the capital at the celebration of the *Nowrooz.*"

This festival is one of the few which have survived the change introduced in the national religion by the Mohammedan couquerors. Its institution, ascribed to

* Porter, vol. L pp. 306—312. " In summer, when the excessive heats compel the king to move from this place, and to pitch his tents either in the plains of Sultanea or Oujan, the majority of the inhabitants follow the royal camp ; and I have been given to understand that, in the months of June, July, and August, the capital cannot boast above 10,000 people. In winter, the population is supposed to amount to 60,000 souls."—KINNEIR, p. 119. Mr. Morier was informed, that it contains 12,000 houses, which, adopting Olivier's estimate of seven or eight persons to a house in Persia, would give a population of between 80 and 90,000. It has risen rapidly. In 1797, Olivier describes it as little more than two miles in circumference, the palace occupying more than a fourth of the area; and the population, including the royal household of 3000 persons, amounted to only 15,000.

Jémsheed, certainly dates from the earliest ages. It originally partook of a religious character, and was intended to solemnize the commencement of the solar year, when the sun enters Aries. The festival lasted six days; and Sir R. K. Porter suggests, that this might have some reference to the six days in which the world was created.* Since the introduction of Mohammedism, it has changed its character in these respects. It no longer commences the civil year of the Persians, who, like all other Mohammedans, adopt the lunar calculation. It lasts only three days, instead of six. It is unconnected with any religious observances; there are no solemn processions, still less any offerings of viands to the spirits of departed friends and heroes, as in the times of Magianism. Still, however, every one, on meeting his friend in the morning, salutes him with *Ayd mobárek* (happy festival), or *Ayd-i-shumah mobárek báshed* (may your festival be auspicious!); as we, in England, wish our friends a merry Christmas, or a happy new year. The rich still send donations to the poor; and the common people interchange little presents of oranges, flowers, and other trifles; all are dressed in their holiday clothes; pistols and muskets are continually discharged as *feux de joie;* and there is a general appearance of festivity. " Among other gratulatory testimonies of good will," Sir Robert K. Porter says,

* " It is said, that on this day the Almighty created the world, and that, by Divine command, the seven planets first began to move in the sign of Aries; Adam also was created on this day, and therefore it is entitled *Naw-rúz*, the New Day."—MS. cited by Ouseley, vol. iii. p. 342. The learned Traveller has shewn that Dr. Hyde is mistaken in supposing that the institution originated with Jelad-ad-Din, third sultan of the Seljoukian family, in the eleventh century. Before he was born, Tabri and Ferdousi had already described the festival, ascribing it to Jemsheed.

"eggs, dyed or gilded, are mutually presented by the assembled multitude at this feast, in the same way that they are interchanged at the festival of Easter, by the members of the Greek Church." * This Traveller was present at the festival, as held in the capital on March 21, 1818; and we shall avail ourselves of his description of the scene; premising, on the authority of another traveller, that, a little before midnight, a signal gun fired from the *areg* or citadel, announces the moment of the supposed entrance of the Sun into the zodiacal sign of the Ram. This is followed by the obstreperous burst of the royal drums and trumpets, which continue their rude music for some hours.

" It was a fine morning, and at eight o'clock we mounted our horses; proceeding through narrow streets, and a part of the bazar, which terminated at the outer gate of the Ark. After passing over an open space, we crossed the bridge of the citadel, and thence were conducted into a very large square. A dome-shaped building of wood, open to the eye, appeared in the middle of the place; and under its roof stood the enormous brass cannon which Chardin mentions having seen in the Maidan-shah, at Ispahan. It was brought from that capital several years ago, and stationed here, on a huge and apparently immoveable carriage. Old guns, of various calibre, all equally awkward and unmanageable, and mingled with a few of modern fabric, stand round the sides of this central structure. Not far distant, about 200

* " I recollect the same custom," adds Sir Robert, " at the same sacred anniversary, in the northern counties of England; but I have never been able to obtain any explanation of the usage. The only conjecture I can offer, is, that eggs of gold having been a very ancient mode of tribute in the East,····this sign of homage might (on the introduction of Christianity) change its direction, and become a mark of brotherhood."—PORTER, i. 320.

swivels lay in rows on the ground. They belonged to the camel corps, who were on duty to salute the king on his entrance into the great assembly of his people. And, indeed, it might well have that title; for persons of all ranks were thronged together, within the walls of this outer court. Persians of the lowest orders, some decently attired, others in the rags of mendicity; khans in *kaalats* (the robe of honour) covered with gold and brocade; servants in gorgeous coats; and soldiers in their military garbs; all pressed on each other in one equalizing mob. It was not practicable to get our horses through such a mass of human beings; so we dismounted at the entrance of the square, and following the necessity of shouldering our way to the opposite egress, tried by that wedge-like motion to make a passage to the royal portal. Awe of the chief headsman did not widen the path an inch; neither did the hard-plied sticks of the *chargé d'affaires'* domestics in front, effect the slightest breach; they might as well have battered a wall. However, we got through at last, with no small impression made upon our court-apparel, and the shawls of our waists rent into as many strips as we had had tugs in our passage. Leaving the throng behind, we turned under a narrow and dark archway, to a low and very small door, and entered through it at once upon the quarter of the palace. It shewed a spacious area, shaded with trees, and intersected by water. In the centre stood the splendid edifice where his majesty was to sit to receive the homage of his subjects. We were led towards the southern aspect of this place, the grand saloon fronting that way, where the ceremony of royal presentation was to be performed, and were carefully stationed at the point deemed the best for seeing and hearing the Great King.

Before his Majesty appeared, I had time to observe the disposition of the scene, in which this illustrious personage was to act so conspicuous a part.

" Rows of high poplars and of other trees, divide this immense court, or rather garden, into several avenues. That which runs along the midst of the garden, is the widest; inclosing a narrow piece of still water, stretching from end to end, and animated, here and there, with a few little *jets d'eau;* the margins of which were spread with oranges, pears, apples, grapes, and dried fruit, all heaped on plates, set close together, like a chain. Another slip of water faced diagonally the front of the palace; and its fountains being more direct in the view of the monarch, were of greater magnificence and power, shooting up to a height of three or four feet! a sublimity of hydraulic art, which the Persians suppose cannot be equalled in any other country. Along the marble edges of the canal and fountains, were also placed fruits of every description, in pyramids; and between each elevated range of plates, with these their glowing contents, stood vases filled with flowers, of a beautiful fabric, in wax, that seemed to want nothing of nature, but its perfume. In a line, beyond these, was set a regular row of the finest china bowls, filled with sherbet. In two parallel files, down the sides of the wide central avenue, stood the khans and other Persians of rank, arrayed in their most costly attire, of gold or silver brocade; some of them wearing, in addition, the royal *kaalat,* which usually consists of a pelisse lined with fine furs, and covered with the richest embroidery; their heads bound with Kashmere shawls of every colour and value.

" The royal procession made its appearance. First, the elder sons of the king entered, at the side on which we stood; Abbas Mirza taking the left of the whole, which brought him to the right of the throne. His brothers followed, till they nearly closed upon us. Directly opposite to this elder rank of princes, all grown to manhood, their younger brothers arranged themselves on the other side of the transverse water. They were all superbly habited, in the richest brocade vests and shawl-girdles, from the folds of which glittered the jewelled hilts of their daggers. Each wore a sort of robe of gold stuff, lined and deeply collared with the most delicate sables, falling a little below the shoulder, and reaching to the calf of the leg. Around their black caps, they also had wound the finest shawls. Every one of them, from the eldest to the youngest, wore bracelets of the most brilliant rubies and emeralds, just above the bend of the elbow. The personal beauty of these princes, was even more extraordinary, to the eyes of a traveller, than the splendour of their dresses; there was not one of them, who might not have been particularised any where else, as most eminently handsome.

" At some distance, near the front of the palace, appeared another range of highly-revered personages; moullahs, astrologers, and other sages of this land of the East, clothed in their more sombre garments of religion and philosophy. Here was no noise, no bustle of any kind; every person standing quietly in his place, respectfully awaiting the arrival of the monarch. At last, the sudden discharge of the swivels from the camel-corps without, with the clangor of trumpets, and I know not what congregation of uproarious sounds besides, announced that his majesty had entered the gate of the citadel. But the most extraordinary part of this clamour, was the

appalling roar of two huge elephants, trained to the
express purpose of giving this note of the especial
movements of the Great King.

" He entered the saloon from the left, and advanced
to the front of it, with an air and step which belonged
entirely to a sovereign. I never before had beheld
anything like such perfect majesty; and he seated
himself on his throne with the same undescribable,
unaffected dignity. Had there been any assumption
in his manner, I could not have been so impressed.
I should then have seen a man, though a king, thea-
trically acting his state: here, I beheld a great sovereign feeling himself as such, and he looked the
majesty he felt.

" He was one blaze of jewels, which literally dazzled
the sight on first looking at him; but the details of
his dress were these. A lofty tiara of three elevations
was on his head, which shape appears to have been
long peculiar to the crown of the Great King. It was
entirely composed of thickly-set diamonds, pearls,
rubies, and emeralds, so exquisitely disposed, as to form
a mixture of the most beautiful colours, in the brilliant light reflected from its surface. Several black
feathers, like the heron-plume, were intermixed with
the resplendent aigrettes of this truly imperial diadem,
whose bending points were finished with pear-formed
pearls of an immense size. His vesture was of gold
tissue, nearly covered with a similar disposition of
jewellery; and, crossing the shoulders, were two
strings of pearls, probably the largest in the world.
I call his dress a vesture, because it sat close to his
person, from the neck to the bottom of the waist,
shewing a shape as noble as his air. At that point,
it devolved downwards in loose drapery, like the usual

Persian garment, and was of the same costly materials with the vest. But, for splendour, nothing could
exceed the broad bracelets round his arms, and the
belt which encircled his waist: they actually blazed
like fire, when the rays of the sun met them; and
when we know the names derived from such excessive
lustre, we cannot be surprised at seeing such an effect.
The jewelled band on the right arm was called *The
Mountain of Light;* and that on the left, *The Sea of
Light.*[*]

"The throne was a platform of pure white marble,
raised a few steps from the ground, and carpeted with
shawls and cloth of gold, on which the King sat in the
fashion of his country, his back supported by a large
cushion encased in a net work of pearls. The spacious apartment in which this was erected, is open in
front, and supported by two twisted columns of white
marble, fluted with gold.[†] The interior was profusely decorated with carving, gilding, arabesque
painting, and looking-glass, which latter material
was interwoven with all the other ornaments, gleam-
ing and glittering in every part from the vaulted roof
to the floor. Vases of waxen flowers, and others containing rose-water, were arranged about the apartment.

"While the Great King was approaching his throne,
the whole assembly continued bowing their heads to
the ground, till he had taken his place.[‡] A dead

---

[*] These superb diamonds were placed in the Persian regalia by
the rapacious conquests of Nadir Shah. The *bazu-bends* or armlets
(*armillæ*) are worn only by the Shah and his sons. They appear to
have been an ancient symbol of royalty. See 2 Sam. i. 10.

[†] These pillars are said to have been brought from the palace of
Kureem Khan at Shiraz.—OUSELEY, vol. iii. p. 118.

[‡] "We approached him, bowing after our own manner; but the
Persians bowed as David did to Saul, who 'stooped with his face

silence then ensued, the whole presenting a most
magnificent and, indeed, awful appearance; the
stillness being so profound amongst so vast a concourse, that the slightest rustling of the trees was
heard, and the softest trickling of the water from the
fountains into the canals. As the motionless state of
every thing lasted for more than a minute, it allowed
me time to observe particularly the figure of the Shah.
His face seemed exceedingly pale, of a polished marble
hue; with the finest contour of features; and eyes
dark, brilliant, and piercing; a beard black as jet,
and of a length which fell below his chest, over a
large portion of the effulgent belt which held his dia-
mond-hilted dagger. This extraordinary · amplitude
of beard appears to have been a badge of Persian
royalty, from the earliest times; for we find it attached to the heads of the sovereigns, in all the ancient
sculptured remains throughout the empire.

"In the midst of this solemn stillness, while all
eyes were fixed on the bright object before them,
which sat, indeed, as radiant and immoveable as the
image of Mithrus itself, a sort of volley of words,

to the earth, and bowed himself.' (1 Sam. xxiv. 8.) That is, not
touching the earth with the face, but bowing with the body at
right angles, the hands placed on the knees, and the legs somewhat
asunder. It is only on remarkable occasions that the prostration
of the *Rouee Zemeen* (the face to the earth) is made; which must
be the falling upon the face to the earth and worshipping, as Joshua
did. (Josh. v. 14.) Stated distances were fixed for taking off our
shoes; some of the ambassador's suite being obliged to take off
theirs at a considerable distance from the king, while others,
whose rank gave them more privilege, kept theirs on until near
the stairs which led into the room. As the Persians allow to their
monarch a great character of sanctity, calling him the *Sil Allah*,
the shadow of the Almighty, they pay him almost divine honours.
See Josh. v. 15."—MORIER, vol. ii. pp. 172, 3. See, for an account of the ceremonial of the Indo-Chinese courts, Mod. Trav.
Birmah, pp. 219—26; 281, 5. Also, *Turkey*, p. 215, *note.*

bursting at one impulse from the mouths "of the moullahs and astrologers, made me start, and interrupted my gaze. This strange outcry was a kind of heraldic enumeration of the Great King's titles, dominions, and glorious acts; with an appropriate panegyric on his courage, liberality, and extended power. When this was ended, all heads still bowing to the ground, and the air had ceased to vibrate with the sounds, there was a pause for about half a minute, and then his Majesty spoke. The effect was even more startling than the sudden bursting forth of the moullahs; for this was like a voice from the tombs, so deep, so hollow, and, at the same time, so penetratingly loud. Having thus addressed his people, he looked towards Captain Willock, the British *chargé d'affaires*, with whom I stood; and then we moved forward to the front of the throne. The same awful voice, though in a lowered tone, spoke to him, and honoured me with a gracious welcome to his dominions. After his Majesty had put a few questions to me, and received my answers, we fell back into our places; and were instantly served with bowls of a most delicious sherbet, which very grateful refreshment was followed by an attendant presenting to us a large silver tray, on which lay a heap of small coin, called a *shy*, of the same metal, mixed with a few pieces of gold. I imitated my friend in all these ceremonies, and held out both my hands to be filled with this royal largess; which, with no little difficulty, we passed through our festal trappings into our pockets.

" When the rest of the gratulatory compliments of the day had been uttered between the monarch and his assembled nobles, the chief executioner, our former herald, gave us the signal that all was over for that morning. We then retired, as we came, under his auspices ; but, if possible, with still more pressure and heat than we had battled through in our approach."[*]

The throne described by this Traveller, is probably the celebrated *takht-i marmer* (marble throne) of which the materials were brought from Yezd : it is adorned with handsome reliefs. His Majesty received Sir Gore Ouseley, sitting on the gorgeous *takht-i-taous* or peacock throne, which Nadir Shah brought as a trophy from Delhi. It occupied a corner, not the centre of the room. Next to it, immoveable as statues, stood two little princes, five or six years of age. More remote from the throne, but in the same line, were five other princes. On the same side, but in a recess formed by large windows, appeared three *mastowfies* (secretaries). About two yards from the door, and five or six from the throne, in a diagonal direction, was the ambassador's chair, with his suite behind him, standing. Four of the principal ministers stood near the door. Beyond them, extending in a line towards the left of the throne, were five or six officers in attendance. One held a most beautiful *taje* or crown, not inferior in the lustre of the jewels to that which decorated the head of the Shah ; another bore the scimitar of state ; a third, the royal bow, in case ; a fourth, the shield ; and the fifth, a golden tray filled with diamonds and precious stones of wonderful size and dazzling brilliancy. The golden throne seemed studded at the sides with precious stones of every possible tint ; and the back resembled a sun or glory, of which the radiation was imitated by diamonds, garnets, and rubies. Of such also were composed the two birds which give name to the throne, one perched on each of its enamelled shoulders.[†] The King's dress

* Porter, vol. i. pp. 320—9.

† Ouseley, vol. iii. p. 130. See also, for a minute description of

on this occasion, was scarlet; but it was difficult to discover either the colour or the texture, from the profusion of large pearls and sparkling jewels with which it was·embroidered. At the audience given to Sir John Malcolm in 1800, the ground of his Majesty's robes was white, covered in like manner with jewels of an extraordinary size; and " their splendour, from his being seated where the rays of the sun played upon them, was so dazzling, that it was impossible to distinguish the minute parts which combined to give such amazing brilliancy to his whole figure."* His more ordinary dress is thus described by Sir Robert K. Porter, who had the transcendent honour of taking the Shah's portrait in this costume. " His head was covered with the cap of his country; a black lamb-skin, worn alike by prince and peasant. His robe was of fine gold brocade, having a deep cape of dark sable falling on his shoulder. His under garments were composed of red Kashmere shawls of the richest work. Another shawl, of deeper hues, but of greater value, bound his waist, in which was stuck a curved dagger, blazing with diamonds, rubies, and emeralds, and hung with a tassel of the largest pearls, with which

this throne, Johnson, p. 167. His majesty possesses an assortment of thrones, each having its distinguishing name. Mr. Morier, describing either the *takht-i-taous* or another, says: " The throne upon which the king sat, was ascended by steps, upon which were painted dragons. It is surrounded with a balustrade; and the whole of it, which is overlaid with fine gold, beautifully enamelled, we were told, cost 100,000 tomauns. The throne of Solomon was ascended by steps; there were stays on each side the sitting place; and, what is its principal feature of resemblance, was overlaid with pure gold.—2 Chron. ix. 17, 18."—MORIER, vol. II. p. 174. See also p. 46 of this volume.

* Sketches of Persia, vol. ii. p. 129. See note † at p. 66 of this volume.

he occasionally played while he discoursed. Behind him was placed one of his magnificent cushions, totally covered with orient net-work, and tasselled also at its corners with bunches of the same costly ornaments. Two Persian noblemen stood a few paces from him; one bearing the royal mace or sceptre; the other, the shield and sword; each of the insignia of empire being thickly studded with every kind of precious stone. The boss of the shield was one entire ruby, which, for size, colour, and perfection, is probably not to be matched in the world."[*]

The Shah gave audience to the British Envoy, Col. Macdonald Kinneir, in 1826, at the royal camp near Achar; and although the ceremonial was nearly similar, the circumstances give interest to the scene, as they approach still nearer to the customs of ancient times. On the day appointed, the Envoy and his suite proceeded on horseback, " in gay apparel and scarlet *shakshoors*," attended by an escort and a large body of servants, to the royal tent. Before the first entrance, the corps of *zomboorekchees*, or camel-artillery men, were drawn up in three sides of a square. Their uniform is most fantastic, consisting of a yellow hussar jacket, white *shulwas*, and boots; a scarlet sugar-loaf cap, edged with black fur, with a brass plate and feather, forms the head-dress. Here, the party dismounted, and entering the receiving tent, were regaled with *kaleouns*, coffee, tea, and other refreshments. " After waiting some time," proceeds Lieut. Alexander, " his Majesty was announced to be on his throne. We rose and passed through the first entrance, the Envoy carrying the letter from the Governor-general, inclosed in silk and cloth of gold.

* Porter, vol. i. p. 355.

We found all the troops in camp drawn out in a large square, who, in compliment to us, were dressed in scarlet jackets. We walked onwards, passed through the immense tent in which was the judgement-seat, a small throne adorned with pearls and precious stones, and then through the entrance to the enclosure formed by the *serai purdah*. Over this, as over the first entrance, was the favourite representation of the hero Rustum killing the white demon, and liberating his sovereign from confinement. Within was a line of battle-ax and mace bearers. At the upper end of the inclosure, was a splendid open tent supported by flowered and gilded poles; we advanced towards it, led by the master of the ceremonies, with wand of office, high turban, and scarlet and furred robe. Half way up the walk, we stopped, threw off our slippers, and made a low obeisance towards the tent, from which issued a clear and solemn voice, saying, *Khoosh amudeed*, You are welcome. We made two other obeisances, passed through a guard of richly dressed musketeers, and entered by a door in the side wall of the royal tent. Opposite to us, on a high and magnificent throne, sat his Persian Majesty, or, as the master of the ceremonies designated him, *Kebleh Alum, Shahein Shah, Zil Ullah;* the Centre of the Universe, the King of Kings, and Shadow of God.

" He appeared a hale man and tall, sixty-five years of age, and had lost some of his front teeth. He had on the usual Persian cap, encircled by the *toorah*, a rich bandeau of jewels, and was clothed in a close red dress; his *basoo-bunds*, or armlets, were splendid, as were his girdle and dagger; all these were closely set with gems of rare beauty and immense value. His beard flowed below his girdle. On his right stood a line of twelve princes of the blood royal, all possessing

the fine aquiline nose which distinguishes the Kujurs ;
below them and near us, stood several of the ministers ;
among others, our friend Mirza Abool Hussein Khan,
adorned with the first and second orders of the [Sun
and the] Lion and the Sun.* He marshalled us along
the wall opposite his Majesty, according to our rank.
The Envoy was in front of us near a gilt chair. The
letter of the Governor-general was laid at his Majesty's
feet. After again bowing low, and receiving the
Khoosh amudeed, the Mirza introduced us to the king,
who was amusing himself with dangling in his hand
a heavy dagger-knot of large pearls. Outside the tent,
and on his Majesty's left, splendidly attired, were
three young men, the shield, sword, and cupbearers,
all which insignia glittered with jewels. On the King's
right, and on the ground, upon the carpet, was the
lofty cylindrical crown, on which the plume or *jika*
nodded ; also, the *kara-nai* or Turkish caleoon, and
an immense pillow studded with pearls. Altogether,
there was a great display of pearls : the throne, high-
backed and with arms, was one mass of them. It is
said that his Majesty has a mule-load of these precious

---

* " Nothing can be more curious than the fact of Mahomme-
dan princes creating honours of knighthood to confer distinctions on Christians. The usage commenced with the court of
Constantinople, and was followed by that of Teheran. The King
of Persia created the order of the Sun, for General Gardanne, the
ambassador from Buonaparte. This order was offered to Sir Harford Jones, envoy from the King of England, but was declined on
account of the circumstances attending its origin. It was subsequently pressed upon the acceptance of General Malcolm, but he
deemed it proper to follow the example of the envoy of the King
of England. The King of Persia determined, however, as he said,
that his first European friend should wear an order of his creation,
and instituted that of the Lion and Sun, which had been from
very ancient times the arms of Persia."—*Sketches of Persia,* vol. ii,
p. 163.

articles in his treasury, besides a vast quantity of jewels, and thirty millions sterling in specie: no other monarch in the universe is possessed of so much treasure. His Majesty was in excellent spirits, or *damaughish chak bood*, as the Persians express it, and was exceedingly affable and polite. His personal attentions to the Envoy were very marked; he twice pressed him to sit, which the Envoy declined doing. This mark of respect on the part of the latter, raised him in the good opinion of the Shah and his ministers. His Majesty's manner to the Russian envoy, Prince Menzikoff, was cold and distant; he did not ask him to sit, and would not permit his suite to enter the tent; they stood in a line outside. The Russians had themselves alone to blame for all this, for they still insist on wearing their boots.

" The Shah said, that he had been anxiously expecting the Envoy for some time, and that ' his place had been long empty.' The latter replied that, after leaving Shiraz, the sickness which prevailed in camp, prevented his making such rapid progress as he wished, but that, after quitting Isfahan, he had hastened to the royal stirrup. His Majesty said, it was fortunate he had not arrived sooner, or he would have been involved in disputes with the Russians; adding, ' *poof reksha pur*,' I spit on their beards. He then drew comparisons between the English and the Russian nations, and was complimented by the Envoy on the successes which had attended the Persian arms. In return to this compliment, he said: ' Whose dogs are they, that they should attempt to compete with the *Kizil-bashees*? (golden-heads, as the Persians call themselves.) Upon this, Mirza Aboul Hussein Khan, who had been long anxiously waiting an opportunity to join in the conversation, exclaimed, ' *Aferin!*

aferin ! la illah illulah : koorbanut-i-shumah.' Excellent ! there is but one God : I am your sacrifice. *Mashalla !* God be praised ! The victorious army of the Shah has already driven the Russians out of Georgia.' Then, turning to the Envoy, he said; ' Your face is whitened : your consequence is increased by the condescension of his Majesty.' The Envoy merely answered, ' *Barek Ullah*,' Praise be to God. When the Shah had drunk coffee, and smoked from a diamond-covered caleoon brought in by a khan, we took leave, after half an hour's desultory conversation. The introduction was well conducted and very impressive, and the exhibition grand and imposing."*

Mr. Morier's description of the entertainment given by the Shah on the fourth day of the festival of Norooz, to which the Envoy was invited, is interesting, both as an illustration of the manners of the modern Persians, and on account of the conformity of some of the existing customs to the institutions of remote antiquity.

" The court in which the various exhibitions were to take place, appeared to us to be nearly 200 feet square. On each side of the great gate, were sixteen arched compartments, each of which opened into a small room. In the centre was a high pole, with a truck at the top, and small projections, for the convenience of ascending it. This pole is for the purpose of horse-exercises and shooting at the mark. Close under the room in which the Shah was seated, was a basin of water, on the other side of which were erected the poles and ropes of a rope-dancer. In a circle round these, were placed fire-works in various forms and quantities. Four figures, composed of paper and

* Alexander's Travels, pp. 205—6.

linen, and dressed like Europeans, were erected on high, and surrounded with fire-works. At a distance were elephants of paper, stuck all over with rockets; on all the walls were rockets, and fire-works were placed in every direction. Opposite to the Shah, in two lines, were the newly-raised troops, with drum- mers standing in a row at the furthest extremity. In the centre of these was the *Nasakchee Bashee*, who appeared as the director of the entertainment. He had a stick in his hand, and wore on his head a *jika*, a distinguishing ornament borne by 'particular people only, to whom the King grants the liberty.

" The first ceremony was the introduction of the presents from the different provinces. That from Prince Hossein Ali Mirza, governor of Shiraz, came first. The master of the ceremonies walked up, having with him the conductor of the present, and an at- tendant, who, when the name and titles of the donor had been proclaimed, read aloud from a paper the list of the articles. The present from Prince Hossein Ali Mirza, consisted of a very long train of large trays placed on men's heads, on which were shawls, stuffs of all sorts, pearls, &c.; then, many trays filled with sugar and sweetmeats; after that, many mules laden with fruit, &c. &c. The next present was from Ma- homed Ali Khan, prince of Hamadan.[*] He was the eldest born of the king's sons; but he had been de- prived by his father of the succession, because his mother, a Georgian slave, was of an extraction less noble than that of the mothers of the younger princes. His present accorded with the character which is assigned to him; it consisted of pistols and spears, a string of one hundred camels, and as many mules.

* Since dead.

After this, came the present from the prince of Yezd, another of the king's sons, which consisted of shawls and the silken stuffs, the manufacture of his own town. Then followed that of the prince of Meshed. The last of all, and the most valuable, was that from Hajee Mohamed Hossein Khan, *Ameen-ed-doulah.* It consisted of fifty mules, each covered with a fine Cashmire shawl, and each carrying a load of a thousand *tomauns.* The other offerings had been lodged in the *Sandeck-Khonch.* This was conveyed in a different direction to the treasury. Each present, like the first, contained a portion of sugar and sweetmeats.

" When all the train had passed in procession, one by one, before the King, the amusements commenced. First came the rope-dancer : a boy about about twelve years old ascended the rope, and paced it backward and forward. The same rope was continued to the roof of the room in which the King was seated, making first an angle of 40°, and then, in a second flight, an angle of 50°, with its horizontal extension. The boy, balancing himself with his pole, walked up the first steadily, and with very little more difficulty ascended the second, while the music below animated him in his progress. He then, with the same steadiness, descended, walking backward, and safely reached the horizontal rope. After this, a man in a kind of petticoat began a dance of the most extravagant attitudes. A large elephant, which had been in waiting amid the crowd, was next brought forward, and was made to give a shriek, and then to kneel down, paying, as it were, his *selaam* to the king. A company of wrestlers succeeded; and every one who threw his antagonist on his back, ran before the king, and received a *tomaun.* When ten such feats had been successively performed, a man led in a bear, with which in his turn he wrestled. But the bear always had the advantage; and when his antagonist attempted to throw him into the basin of water, the bear became so much out of humour, that, if he had not been deprived of his teeth, he would probably have demolished the unlucky assailant. Then rams were brought into the arena, and, in several couples, fought for some time with much obstinacy. A poor ox was next introduced, and after him a young lion. The ox was scarcely suffered to walk, before the lion was let loose upon him. Twice was the lion dragged off, and twice permitted to return to the charge, which he always made in the rear, and of which the success was secure and easy. A less sanguinary display succeeded: a bear was brought forward by a company of *looties* or mountebanks, and danced for some time to the rude noise and music of its leaders. Then came a man who, on his bare head, balanced, among other things, two high vases full of water, which another was to break with his cane. To all these different performers the King threw different sums, as he was pleased with their several tricks and feats. At sunset, his Majesty retired to say his *namaz* (vespers), when his *Nokara Khanah* (drums and trumpets) played as usual. At this moment the Envoy retired, happy to escape the noise and smoke of the fire-works which were to close the entertainment.

" On the 25th, the King held the races, at which also the Envoy was desired to be present. From the Casvin gate, at which we left the city, we proceeded about half a mile, to a fine even part of the country, where a tent was pitched for the king. All his new-raised troops were arranged on the right and in front of it. On the left, facing the tent, we stood in a line near the ministers, Mirza Sheffeea and the

Ameen-ed-doulah. Directly opposite his Majesty were eight of his sons, richly dressed in velvet and gold brocade coats, all glittering with gold and jewels. One of these carried by his side his father's bow and his quiver thickly set with precious stones. The master of the ceremonies in the field was a young Persian, who carried an ornamented and gilded spear. One or two of the princes were mounted on white horses, the lower parts of which were dyed a rich orange colour, terminated at the top by little flowers. The Persians much admire this species of disfigurement, and their taste is not singular in the East. At about fifty paces' distance from the princes, stood the king's band of music, with a troop of *looties* and their monkeys. The state elephants were on the ground, on the largest of which the King, seated in a very elegant *howdar*, rode forth from the city. When he alighted, he was saluted with a discharge of *zembooreks*; the salute, indeed, is always fired when the King alights from his horse, or mounts. In one of the courts of the palace at Shiraz, we had previously noticed this artillery. The *zemboorek* is a small gun mounted on the back of a camel. The conductor, from his seat, behind guides the animal with a long bridle, and loads and fires the little cannon without difficulty. He wears a coat of orange-coloured cloth, and a cap with a brass front; and his camel carries a triangular green and red flag. Of these, there were one hundred on the field; and when their salute was fired, they retreated in a body behind the King's tent, where the camels were made to kneel down. Collectively, they make a fine military appearance. This species of armament is common to many Asiatic states; yet, the effect, at best, is very trifling. The Persians, however, place great confidence in their execution; and Mirza Sheffeea, in

,speaking of them to the Envoy, said: ' These are
what the Russians dread.'

" No exhibition could be more miserable than the
races, the immediate object of our excursion. The
prize is what the king may be pleased to give to the
first jockeys. On this occasion there were two sets,
which came severally from a distance of twelve and
twenty-one miles. Each consisted of about twelve
ill-looking horses, mounted by boys of ten or twelve
years old, who were wretchedly dressed in a shirt and
pair of breeches, boots and cap. In each race, the
king's horses won, of course. Horses are trained in
this manner for a reason sufficiently obvious, in a
country where the fortunes of the state and of every
individual are exposed to such sudden changes. Every
one likes to be prepared with some mode of escape, in
case of pursuit. Now horses thus inured to running,
will continue on the gallop for a day together, while a
high-conditioned and well-fed animal would drop at
the end of ten miles. For this reason, the King always
keeps himself well supplied with a stud of this description, as a resource in the event of an accident.
When, on the death of his uncle, Aga Mahomed
Khan, he was summoned (by Hajee Ibrahim, the
minister of the late king) to assume as heir the sovereignty, he thus travelled from Shiraz to Teheran, a
distance of 500 miles, in six days.

" In the interval of the race, the King sent the
master of the ceremonies to desire the Envoy and his
suite to come before him. We dismounted from our
horses, and proceeded with the prime minister and the
Ameen-ed-doulah, before the King's presence, making
low bows as we advanced. When we were about
twenty steps from his Majesty, we stopped, and made
our final low bow. The King was seated on a high

chair under a canopy, the sides of which were formed of gold cloth and of looking-glasses. The chair itself was beautifully embroidered with enamelled flowers and other ornaments : on one of the arms was a pot of flowers, and on the other a vase of rose-water. On one side was spread a velvet and gold cloth carpet, with the pearl pillow. The King was in his riding-dress, a close coat of purple velvet embroidered in pearl, the sheep-skin cap, and a pair of Bulgar boots. His manners are perfectly easy and unconstrained, with much dignity and affability. He first inquired after the Envoy's health, of whose good qualities the two ministers then entered into an immense eulogy, praising him in terms the most extravagant. Then, the names of all the party were mentioned to the King, and each was asked how he did. All the conversation was complimentary. After the whole was over, we returned to our horses. The king then mounted, and the salute was fired from the *zombooreks.* His infantry first marched off the ground; they were dressed differently, in black or crimson velvet jackets, with loose breeches of crimson or yellow silk, black sheep-skin caps, and light boots. The King passed us at a distance on horseback, preceded by a body of *chatters,* who were dressed with fantastical caps on their heads, and lively-coloured clothes. No person was near him, nor, indeed, is any one permitted. The King of Persia is an insulated being, alone in his court. How different is the state of the sultan at Constantinople, who is almost concealed by the crowds of his attendants ! The princes followed, and then the mob." *

The same Traveller was present, during his second residence in the Persian capital, at the celebration of

* Morier, vol. I. pp. 207—212. See plate at p. 197.

the annual solemnity in commemoration of the murder
of Hossein, the royal martyr of Persia. This takes
place during the first ten days of *Moharrem*, the first
month of the Mohammedan year. The last tragical
scenes of his life, commencing with his flight from
Medinah, and terminating with his death on the plains
of Kerbelah, on the road to Kufah, form the subject
of a drama in ten parts, one of which is performed on
each successive day of the mourning. The last part,
which is reserved for the tenth day, called the *Roos
Katl* (day of murder), or *Roos Hossein*, comprises
the events of the day on which he met his death, and
is acted with great pomp before the king in the largest
square of the city. The enthusiasm with which the
Persians dwell upon the character of Hossein, and
every incident of the closing scenes of his life, is un-
diminished by lapse of time. Their strongest religious and national feelings are on this occasion brought
into play. They execrate Yezid, the usurper, and
Omar, with such rancour, that it is necessary, Mr.
Morier says, to have witnessed the scenes that are exhibited in their cities, to judge of the degree of fana-
ticism which at this time possesses them. " I have
seen," he adds, " some of the most violent of them,
as they vociferated *Ya Hossein !* walk about the
streets almost naked, with only their loins covered,
and their bodies streaming with blood from the cuts
which they have voluntarily given to themselves,
either as acts of love, anguish, or mortification." *

* " Such must have been the cuttings which were forbidden to
the Israelites by Moses, Levit. xix. 28; Deut. xiv. 1. And these
extravagancies, I conjecture, must resemble the practices of the
priests of Baal, who ' cried aloud and cut themselves, after their
manner, with knives and lancets, till the blood gushed out upon
them.' 1 Kings xviii. 28. See also Jer. xvi. 6, 7."—MORIER, vol.
ii. p. 177.

The preparations made throughout the city, consist in erecting large tents (called *takieh*), fitted up with black linen, and the emblems of mourning, for the performance. This expense, together with the hire of a *moollah*, the actors, and the needful theatricals, is borne either by the *mahal* (district), or by men of consequence, as an act of devotion. Besides these *takiehs* in different open places and streets, a wooden pulpit, without any such appendage, is sometimes erected, from which a *moollah* harangues the crowd.

On the 8th night of the *Moharrem*, the Grand Vizier invited the whole of the embassy to attend his *takieh*. " On entering the room," says Mr. Morier, " we found a large assembly of Persians clad in dark-coloured clothes, which, accompanied with their black caps, black beards, and their dismal faces, looked really as if they were ' afflicting their souls.' We observed that ' no man did put on his ornaments.' * They wore neither their daggers nor any other part of their dress which they regard as ornamental. A *moollah* of high consideration sat next to the Grand Vizier, and kept him in serious conversation, while the remaining part of the company communicated with each other in whispers. After we had sat some time, the windows of the room in which we were seated, were thrown open, and we then discovered a priest placed on a high chair, under the covering of a tent, surrounded by a crowd of the populace, the whole place being lighted up with candles. He commenced with an exordium, in which he reminded them of the great value of each tear shed for the sake of Imam Hossein, which would be an atonement for a past life of wickedness; and also informed them, with much solemnity,

* See Exod. xxxiii. 4.

that ' whatever soul it shall be, that shall not be afflicted in the same day, shall be cut off from among the people.' * He then began to read from a book, with a sort of nasal chant, that part of the tragic history of Hossein appointed for the day, which soon produced its effect upon his audience ; for he had scarcely turned over three leaves, before the Grand Vizier began shaking his head to and fro, and to utter, in a most piteous voice, the usual Persian exclamation of grief, ' *Wahi! wahi! wahi!*' both of which acts were followed, in a more or less violent manner, by the rest of the audience.

" The chanting of the priest lasted nearly an hour, and some parts of his story were, indeed, pathetic and well calculated to rouse the feelings of a superstitious and lively people. In one part of it, all the company stood up; and I observed that the Grand Vizier turned himself toward the wall, with his hand extended before him, and prayed. After the priest had finished, a company of actors appeared, some dressed as women, who chanted forth their parts from slips of paper, in a sort of recitative, that was not unpleasing even to our ears. In the very tragical parts, most of the audience appeared to weep very unaffectedly ; and as I sat near the Grand Vizier and his neighbour, the priest, I was witness to many real tears that fell from them. In some of these mournful assemblies, it is the custom for a priest to go about to each person at the height of his grief, with a piece of cotton in his hand, with which he carefully collects the falling tears, and then squeezes it into a bottle, preserving them with the greatest caution. This practically illustrates that passage in Psalm lvi. 8,

* See Levit. xxiii. 29.

' Put thou my tears into thy bottle.' Some Persians believe, that, in the agony of death, when all medicines have failed, a drop of tears so collected, put into the mouth of a dying man, has been known to revive him; and it is for this use that they are collected.

" On the *Roox Catl*, the tenth day, the Ambassador was invited by the King to be present at the termination of the ceremonies, in which the death of Hossein was to be represented. We set off after breakfast, and placed ourselves in a small tent that was pitched for our accommodation, over an arched gateway, which was situated close to the room in which his Majesty was to be seated. We looked upon the great *maidan*, or square, in front of the palace, at the entrance of which we perceived a circle of *Kajars*, or people of the king's own tribe, who were standing barefooted, and beating their breasts in cadence to the chanting of one who stood in the centre, and with whom they now and then joined their voices in chorus. Smiting the breast is a universal act throughout the mourning; and the breast is made bare for that purpose, by unbuttoning the top of the shirt. The King, in order to shew his humility, ordered the *Kajars* (among whom were many of his own relations) to walk about, without either shoes or stockings, to superintend the order of the different ceremonies about to be performed; and they were to be seen stepping tenderly over the stones, with sticks in their hands, doing the duties of menials; now keeping back a crowd, then dealing out blows with their sticks, and settling the order of the processions. Part of the square was partitioned off by an inclosure, which was to represent the town of Kerbelah, near which Hossein was put to death; and close to this were two small tents, which were to represent his encampment in the desert with his family. A wooden platform covered with carpets, upon which the actors were to perform, completed all the scenery used on the occasion.

" A short time after we had reached our tent, the King appeared; and although we could not see him, yet, we were soon apprised of his presence by all the people standing up, and by the bowing of his officers. The procession then commenced as follows.

" First came a stout man, naked above the waist, balancing in his girdle a long, thick pole, surmounted with an ornament made of tin, curiously wrought with devices from the Koran; in height altogether about 30 feet. Then an other, also partly naked, balanced in his girdle an ornamented pole still more ponderous, though not so high, upon which a young dervish, resting his feet upon the bearer's girdle, had placed himself, chanting verses with all his might in praise of the king. After him, a still stronger man, a water-carrier, walked forward, bearing an immense leathern sack, filled with water, slung on his naked back, on which, by way of bravado, four boys were piled one over the other. This personage, we were told, was emblematical of the great thirst which Hossein suffered in the desert.

" A litter in the shape of a sarcophagus succeeded; this was borne on the shoulders of eight men, and is called the *Kaber Peighember*, or the tomb of the prophet. On its front was a large oval ornament entirely covered with precious stones, and just above it, a great diamond star. On a small projection were two tapers, placed on candlesticks enriched with jewels. The top and sides were covered with Cashmere shawls, and on the summit rested a turban, intended to represent the head-dress of the prophet. On each side walked two men bearing poles, from which a variety of beautiful shawls were suspended, at the top of which were representations of Mahommed's hand, studded with jewellery.

" After this, came four led horses, caparisoned in the richest manner. The fronts of their heads were ornamented with plates, entirely covered with diamonds, which emitted a thousand beautiful rays. Their bodies were dressed with shawls and gold stuffs ; and on their saddles was placed some object emblematical of the death of Hossein. When all these had passed, they arranged themselves in a row, to the right of the king's apartment.

" After a short pause, a body of fierce-looking men, with only a loose white shirt thrown over them, marched forward. They were all smeared with blood, and each brandishing a sword, they sang a sort of hymn, the tones of which were very wild. These represented the sixty-two relations, or the martyrs, as the Persians call them, who accompanied Hossein, and were slain in defending him. Close after them was led a white horse, covered with artificial wounds, with arrows stuck all about him, and caparisoned in black, representing the horse upon which Hossein was mounted when he was killed. A band of about fifty men, striking two pieces of wood together in their hands, completed the procession. They arranged themselves in rows before the King; and marshalled by a *maître de ballet*, who stood in the middle to regulate their movements, they performed a dance, clapping their hands in the best possible time. The *maître de ballet* all this time sang in recitative, to which the dancers joined at different intervals with loud shouts, and reiterated clapping of their pieces of wood.

" The processions were succeeded by the tragedians. Hossein came forward, followed by his wives, sisters, and relatives. They performed many long and tedious acts; but, as our distance from the stage was too great for our hearing the many affecting things which no doubt they said to each other, we will proceed at once to where the unfortunate Hossein lay extended on the ground, ready to receive the death-stroke from a ruffian dressed in armour, who acted the part of executioner. At this moment, a burst of lamentation issued from the multitude, and heavy sobs and real tears came from almost every one of those who were near enough to come under our inspection. The indignation of the populace wanted some object upon which to vent itself, and it fell upon those of the actors who had performed the parts of Yezid's soldiers. No sooner was Hossein killed, than they were driven off the ground by a volley of stones, followed by shouts of abuse. We were informed that it is so difficult to procure performers to fill these characters, that, on the present occasion, a party of Russian prisoners were pressed into the army of Yezid; and they made as speedy an exit after the catastrophe as it was in their power. The scene terminated with the burning of Kerbelah. Several reed huts had been constructed behind the inclosure before-mentioned, which, on a sudden, were set on fire. The tomb of Hossein was seen covered with black cloth, and, upon it, sat a figure disguised in a tiger's skin, which was intended to represent the miraculous lion, recorded to have kept watch over his remains after he had been buried.

" The most extraordinary part of the whole exhibition, was the representation of the dead bodies of the martyrs, who, having been decapitated, were all placed in a row, each body with a head close to it.

To effect this, several Persians buried themselves alive, leaving the head out just above ground; while others put their heads under ground, leaving out the body. The heads and bodies were placed in such relative positions to each other, as to make it appear that they had been severed. This is done by way of penance; but in hot weather, the violence of the exertion has been known to produce death. The whole ceremony was terminated by the *khotbeh*, which is an action of prayer for Mohammed and his descendants, and for the prosperity of the King. This was delivered in a loud voice by a man, the best crier of his time, (as Xenophon calls Tolmides,) who is celebrated for his strong voice, and indeed deservedly so; for at about fifty yards' distance from us, we heard every word he said, notwithstanding the noise of the multitude which surrounded us." *

The costume of the modern Persians has already been described in our account of the Shirazees; but a few particulars must be added from the pages of Mr. Morier. " The dress of the Persians," he remarks, " has been much changed since the time of Chardin. It never possessed the dignity and solidity of the Turkish dress, and much less now than ever. So materially, indeed, have their fashions altered, that, in comparing with the modes of the present day, the plates and descriptions in Chardin and Le Brun, we can recognise no longer the same people. It is extraordinary that an Asiatic nation so much charmed by show and brilliancy, should have adopted in their apparel the dark and sombre colours which are now universal among all ranks. In the reign of the Zund family, light colours were much in vogue; but the present race,

* Morier, vol. ii. pp. 178—184.

perhaps from a spirit of opposition, encourage dark ones. A Persian, therefore, looks a most melancholy personage, resembling closely some of the Armenian priests and holy men whom I have seen in Turkey. Browns, dark olives, bottle-greens, and dark blues, are the colours mostly worn. Red they dislike; and it is singular, that this is a hue which fashion seems to have discarded even in' the countries far be-yond the northern and eastern confines of Persia; for the merchants of Bokhara, who come down annually to Busheer to. buy cloths, totally disregard scarlets, and will not give any thing like the price for that colour, which they will pay for others. *

" The head-dress of every Persian, from the king to the lowest subject, is composed of the same material, and consists of a black cap about a foot and a' half high': these caps are all jet black, and all made of skins of the same animal. The finest are taken from the lamb in the moment of its birth; and they decrease in value down to the skin of the full-grown sheep, which the common *rayut* wears. The lamb-skins are also used to line coats and pelisses. The only distinction in the head-dress of Persia, is that of a shawl wrapped round the black cap; and this distinction is confined to the king, his sons, and some of the nobility and great officers of state. Cashmeer shawls have been discouraged of late, in order to promote the domestic manufactory of brocade shawls.

" Like the Turks and most other Asiatics, the Per-

---

* This taste for sombre colours would seem, indeed, to be a Kujuree fashion, introduced and enforced by sumptuary laws, by the present family, who are of Turkish origin. See vol. i. p. 359. The king himself and his sons, however, occasionally wear crimson or scarlet. *Zeer-jumahs* of red silk are not uncommon, and scarlet cloth boots are *dress.*

sians are very careful in preserving warmth in the
feet. In winter, they wear a thick woollen sock;
and in a journey, they bind their feet and legs with a
long bandage of cloth, which they increase with the
advance of the cold. They have three different sorts
of shoes, and two sorts of boots. 1. A green slipper,
the heel about an inch and a half high, with a painted
piece of bone at the top: these are worn by the higher
classes, and by all before the king. 2. A flat slipper
of red or yellow leather, with a little iron shoe under
the heel, and a piece of bone over that shoe, on which,
as in the former, the heel rests. 3. A stout shoe,
with a flat sole, turning up at the toe, which covers
the whole foot, and is made either of leather or of
thick-quilted cotton: it is worn by the peasants and
by the *chatters* or running footmen. The boots are,
1. A very large pair, with high heels, turned up at
the toe, generally of Russia leather, and covering the
leg. 2. A smaller and lighter kind, buttoning at the
side and reaching only to the leg. When the Persians ride, they put on a loose trowser of cloth, called
shalwar, into which they insert the skirt of the *alkalok* (or vest), as well as the silken trowsers (*zeer jumah*); so that the whole looks like an inflated bladder.
The *shalwar* is very useful in carrying light baggage.*

* Although the climate requires full as much clothing in winter
as that of Turkey, the Persians do not load themselves by any
means with so many clothes as the Turks. Mr. Morier gives the
following general inventory of a Persian's wardrobe: 1. The *zeer-
jumah;* wide trowsers of red silk or blue cotton. 2. The *peera-
hān,* or shirt, generally of silk. 3. The *alkalok,* a tight vest of
chintz quilted with cotton, descending below the calf of the leg,
and with sleeves open from the elbow. 4. The *kāba* (or *kouba*);
an outer vest, fitting tight to the hips, and closed from the elbow
by buttons. There is a double-breasted sort, made of cloth or
quilted cotton, called *bagalee,* which is worn in winter. 5. Over
the *kāba* comes the *shāl-kemer,* a shawl or bandage about eight

" The Persians shave all the head except a tuft of hair just on the crown, and two locks behind the ears; but they suffer their beards to grow to a much larger size than the Turks, and to spread more about the ears and temples. They almost universally dye them black, by an operation not very pleasant, and necessary to be repeated generally once a fortnight. It is always performed in the hot-bath, where the hair, being well saturated, takes the colour better. A thick paste of *henna* is largely plastered over the beard, which, after remaining an hour, is washed off, and leaves the hair of a very strong orange colour, bordering upon that of brick-dust. After this, a thick paste is made of the powdered leaf of the indigo, and a deep layer is put upon the beard: this second process, to be taken well, requires full two hours. During all this operation, the patient lies quietly upon his back, while the dye (more particularly the indigo, which is a strong astringent) contracts the features of his face in a very mournful manner, causing the lower part of the visage to smart and burn. When the indigo is at last washed off, the beard is of a very dark bottle-green, and becomes a jet black, only when it has met the air for twenty-four hours. Some, more fastidious, prefer a beard quite blue. The people of Bokhara are famous for blue beards. It is inconceivable how careful Persians are of this ornament: all the young men sigh for it, and grease their skins to hasten the growth of the hairs; because, until they

yards long and one broad, wrapped round the waist: this is either the Cashmeer or common Kerman shawl, or an English chintz or flowered muslin. To this is fastened, by a string, the *kunjur* or dagger. 6. Various sorts of outer coats, worn or thrown off according to the season; the *tekmch*, the *oymee*, the *baroonee*, the splendid *katebee*, and the sudorific *hummum* or *pooshtee*

have a respectable covering, they are supposed not fit
to enjoy any place of trust." *

To the northward and westward of Isfahan, the
Turkish language prevails. " The natives," Lieut.
Alexander says, " hardly understood a word of Persian in some of the villages" which he passed in his
route to Hamadan. A remarkable difference of pronunciation also distinguishes the southern Persians
from the inhabitants of the northern provinces.
" Having hitherto been accustomed," says Sir W.
Ouseley, " to hear Persian spoken with the southern
accent, considered at Shiraz and Isfahan, and even in
many places of the north, as extremely soft and melodious,—my ear was surprised, not very agreeably, by
the broad, though more correct sound which Prince
Ali Shah (at Tehraun) gave to the *a* before *n*, in such
words as *Iráni* and *Isfaháni*. These, an Italian would
have pronounced exactly like the prince, while we had
learned to express them as if written Iroony, Isfa-
hoony."*

* Morier, vol. i. pp. 243—7.

† Ouseley, iii. 127, note. This softer pronunciation is called
shirein. Lieut. Alexander, who had studied Persian in India,
where the broad accent prevails, was much struck with the different pronunciation of Southern Persia; *noon* for *nán* (bread),
Iroon for *Irán*, *Ulee* for *Ali*. To avoid ambiguity, however, the
title of *Khán* is never sounded like *khoon*, which signifies blood.
The Indian and Persian pronunciations differ in other respects,
the long *o*, which the Persians can scarcely pronounce, being substituted in India for the *a* and *u* (oo.) Thus, *rooz* (a day), *kuh* or
kooh (a mountain), and *roo* (the face), are pronounced in India,
roze, koh, ro. See OUSELEY, v. i. pp. xii—xvi. WARING, p. 147.
This will explain the various orthography which occurs in writing
Persian words, some travellers giving them as pronounced, others
as written by the best authorities. It was our wish to observe a
greater uniformity in the orthography adopted in our text; but
this has been found impracticable, and we have generally followed
the Traveller cited, giving, in most cases, the variations.

We had intended in this place to give some additional particulars relating to the customs and habits of the modern Persians, but our limits will not admit of going further into these amusing but unimportant details ; * and we can make room only for the following description, taken from the pages of Sir W. Ouseley, of a Persian feast, given by the vizier to the British ambassador.

" We partook, on Dec. 7th, of a magnificent dinner at Mirza Shefia's house, to which we rode about seven o'clock in the evening, by the light of many *fanoos*, or lanterns made of paper or linen ... Our slippers having been left outside the door of a large handsome room, illuminated by means of lamps and candlesticks placed on the floor, the usual salutations and welcomes, and all the regular series of inquiries concerning health, and thanks for the honour conferred in visiting, began immediately on the Ambassador's entrance ; were continued while Mirza Shefia conducted him to a corner ; and did not end for some minutes after we were all seated on *nammeds* (*nummuds*) spread over the splendid carpet close to the walls. The guests were then furnished with *kaleáns* (*kaleoons*), mostly their own, and by their own servants ; for, on these occasions, the *pish-khydmet* or *valet de chambre* generally accompanies his master, to prepare and present the implements of smoking, and to hold the slippers for him when taking leave. Coffee, without milk or sugar, was next introduced by the servants of our

* On this subject, the general reader may be referred, for ample satisfaction and amusement, to Mr. Morier's spirited work, " The Adventures of Hajji Baba." 3 vols. 1824. The indices to the Author's Travels and to Sir W. Ouseley's elaborate volumes, will also guide those who wish for further information, to some curious details. Nor must we forget to refer them to the Sketches of Persia so often cited in these pages.

host ; one bringing, on a tray, several fine China cups
without handles, each in a fillagree receptacle, silver
or silver-gilt, of the same form ; and another, from a
large coffee-pot, filled three or four cups, one of which
Mirza Shefia handed to the Ambassador, who sat on
his right.   The servants, having distributed coffee to
every person, collected the empty cups, and retired.
Kaleáns were again presented ; and to them succeeded tea, in porcelain cups larger than those which
had contained the coffee, but without saucers.   After
this appeared what in Europe would have constituted
the dessert, but which was here the forerunner of
dinner ; apples, pears, melons, the grains of pomegranates in bowls, ices and sweetmeats, placed before us
on capacious trays. These having been removed, after
ten or twelve minutes, preparations were made for the
display of a more substantial meal ; while, from sitting cross-legged on the floor so long, my situation
had become already extremely irksome.

" The servants now held before us silver basins,
having covers grated or pierced with open work in
several places, and ewers resembling large coffee-pots,
from which they poured on our hands lukewarm water ;
this fell through the grated covers, and disappeared ;
the basins were then transferred to other guests for
similar ablutions.   Next were spread on the carpet,
close to our knees, long narrow strips of flowered linen
or chintz, the borders of which contained, in small
compartments, some Persian verses inculcating hospitality to strangers and gratitude to God for the
blessings of abundance.   On these strips the bread
was placed ; it consisted of circular cakes large as our
common dinner plates, flat, and not much thicker
than a crown piece.   A multitude of servants then
entered, bringing various trays, which they laid down

near the cakes of bread ; each tray containing at first only five or six bowls and dishes of lamb, fowl, fish, and vegetables,* besides two or three ample porcelain basins, filled with different sherbets, a long-handled spoon floating on the surface. One tray accommodated two guests, and between the trays were lofty pyramids of rice in its various forms, as *chillaw*, boiled simply, or as *pillaw*, mixed with meat and fruit, highly seasoned with spices, and enriched with unctuous sauces at once sweet and acid. Having laid before us the trays already described as amply furnished, the servants were nevertheless employed for a considerable time in loading them with additional bowls and dishes of viands, placed over or between the first, and others over them, so that at last, the pile accumulated on each tray amounted to fifteen or sixteen ; and with the intermediate *pillaws* and sherbets, there must have been, before the conclusion of the feast, above three hundred china bowls and dishes at one moment on the floor.† The meat was chiefly saturated with oil or liquefied fat, corrected in some instances by vegetable acids.

" Being without knives and forks, we necessarily grasped with our fingers, not only solid meat, but even

---

* Mutton, at Tehraun, is excellent and cheap ; beef is sometimes good, but is seldom eaten by the Persians. Delicious herrings, of a large species, called *shah-mahce* (king of fishes), and fine salmon, are obtained from the Caspian. Hares abound in the plain, but its flesh is deemed unclean by the Persians, in opposition to the Turks, who eat it without scruple.—MORIER, vol. i. p. 230.

† The display of beautiful porcelain has long been a favourite luxury of the Persians. At a dinner given by the *Ameen ad Douleh* at Isfahan, the floor was covered with ten large trays, each containing twenty-five china bowls and dishes of various sizes. A Persian writer notices a banquet given by a private individual at the beginning of the fourteenth century, when 400 china dishes and vessels were at once placed before the guests.—OUSELEY, iii. 23.

moist and 'clammy substances. For plates, the only
substitutes were the flat cakes. Of these, it did not
appear that much was eaten, but such bones and fragments were collected on them, as would, in France or
England, have been removed by a servant. On those
cakes, too, I noticed many of the Persians wiping,
from time to time, the greasy fingers of their right
hand, the left not being employed. When preparing
to eat, they stooped forwards, kneeling, until their
heads were nearly over some dishes, which the long
beards of several almost touched; and I have often
been surprised at the ingenuity which they evinced in
scooping from a gelatinous mass, with the first finger
only, or the first and second united, exactly such a
quantity as they required for a mouthful; studiously
contriving that their clothes should not be defiled by
any particle.

" Towards the close of this feast, a lamb roasted
entire, was brought to Mirza Shefia. On his recom-
mending it to the Ambassador, two or three servants
immediately tore the limbs and joints asunder, using
in this simple operation their hands alone; which
being stained, according to custom, with the reddish-
brown tint of henna, excited some suspicion of dirti-
ness, perhaps not altogether false. With their hands
alone, how impure soever they were, or seemed to be,
those servants also restored to their places in the bowls
and dishes, any meat, fish, or rice, that had fallen on
the cloth; while their skirts, as they passed to and
fro in crowds along the floor, which scarcely afforded
room for their feet between the trays and lamps, often
flapped against the *pillaws*, or into the bowls of sherbet.
Such trifling accidents were probably inevitable; none
more serious occurred; and our venerable host, although a man of impaired vision, had acquired the

habit of observing instantaneously, and could indicate to his servants, by a nod, any little want or embarrassment of a guest, even the most remote, without interrupting, for one moment, either his own, or another person's discourse.

" The trays and their contents were at last removed; and next, the chintz *sufrehs* (napkins), with all the morsels of bread, meat, and rice, that had been scattered on them. Basins were then brought, and ewers containing lukewarm water, strongly impregnated with the smell of roses. This was poured on our hands as at the former ablution. Kaleáns, which had begun the feast, now terminated it; and we, having smoked and chatted for a few minutes, took leave of the Persians, receiving our slippers from the servants who waited near the door, and returned on horseback, as we had gone, by the light of *fánoos*. The entertainment which I have thus described, was enlivened, without the help of wine, by facetious anecdotes, and sallies of wit. The powers of agreeable conversation, Mirza Shefia seemed to possess in a very extraordinary degree; and his manners would have been reckoned easy and polished at any court in Europe." *

The *Takht-i Kajar*, a summer palace built by the present Shah, about three miles to the N.E. of Tehraun, on the acclivity of a detached hill, on the great slope of Mount Elborz, claims a passing notice. At a distance, it presents a magnificent elevation, apparently of several stories; but these, on a nearer view,

---

* Ouseley, vol. iii. pp. 141—8. An amusing description of an entertainment given to the Shah by the chief physician, is given by Hajji Baba, vol. ii. ch. 3; and Sir R. K. Porter describes the luxuries and penalties (to a European) of a Persian feast, much in the same terms as Sir W. Ouseley, vol. i. pp. 236—239.

prove to be the fronts of successive terraces.[*]　The spacious gardens are planted with poplars, willows, and fruit-trees; and from the upper terrace is obtained a beautiful prospect.　The structure itself, however, which is of brick, is much inferior, Mr. Morier says, to any of the buildings erected by Kureem Khan or the Sefi monarchs.　The site, too, is ill chosen, the soil being impregnated with salt, which " oozes out through the walls, and undermines their solidity." Futeh Ali Shah has also built another summer residence, called the *Negauristan*, half a mile from the city in the same direction, which is his favourite residence at the beginning of summer.　The gardens, at that season, fragrant with the rose, and vocal with the nightingale, must, according to Sir R. K. Porter's flowery description, then form a Persian paradise.[†]

We are indebted to this Traveller for the fullest account of the remains of the ancient city of Rhey (Raï), the Rhages of Arrian and the book of Tobit, and contemporary, therefore, with Nineveh and Ecbatana.　Here, Alexander arrived on the eleventh day of his march from the latter city, in pursuit of Darius, and rested for five days.[‡]　It subsequently received from Seleucus Nicator the appellation of *Europos*, and under the Parthian monarchs was named *Arsaké* (or *Arsace*) in honour of Arsaces Tiridates, who died 217 years B.C.[§]　In the second century of our era, it had resumed its ancient name, under which it is men-

---

[*] See Morier, vol. i. p. 226, and plate. Johnson, p. 160. Porter, vol. i. p. 335.

[†] Porter, i. 336—8. This Traveller noticed, in these delicious gardens, two rose-trees full fourteen feet high, laden with thousands of flowers.

[‡] It was a day's journey from the Caspian Straits.—ARRIAN, b. iii. c. 20.

[§] Ouseley, vol. iii. p. 177—180.

tioned as the residence of the Parthian kings during the vernal season, and the capital of *Media Rhagiana.* Under the Mohammedan sovereigns, it has undergone many vicissitudes, having been repeatedly ruined by wars and earthquakes, and as often restored. It was the birth-place of Haroun al Rashid, and one of the favourite seats of his magnificence. In the tenth century, it ranked next to Nishapore in size, occupying a square of one *farsang* and a half, and was more populous and better supplied with the necessaries and luxuries of life, than any other city in Irak. Even then, however, the greater portion of Raï was in a state of ruin; and while its commercial greatness was at its height, its walls and fortifications were going to decay. It was still a considerable city when it was surrendered to the generals of Chenghiz Khan by the Shafei sect, in 1221; on which occasion, almost every person of the rival sect of Hanifi (amounting to several thousands), was massacred. Under Ghazan Khan, it was partly rebuilt and repeopled; and it was the occasional residence of Shah Rokh, about the middle of the fifteenth century.* The only inhabited part, at present, is the village of Shah Abdulazim, which takes its name from the tomb of a celebrated Mohammedan saint, whose memory is held in high veneration. This village, containing a handsome old mosque, a bazar, two caravanserais,† some baths, and between three and four hundred families, has a pleasing appearance, with its verdant gardens, amid the surrounding desolation.

* See authorities in Ouseley, vol. iii. pp. 186—199. Morier, vol. i. p. 403.

† Though only between four and five miles from Tehraun, caravans proceeding towards Isfahan, generally halt here as a rendezvous on the first night.

Sir W. Ouseley considers as among the most ancient ruins of Rhey, the ramparts and turrets on a rocky height which closes and commands the plain at its eastern extremity; offering a situation so favourable for defence and so well provided with water, that it must have been at all times chosen as the site of the citadel. The walls and towers are of brick and clay, the lower parts being in a few places fronted and strengthened with stone. " But, of whatever age may be the materials of these buildings, or of the tumular masses that appear scattered for many miles along the plain, one object only," continues the learned Traveller, " among all that I examined, can with certainty be pronounced a work of art more ancient than the Mohammedan era. This is a sculptured tablet, carved in the usual manner of the Sassanian ages, on a face of the rock imperfectly squared and smoothed for the purpose." It represents an equestrian figure of Shahpoor, advancing at full gallop to close combat, having a globe on his head and a ball on each shoulder. The performance is rude and imperfect, and the subject has never been finished, as the outlines of another figure are traced on the same rock.[*]

Directly from the base of the castle rock, runs a line of massy fortification inclosing a triangular area, which has perhaps, in modern times, been the *areg*, or a lower citadel. Three enormous towers yet remain, which probably commanded the gates. One lofty brick tower, of admirable masonry and singular form, is encircled, near the top, with a Kufic inscription rudely executed in the brick. A similar inscription, executed

---

[*] Ouseley, vol. iii. pp. 182, 3. Morier, vol. ii. p. 199. Porter, vol. i. p. 163.

in brick, encircles a round tower of stone. Another
wall, exterior to the ramparts of the town, connects
the height on which the great citadel stands, with
another rocky projection, where every tenable spot
has been strongly guarded by outworks ; linking
themselves, across the gorge of a deep ravine, to the
side of a third fortress, finely built of stone, on the
summit of a 'rock which commands the open country
to the south. Within this fortress stands a low circular building decorated with tiles of various colours,
evidently a Mohammedan tomb or chapel ; * and the
mouldering relics of two or three mosques are discoverable among the hillocks of ruins within the walls
of the modern inclosure. Mounds and hollows, tombs
and wells, are scattered all over the plain ; but, as the
materials used have been either brick or clay, they are
of little interest, and can in many instances be with
difficulty distinguished from mounds of earth. The
ancient Rhages has shared the fate of Nineveh and
Babylon ; and the convulsions of nature have aided
the devastation of war and the slow dilapidations of
time.

From Tehraun, Sir W. Ouseley, in the months of
February and March, 1812, made an excursion into
Mazanderan, passing through Firoozkuh † and the

---

* This is apparently what Mr. Morier refers to as the tomb of
one of the wives of Imaum Hossein, i. 233.

† Firoozkuh (or Piruzkuh) is considered by the inhabitants as
the last town of Persian Irak. At this town, the *Pylæ Caspiæ* are
supposed to terminate northward, the 'other extremity being at
Khuar, the ancient Choara. Sir W. Ouseley was prevented from
pursuing the defile to Khuar, but he inclines to the opinion of
Rennell and other geographers, that this was the strait through
which Alexander entered Parthia in pursuit of Darius. See a
learned note at vol. iii. 545—50. Mr. Frazer, however, who devotes
a long note to this subject (pp. 291—3), adduces strong reason for

forests of Hyrcania, to Saree, the ancient Zadracarta;
and thence through Ashraff, (now reduced to a mean
village,) Furahabad, and Balfurush, to Amool, formerly
regarded as the capital of Tabristan, but now wearing
an air of poverty, gloom, and progressive decay. In
returning, he took a different route from Firoozkuh,
through Damawend, "a very ancient and celebrated
city," now in decay, which gives its name to the lofty
mountain. The details of this journey, though illustrative of the geography of the country, furnish no
matter of particular interest.

FROM TEHRAUN TO MUSHED.

OUR contracting limits compel us also to confine ourselves to a brief notice of the longer and more adventurous journey undertaken by Mr. Fraser into Khorasan and the Caspian provinces. The Shah is extremely jealous of permitting any European to explore
the country eastward of the usual line of road between
Shiraz and Tehrauns; owing, it is supposed, to an
unwillingness that any stranger should see the naked-
ness of the land, and discover the disaffection of its
inhabitants. Mr. Fraser goes so far as to avow his
belief, that the murder of Mr. Browne, the celebrated
Traveller, was perpetrated at his Majesty's instiga-
tion: his gold chronometer is ascertained to have
found its way into the possession of the Shah. Cer-

the opinion, that the *Feeroze-cooes* defile (as he strangely spells it)
leading into Mazanderan by the steep and difficult pass called
Sawachee, was not that through which Darius was pursued. He
supposes it to have been the pass of *Gurdunee Sirdara*, two *farsangs*
in length, leading through a ridge projecting southward from the
Elborz range, and dividing the plains of Khawr and Vuromeen;
Darius having taken the high road towards Mushed. See also on
this subject, Morier, vol. ii. 365, 6.

tain Europeans, who had penetrated to Mushed, are, moreover, stated to have died under suspicious circumstances. Mr. Fraser, therefore, determined on leaving Tehraun without asking the royal permission, assuming the native dress, and travelling with the caravans. As an ostensible object, he provided himself with a few commodities suited to the markets of the towns he intended to visit, not forgetting a stock of medicines, that he might, on occasion, enact the physician; a character under which the Frank has often obtained protection and favour in eastern countries, where he would otherwise have been exposed to insult and danger. In Dec. 1821, he left Tehraun, attended by a faithful negro *valet* and four Persian servants, together with a young Persian of good family, considerable liberality of sentiment, and respectable mental endowments, whom he engaged as his travelling companion. The party, after encountering various detentions and some hazards, reached Mushed early in February, where Mr. Fraser remained six weeks, in the hope of being able to cross the desert to visit Bokhara and Samarcand. But the disturbed state of the country, which had put a total stop to all intercourse by caravans, rendered further progress in that direction impossible.

Mr. Fraser's route to Mushed led him through Semnoon, Dowlutabad, Damghan, Shahrood, Bostam, and Nishapore. The latter city, one of the most ancient in the country, and for a long time the favoured capital of the Seljoukian dynasty, does not now contain above 2000 inhabited houses, but is surrounded with ruins and obscure vestiges of its former extent and consequence. Its fertile plain, however, in spite of the desolating effects of savage invasions and an oppressive government, can still boast of more cultivation than any other part of Persian Khorasan. Our Traveller visited the celebrated turquoise-mines near this city; and he gives some interesting details relative to the various forms in which the gem and its *nidus* present themselves.

Mushed, built originally of sun-dried brick or mud, and now exhibiting the usual appearance of depopulation and decay, has nothing to interest the Traveller, except the mausoleum of Imaum Reza and the magnificent groupe of buildings connected with it. All the pomp of eastern architecture has been lavished upon this edifice, where silver gates, jewelled doors, rails of solid gold, glittering domes and beautiful minarets, lofty gateways and handsome arcades, seem to realize the most gorgeous descriptions of Arabian romance. The mosque built by the queen of Shah Rokh, is pronounced to be by far the most beautiful and magnificent which the Author had seen in Persia. Yet, this shrine has been often plundered, and its revenues are greatly reduced. Of the sixteen *medressas,* the greater part are either deserted or in decay. Mushed contains the tomb also of the far-famed Haroun al Rashid.

Forced reluctantly to turn his steps homeward, Mr. Fraser resolved to vary his route, and accordingly proceeded by Kourdistan, (a district of Khorasan bordering on the great desert,) through the once populous and fertile plains of Gourgaun, to Astrabad, at the south-east corner of the Caspian. He left Mushed on the 11th of March, and on the 6th of April entered Astrabad; having every where found, both among the Kourdish and Turkoman *Eels*, who occupy, with

---

* *Eel*, Mr. Fraser says, is, in Persian, the singular, of which Eelhaut (Illeyaut, Illiât) is the plural: he, therefore, forms the English plural in the usual way, and writes it *eels.*

doubtful allegiance, the northern frontier of Persia, a hospitable reception. *

Astrabad (called, from the number of its *seyeds*, *Dar el Moumenin*, the gate of the faithful,) is a walled town nearly four miles in circumference, and containing about 1000 families. Mr. Fraser gives a much more favourable account of its picturesque appearance, its well-paved and clean streets, and flourishing gardens, than Mr. Morier. † It can boast, however, of but little trade, and the sallow looks of the inhabitants afforded a too unequivocal confirmation of the reputed unwholesomeness of the place, arising from the noxious exhalations of the surrounding swamps and untrimmed forests or jungle.

From Astrabad, Mr. Fraser proceeded through Saree, Ashraff, and Balfroosh, to Resht, the capital of Ghilan ; whence, after some personal adventures of no ordinary interest, connected with an unsuccessful endeavour to make his escape from a suspicious detention by the prince, he ultimately reached Tabriz by way of Ardebeel.‡

* Here, Mr. Fraser's " Narrative of a Journey into Khorasan " terminates. In an appendix is given a very valuable geographical sketch of Khorasan, of which use has been made in our introductory matter.

† Morier, vol. ii. p. 375.

‡ These adventures are detailed in Mr. Fraser's " Travels and Adventures in the Persian Provinces on the Southern Banks of the Caspian Sea." 4to. 1826. This volume contains a very valuable appendix relating to the geology and commerce of Persia. The position of the following places was ascertained by the Author's observations. In Khorasan: Semnoon, lat. 35° 33′ 30″ N., long. 53° 28′ 18″ E. Damghan, lat. 36° 10′ N., long. 54° 35′ 32″. Nishapore, lat. 36° 12′ 20″ N., long. 58° 49′ 27″ E. Mushed, lat. 36° 17′ 40″ N., long. 59° 35′ 27″ E. (a difference of nearly 3° further E. than has hitherto been assigned to it.) In the Caspian provinces : Astrabad, lat. 36° 51′ N., long. 54° 25′ 33″ E. Saree, lat. 36° 34′ 10″ N., long. 53° 6′ 20″ E. Reshd, lat. 37° 17′ 30″ N., long. 49° 42′ 53″ E.

We must now very hastily sketch the remainder of the route from Tehraun to that city.

FROM TEHRAUN TO TABRIZ.

From Tehraun to the Russian frontier, at regular distances of from 24 to 32 miles, there are posts of eight, ten, or twelve horses established by Government. The first station is at Songoorabad, about 41 miles from Tehraun; the second at Suffer Koja, 22 miles; the third at Kazvin, 30 miles.*

Kazvin (Casbin, Kazween) is a larger town in circumference than Tehraun, though not so populous, containing about 25,000 male inhabitants. It is surrounded with a mud-wall and towers, but has no ditch. All round the walls to a considerable distance extend vineyards and orchards: the former yield a grape celebrated throughout Persia. The soil is clay, fertilized by irrigation. Water is scarce, and is conducted by *kanauts* from a distance. The palace of the Sefi kings, who once held their court here, is still standing, but in faded splendour, surrounded with ruins; and the greater part of its once magnificent buildings are almost totally abandoned.

A fine level road on a hard gravel runs S. 40° W. to Siah-dehan (pronounced Siadeeon), a decayed village, distant 21 miles (6 *farsangs*). The next station is Aubhaur (Avher), distant 28 miles. This place presents a more respectable and pleasing aspect than

---

* Johnson, p. 170—3. Sir W. Ouseley halted, the first day, at Caredje (or Karatch), a stage of 23 or 24 miles: near this village, the King was at that time erecting a new city, to be called Sulimaniah, from the city of that name, taken from the Kourdish chief. (Morier, vol. ii. p. 199.) The second stage was Nasrabad, 22 or 23 miles; the third was to Saffer Khuajeh (Suffer Koja), 13 miles; the fourth, to Hassanabad, 19 miles; the fifth, about 11 miles, to Casvin.

most Persian towns, being situated in the midst of gardens and groves, on a winding stream of the same name. Rising above the trees, are seen some ruined walls, occupying a height, which are called *Kalaa-i-Darab*. The castle of which they formed part, must once, Sir W. Ouseley says, have been as strong as brick and clay could make it, and the ramparts still inclose a considerable area.[*] This tract of country, including the plain and mountains of Sultaneah, is the *Shikar-Jah*, or hunting-place of the present Shah. Antelopes, partridges, and bustards are found in abundance. The King's principal summer palace is at Sultaneah, situated on a conspicuous eminence rising from the plain. The once populous city of Sultaneah, distant from Abhaur two stages of 16 and 18 miles,[†] is now reduced to a straggling village. Nothing remained, when Sir W. Ouseley travelled, but the decaying walls of edifices, some, even in ruin, magnificent and beautiful, and mouldering heaps of brick and clay. Immediately on entering the plain, a splendid edifice is seen towering above the village, its cupola of azure-coloured tile-work rising to the height of above 130 feet. This is the tomb of Sultan Mohammed Khodabunda Aly, one of the most beautiful structures originally in all Persia; yet, notwithstanding its sacred character, it has been almost en-

[*] " The materials are large mud bricks, mixed with straw and baked in the sun, the same which I remarked at Rey, and at the *Atesh Gah* at Ispahan, and the same perhaps as those at Babylon. These circumstances will give greater force to the reasoning of Major Rennel, who only wanted the attestation of some existing remains, to prove it to be the ancient Habor, one of the three places to which the tribes of Reuben, Gad, and Manasseh were sent into captivity."—MORIER, ii. 207.

[†] The intermediate stage is *Sain Kalaa*, written *Sihin Caleh* and *Saingaula*, and by Chardin transformed into *Château de Hassan*.

tirely pulled down for the sake of the materials, which have been used in constructing the paltry palace which forms his Majesty's summer residence. This dilapidation had been going on, in 1817, for the last seventeen years; but still, this noble monument was magnificent in ruin. The central apartment is about 60 feet in diameter, being one arched dome of great symmetry and beauty. A new city has been begun near the palace, which is to be called Sultanabad.

The plain of Sultaneah is about twelve miles broad, bordered by hills backed by snow-capped mountains. It is entirely devoted to the royal pastures. Here, in the month of June, his Majesty generally encamps; and it is here that he receives the Russian ambassador.

The next stage is to Zunjaun, distant about 24 miles. This town appears at a distance a flourishing place, abounding with trees; but, on entering it, Sir W. Ouseley says, he rode at least for a mile through ruins. An ample cemetery attested its former populousness, and the inhabitants still amount to about 10,000. It is the capital of the *bolouk* (district) of Khamseh,* containing 100 villages, which pays no revenue, but furnishes, in lieu, 5000 horsemen. A stage of 24 miles leads to Armeghaneh, a village with a fort, in the same district. The Turkish language, which begins to be spoken more or less after leaving Kazvin, is the only one understood by the boorish inhabitants. The road now lies over a high stony country, intersected by valleys, and bounded by distant mountains, and the change in the climate indicates its increasing elevation. At 26 miles is Aukhund (*Ak-*

* Sir W. Ouseley considers this word (written by Mr. Morier *Hamze*) as answering to the Greek Pentapolis.

kand, white town), an inconsiderable place, with numerous ruins; and about 24 miles further, Meana (or Mianeh), infamous for its poisonous bugs, the bite of which is sometimes mortal. * It is nevertheless a thriving place, being a mart for the carpets made by the neighbouring Eelauts.

The whole country in this part, and especially towards the W. and N., seems to have been formed by some great convulsion of nature. There are lands, Mr. Morier says, of every soil, and of every form and colour. Aukhund is now the frontier town of Azer-bijan. The original boundary was the *Kizzil Oozan,* a deep and rapid stream running through a wild desert of mountains, which is crossed by an ancient bridge about 15 miles beyond. Immediately after passing this river, the road begins to ascend the *Kauflaun Koh* (or *Koplan Kúh*), separating Irak Ajem from Azerbijan. At Shehderabad, about eight miles S.W. of the road, is a copper mine, which, in 1817, an Englishman had begun to work.†

---

* Dr. Campbell, physician to the British Residence at Tehraun, describes the disease as beginning with nausea and vomiting, succeeded by visceral obstruction, and terminating in death within six weeks or two months. In form and colour, the *milleh* resembles the large dog-tick of India. It makes its appearance only in the hot season.—See JOHNSON, p. 106. OUSELEY, iii. 391. At Meana, . Thevenot died in 1667.

† Johnson, p. 214. Lieut. Alexander calls the place Shaik Durah Bad, and says, "Here are, perhaps, the richest veins of copper in the world: silver and lead are also found in considerable quantities. The soil is ferruginous. The veins are at the bottom of a range of hills, running from N.W. to S.E, in front of the *Kofilan Koh.* The river Gharangoo, which is a branch of the Kiziloozun, runs through the district where the veins are met with. An unusual rise of its waters discovered the precious ore, a short time back····Iron is obtained here in great quantity; and the oxide of lead is found on the surface of the ground: the latter is melted by the villagers into bullets. If ever a European colony

From Meana, a road strikes off to Ardebeel, running along the S.W. verge of the Moghaun plains, which was taken by Lieut. Alexander, in proceeding from Isfahan to the royal camp at Achar. His first stage from Shehderabad, was 25 miles, to Herees; ascending, in the way, a steep *kootul*. Kureem, distant 25 miles, was the next stage; and the third day brought him to Ardebeel. The plain of Moghaun, on which it stands, is the winter resort of the Eelauts. It is celebrated for having impeded the victorious career of Pompey, whose army was here attacked by venomous serpents; and this Traveller was assured that some parts of the plain are still infested with an immense number of those reptiles. Ardebeel, at one time the capital of the Turkomans of the Black Sheep, and venerated as the original seat of the Sefi family, has entirely declined from its former importance, and is remarkable only as containing the tombs of Sheikh Suffee and his illustrious descendant, Shah Ismail. Their remains repose under lofty domes, and the ark over the grave of the saint is fenced off by a silver grating. In one of the rooms, which are highly ornamented, is a large collection of China, among which are some beautiful agate cups and dishes; also, a library of splendidly bound books; all the offering of Shah Abbas. A square fort, with four bastions, has been constructed here by Major Menteith, which is garrisoned by a detachment of the *Janbaz*, or disciplined infantry.*

The next stage, from Meana towards Tabriz, is

---

were to be established in Persia, I know not of a better situation for it than this; the climate being good, the soil fertile, rich ores in abundance; and, as it is at a distance from the frontier, the colony would not run the risk of being disturbed during war."— ALEXANDER, pp. 183, 4.

* Alexander, pp. 187—9.

22 miles, to *Toorkmaunshahea* (or *Turkoman Chaï*) :
not a tree is to be seen, nor a human habitation, the
whole way.   The liquorice plant covers the hills ; but,
in the neighbourhood of the village, there has been a
great deal of cultivation.   An undulating country,
covered with grasses, extends for the next 12 miles, to
Usdenshee, an Armenian village,* situated in the
Kara-Chemen, or Black Meadow.   At 25 miles from
Turkoman-chaï is the village of Tekmehdash ; 6 miles
beyond which are found, on an eminence, some large
and upright hewn stones, arranged in lines, of apparently high antiquity, and affording abundant matter
of speculation to the antiquary.†   Whatever was their
original purpose, the square area which they inclose,
has, in later times, been used as a cemetery.   About
6 miles further, is Oojaun, a wretched village in the
midst of rich and extensive plains.   Here, the King
has a summer pavilion, to which he retires in the
hottest weather, Oojaun being considered as the coldest
part of Persia.   Another stage, of 32 miles, over a
bare and disagreeable tract, conducts the traveller to

TABRIZ.

Tabriz, Mr. Morier says, is no more the magnificent
city described by Chardin.   It then ranked as the second
city in Persia, containing, according to his account,

---

* On ascending one of the hills near this place, Col. Johnson
observed a very large spider, which proved to be a very venomous
tarantula, called in Turkish *bheule* : in Georgia, it is known by the
name of *phalang.* Its bite is almost certain death.—Johnson, 206.

† Chardin relates a legend which makes this to have been a
place of assembly for giants in the times of the Kaianian dynasty ;
and a local tradition states, that during the reign of Ghazan Khan,
his nobles used to assemble at these stones, to converse on military
affairs, and therefore called them *Jan-goo,* the place of council.
See Ouseley, vol. iii. pp. 395—7. Morier, vol. ii. p. 210.

15,000 houses, 300 caravanserais, 250 mosques, and
550,000 inhabitants. " At present," adds this Traveller, " if we allow it to be even one-tenth of that
magnitude, we shall probably make an exaggerated
estimate.*

" The modern town is situated nearly in the centre
of the site of the former one; for, on all sides of it, to
a considerable distance, are to be seen the ruins of
houses, streets, &c., which afford a tolerable idea of
the extent of that city which Chardin described.   In
his view of it, the *Mesjid Ali* is placed almost in the
middle of the city: what remains of that building
now forms a part of the fortification.   Tabriz, at this
day, is three miles and a quarter in circumference; it
is surrounded with walls built of sun-burnt bricks,
and with towers of kiln-burnt bricks, placed at irregular distances from each other.   An attempt has
been made to give the shape of bastions to several of
the towers, but no guns are mounted upon them; and
if they were, they could be of little use, as the irregularity of the walls baffles all the rules of science.
There are seven gates, at each of which guards are
stationed: they are closed an hour or two after
sunset, and opened before sunrise.

" No public buildings of any note at present exist
at Tabriz, and few are the remains of those described
by former travellers.   Indications of the great *maidan*
are still to be observed, and the bazar *Kaiserieh* is still
known, but a wooden roof has been substituted for its
former arched one.   The *Ark Ali Shah* (citadel of
Ali Shah) is the most interesting structure at present
in Tabriz; principally because it contains a proof of
what the labour and ingenuity of a few Englishmen

* Sir R. K. Porter thinks it amounts to hardly 100,000. Lieut.
Alexander says, it is estimated at 80,000.

will accomplish, under all the disadvantages of a bad administration and a want of resources. This building comprehends within its limits, the remains of a mosque, (a mass of brickwork as fine, perhaps, as any in the world.) about eighty feet in height; at the top of which, three small chambers have been constructed, whence the town and the surrounding country are seen as if laid out on a chart. The Prince had intended to make the Ark his own place of residence, but he subsequently preferred converting it into an arsenal, where we were delighted to find many of our European trades in full activity.

"A considerable part of the population of Tabriz may be said to live in the suburbs, which are every day increasing, and extend over the site of the ancient city. In all parts of the immediate vicinity, are seen large oblong and square blocks of black marble, which formerly were tombstones, but now are used in many places as stepping-stones over small streams, foundations to houses, channels for water, &c. These, as well as stone rams and stone lions, are constantly met with. Many of the entrances to the gardens and to the houses of the peasantry, like those of Isfahan, Julfa, and Kashan, are formed of one large stone slab. At the village of Shah Gazan, two miles from the walls of Tabriz, is a high mound of brick, the remains of some very considerable building, but of a Mohammedan age." *

Tabriz stands in lat. 38° 5′ 10″ N., long. 47° 17′ 46″ E. † The natives extol the salubrity of the air, to which, according to the native etymology, its name

* Morier, ii. 225, 6; 232. See, for a further description of Tabriz, Porter, i. 220—27; Johnson, 211.

† Fraser. According to the late Mr. Browne, its longitude is 46° 25′, and its latitude, according to Major Menteith, is 38° 4′. Porter, i. 220.

refers.* They complain, however, of the frequent and violent earthquakes: these they attribute to the volcanoes to the eastward, which throw out smoke without flame. The climate is subject also to much thunder and lightning and rain. Between forty and fifty years ago, a dreadful convulsion of nature nearly destroyed the whole city, and caused the death of 80,000 people.† Almost every day, during Sir W. Ouseley's residence here (in June and July), sudden gusts of wind filled the streets with clouds of sand. The thermometer was then constantly below 75°; but it often varies, within twenty-fours, from 56° to 94°. In winter, the cold is so intense, that many instances occur of individuals, accidentally excluded from the city by arriving after the gates were shut, being found frozen to death in the morning.

No vestiges of antiquity have been found in this neighbourhood, that might serve to identify it with the Tabris of Ptolemy or with the Gaza, Ganzaca, or Gazaca of other writers ‡. Sir R. K. Porter mentions, however, a massive and venerable fortress, on a commanding height, which, according to his account, merits examination, although it is probably a Mohammedan structure.

Chardin adopted the strangely erroneous notion, that Tabriz is the site of " the ancient and famous Ecbatana." The true representative of that city is

---

* *Tab* signifies a fever, and *riz* is the participle of *rekhten*, to disperse.

† Ouseley, iii. 406. It is added, on the authority of Major D'Arcy, " that, towards the N.E., at the foot of lofty mountains, several hills of sulphur and arsenic were at that time thrown up; the sulphur being of a deep red colour like ochre, evidently crocus martius or rust of iron, on the pyrites of which the arsenic acting, caused the earthquake."

‡ In Ptolemy, it is written Γαββρις; but this has been supposed to be an error. See Ouseley, iii. 410; D'Anville, ii. 24.

HAMADAN,

Situated, as Herodotus describes it, on a gentle ascent, about 12 *stadia* from the foot of Mount Orontes. The ancient capital of the Medes has dwindled down, however, to a mean, clay-built town, which, till of late, owed all its consequence to the manufacture of a superior sort of leather carried on there. It has been created by the present Shah, a royal government, or provincial capital; and contained, in 1818, about 9000 houses, with a population of between 40 and 50,000 souls, including about 600 Jewish families, and nearly the same number of Armenians. * It lies in the route from Isfahan to Tabriz and Ardebeel, in lat. 34° 53′ N., long. 40° E., and is a great thoroughfare from the north for the trade to Bagdad. It is thus described by M. Morier.

" The situation of this city, at the foot of the mountain of Alwend, resembles that of Brousa, so beautifully situated on the declivity of the Asiatic Olympus; although the former mountain cannot, either in height or in beauty of form, enter into a competition with the latter. It evidently was once an immense city, but at present, it is a confused and melancholy heap of ruins. The roads which lead to its inhabited parts, wind through a long succession of broken walls, which, by the appearance of their fragments, attest the former existence of fine buildings. Like Olympus, Alwend abounds in fine springs of water, a torrent of which constantly flows through the city into the flat country, and renders Hamadan one of the best watered places in Persia. Its present habitations are profusely in-

* Porter, ii. 104. Lieut. Alexander says, 25,000. The latter Traveller took the road leading from Isfahan to Hamadan, in going to Ardebeel.

terspersed with trees, which 'give variety, and even beauty, to what would otherwise be an unpleasing view. Besides the poplar, the *narwend*, a species of the elm, is a very common tree, and grows into shapes so formal, as to raise the supposition that they have acquired them by art."

" The most conspicuous building in Hamadan is the *Mesjid Jumah*, now falling to decay : before it is a *maidan*, which serves as a market-place. Near the mosque, in a court filled with tombs, stands a building called the Sepulchre of Esther and Mordecai. But the whole building does not look of greater antiquity than the Mohammedan age.*

" At about seven miles from our camp, carved on the surface of the rock, on a steep declivity of the mountain of Alwend, are to be seen two tablets, each of which is divided into three longitudinal compartments, inscribed with the arrow-headed character of Persepolis. These inscriptions are called by the Persians, *Genj-nameh*, or tales of a treasure. Close to the foot of the rock runs a stream that issues from the mountain ; and higher up, above the two tablets, is to be traced the commencement of others.

" Another monument of positive antiquity, we discovered casually, in exploring the northern skirts of the city. It consists of the base of a small column of the identical order of the larger bases of the columns at Persepolis, and appears to be of the same sort of stone. This led to a discovery of more importance ;

* A Hebrew inscription, rudely carved on a stone in the wall of the inner chamber, states that the building was erected over the graves of Mordecai and Esther, by two devout Jews of Kashan, A.M. 4474. Two wooden frames, carved all over with Hebrew characters, and shaped liked sarcophagi, are alleged to be the tombs. Pilgrimages are still made by the Jews to this venerated spot. The original structure is said to have been destroyed at the sacking of Hamadan by Timour.

for, adjacent to this fragment, is a large but irregular terrace or platform, evidently the work of art, and perhaps the ground plan of some great building, of the remains of which its soil must be the repository. The situation of this spot agrees with that which Polybius would assign to the palace of the kings of Persia, which he says was below the citadel. Now the position of the ruins of the modern castle, which is most likely the site of that of the ancient, is much more elevated than the platform, and sufficiently near for the latter to be said to be below the former.

" We were conducted to the castle by the Persians; and from the height called the *musellah*, we had a complete view of the whole extent of the city, which, like the palace, might be said to be below it. A strong Persian fort formerly crowned this eminence, but it was destroyed by Aga Mahomed Khan, who has left only one large round tower to attest its former strength. If Ecbatana was situated where Hamadan now is, on this place must have been the fort mentioned by Arrian, in which Alexander ordered all the treasures of Persia to be secured; because common sense points it out as the only spot fit for such a building; and I can credit Polybius, who says, that its fortifications were of wonderful strength. I can also imagine the seven circles of walls mentioned by Herodotus, in the innermost of which the royal treasury was placed.

" On the site of the castle is a small square platform, which the Persians call the *Takht Ardeshir*. It has an exterior facing of white square stones, backed by masonry of common stone and mortar, and has the appearance of a building of the Sassanides, of which dynasty Ardeshir Babegan was the founder. This will lead to the supposition, that, from the time of the

Sassanides at least, to the present day, this spot has been regarded as the situation of the fortress.

" Of Mohamedan antiquities, Hamadan contains a great variety, consisting of sepulchral stones, towers, old mosques, old bazars, and Cufick inscriptions, which are met with at every turn. The burial-place of Avicenna is to be seen here. We were over-whelmed with Arsacidean and Sassanian coins, which are found in great quantities at Hamadan, as well as at a village three *fursungs* off; and we also got several intaglios on carnelion, and numerous Mohamedan talismans. One cylindrical stone with Persepolitan figures and characters upon it, fell into our hands; and several coins of the Seleucides were brought to us, but none of them rare, or in remarkably good preservation. On the whole, we found that Hamadan presented more objects of research to the antiquary, than any other city that we had visited in Persia; and there is every probability that excavations, par-ticularly on the site of what I suppose to be the ancient palaces of the kings, would lead to valuable discoveries." [*]

Here we must terminate our topographical de-scription of Persia. The mountains of Kourdistan, the plains of Mesopotamia, the sources of the Tigris, Ararat and Caucasus, the sites of Susa, Ctesiphon, Nineveh, and Babylon,—these we had hoped to ex-plore; but they would demand another volume, and, after all, do not belong to modern Persia.

* Morier, ii. 264—9. Hamadan, Lieut. Alexander says, is the emporium of coins and antique gems, as Bagdad is of cylinders.

END OF PERSIA.

CHINA.

125
130
40
40
AOTONG
Leaotong G.
Taipi
Peitchira
Kaotchuen
Oula R.
Tchuen
elee
Charlotter I.
Yathau
IANG HAI
Kinkitao
Tengtchoofoo
Sanpoo
NEP. Halle
Group
Nginhaitcho
OR
Angle
NG
C. Clonard
Faichoofog
C.Macartney
Yeng
Nganchanhia
YELLOW
Basil B.
Singtchoo
35
Fooshance
35
Haurchin
Amhersts
Yintayshan
SEA
Isles
Hoang Ho.
Alcestes I.
Strait

CHINA.

THE Chinese empire, inferior in geographical extent only to that of Russia, * presents to our contemplation a vast area of seven millions of square miles, being somewhat less than a tenth part of the habitable globe; governed by one man of foreign race, and containing a dense population, highly civilized, yet carefully secluded from all other nations, and, by their peculiar language and literature, their physical characteristics and national customs, distinguished from every other race. It is not surprising that a people thus circumstanced should be the object of an intense curiosity, or that the mystery which hangs over their history and country, should have led to an exaggerated idea of their antiquity and attainments. It is not, in fact, the immense territory comprised within the " Celestial Empire," that gives it interest and importance in the eye of the philanthropist, so much as the appalling consideration, that it regulates the

* Reckoning from Kashgar to the mouth of the Amoor, the length of the Chinese empire is about 3460 miles, and its greatest breadth, from the Saïanian mountains to the southernmost point of China opposite to the island of Hay-nan, more than 2000 miles. The extent in square miles may be computed at 7,000,000 miles. MALTE BRUN, vol. ii. b. 42. Humboldt assigns to the Chinese empire 463,200 square marine leagues; to the Russian empire, 631,000; to Asiatic Russia, 465,600.

earthly destinies of more than a sixth part of the human race. While the Russian empire contains a scattered population not exceeding fifty-four millions, and Great Britain extends her dominion over about a hundred millions, the population of China Proper is equal to both these put together; and that of the whole Chinese empire is supposed to be not less than 175 millions, being nearly equal to that of all Europe, and more than five times that of both Americas.*

But if, in this point of view, China must be regarded as having strong claims upon our attention, it is, in other respects, one of the most barren and uninviting of countries. Unknown to ancient geography, except by doubtful report, unrelated to history, to either sacred or classic literature, its mountains and plains, its lakes and rivers, are consecrated by no poetic associations, and their barbarous names call up no recollections of the past. The western continent itself has hardly been more entirely separated from the Old World of history, nor is our knowledge of the country of much longer date. In the thirteenth century, Marco Polo penetrated to Cathay or Northern China, from Turkestaun; but in the fifteenth century, it remained to Europeans an unknown country, the accounts of the early travellers being regarded with suspicion. It was from the Portuguese navigators who succeeded Vasco de Gama, and who reached that country across the Indian seas, that Europe first received any certain information of the situation, extent, and resources of China; and some time

---

* Humboldt estimates the population of Europe as far as the Oural, at 195,000,000; that of America, including the West Indies and Newfoundland, at 34,284,000.—*Pers. Narr.* vol. vi. part. i. note 3.

elapsed before it was understood to be the same country as the Kataia or Cathay of Marco Polo and Rubruquis.* "Since that period," remarks M. Malte Brun, "we owe our knowledge of the country to some ambassadors who have seen the court and the great roads, to some merchants who have inhabited a suburb of a frontier town, and a considerable number of (Roman Catholic) missionaries, who have penetrated in every direction, and who being considered as credulous admirers, though artless narrators, inspired little confidence in their judgement; so that the world was left to guess at the truth of numerous facts which these well-meaning persons were ill qualified to appreciate. We have also some Chinese geographers, whose dry tables of nomenclature give us little information. Thus, any extended description of China that could be given, would consist of a series of repetitions."†

These considerations have decided us on confining our account of China within what may be deemed very narrow limits. It is, indeed, a boundless field of indefinite curiosity and vague speculation; but the country is almost unvisited by modern travellers, and therefore cannot claim to fill up any large portion of the present work. Were we to take our rule from the mass of materials relating to the country to be described, our task would not be very soon despatched. The General History of China, as given by Mailla

---

* In August, 1516, Albuquerque caused Rafael Perestrello to proceed from Malacca to Canton in the junk of a native merchant, to collect intelligence respecting the newly-discovered empire; and in the following year, the first unsuccessful attempt was made to open an intercourse with the Chinese.

† Malte Brun, vol. ii. p. 550. For a succinct history of the Portuguese discoveries and the Missions, see Murray's History of Discoveries in Asia, vol. iii. book 5.

and Grosier, occupies thirteen quarto volumes; and
the " Mémoires" of the Missionaries are in fifteen
volumes; exclusive of which, the works published
within the last fifty years, relating to China, would
form a library of themselves.

" In the last century," M. Malte Brun observes,
" China found her interested and ardent panegyrists
in two powerful parties. The French philosophers
and the Jesuits vied with each other in extolling the
laws and the happiness of that country. The philosophers knew nothing of the subject on which they
pronounced a judgement: the Jesuits knew a great
deal. But those who reason with impartiality, will
never prefer the natural religion of Confucius to
Christianity; nor will the free and high-minded
nations of Europe admit the arrangements of a tyrannical police, the annoyance of a childish etiquette, and
the ' great walls' which have been erected for interrupting the communications of the human mind.

" Among these opinions, dictated by enthusiasm
and party-spirit, we must particularize those which
relate to the pretended antiquity of the Chinese empire. We know that the enemies of the Christian
religion have made it an important object of research,
to discover a people whose records are more ancient
than Noah's flood, and more ancient than even the
common term assigned as the epoch of the Mosaic
creation. The pretended antiquity of the Egyptians
and the Babylonians having been reduced to its proper
value, they recurred to that of India and of China.
The wonders of distant countries were fitted to inspire a greater degree of veneration. China was
represented as a highly civilized and flourishing empire 4500 years before Christ; and if due time is
allowed for the formation of such an empire, it must

have existed for a period of ten or twenty thousand years. Some ill-informed missionaries, wishing, from motives of vanity, to display the antiquity of an empire of which they pretended to have made a spiritual conquest, went blindly into the same system, without being aware of the consequences to which it led. A bad historical compilation, translated from the Chinese, * tells us, that Fohi founded the empire of China about 3000 years before Christ, and that, three centuries after this, Hoang-Ti reigned over flourishing states, which were 1660 miles long, and 1100 broad. Unfortunately for such narratives, China has produced historians candid enough to reject all the fables concerning Fohi and Hoang-Ti. They do not even venture to vouch for the traditions respecting the reign of Iao, probably an allegorical person, whose era is fixed twenty-three centuries before Christ. Let us consider in what the great actions of Iao consisted. He drained marshes; he hunted down wild beasts; he cultivated a desert country; and so narrow were the dimensions af his territory, that he surveyed the whole, four times in the year. Ten centuries after this (B. C. 1401), we find the princes of China moving from province to province, accompanied by all their subjects, nomadic like themselves, and living all alike, either in caves of the rocks, or in cabins of earth. In the time of Confucius (B. C. 551), the whole of China, south of the Blue River, was still a desert. Nothing in the Chinese annals of that period affords any evidence of a great nation. There is no authentic monument to attest the power of those who erected it. Their books, written on very brittle paper, and very frequently re-copied,

* *L'Histoire Générale de la Chine.* Trad. par le P. Mailla et l'Abbé Grosier. 12 vols.

can give no information worthy of our confidence. And we further know, that, two centuries before the Christian era, a barbarous monarch caused all the writings then in existence to be destroyed. We must, then, with the learned among the Chinese, give the history of China no further extension than eight or nine centuries at most before Christ. The hypothesis which finds it entitled to any higher antiquity, owes its origin to the caprice of some modern literati, and the vanity of the emperors.

" But we may be told, that astronomical observations, allowed by M. de la Place to be exact, are as ancient as 1100 years before Christ. Laying aside the objections to which the authenticity of these observations is liable, admitting that they are not composed by modern Chinese, they only prove that, 1100 years before Christ, a civilized tribe and town existed, which produced men of science. Eastern Asia may, like Europe, have had her Greeks and her Athenians: there is a great difference between that and the formation of an immense empire. From 1100 to 2300, there is also a long space of time. A shorter interval witnessed the rise, the civilization, and the extinction of Greece and Rome.

" Even subsequently to the commencement of our era, China has been divided into small states; and if her civilization is of more ancient date, it must oftener than once have perished. For, in the thirteenth century, the inhabitants of the province of Fou-kien, in Mangi or Southern China, ate with avidity the flesh of their fellow-creatures, nicely preferring that of persons in good bodily condition; drank the blood of their prisoners of war; and marked their skin with hot irons, like the most savage nations. The person who relates these facts, had the management of a

district of the country. It is a remarkable circumstance, that, from Marco Polo to M. de Guignes, all
who have seen China, have observed facts so universally tending to assuage the enthusiasm of those who
cherished at a distance an admiration of China. We
may praise the character of her policy in some particulars. The politician of Europe may contemplate
with mixed admiration and disappointment, the un-
yielding conviction entertained by the Government, of
the hazard of giving access to the influence of our
political intrigues. And the moral philosopher may
admire the cool and considerate theories by which
they explain and account for the errors both of one
another and of other nations ; so favourably contrasted
with the mysterious reprobation of crime, and boastful
displays of forgiveness, which have so often rendered
European, and especially Spanish manifestos, ridiculous ; and he may view with approbation the firmness
with which they execute such acts as appear expedient
for the safety of the state and social order. How
have they acquired a tone so dignified, and so unlike
that barbarous incapacity for thinking, which in other
particulars they betray, and that inhumanity which
marks many parts of their practical proceedings ?
What are the means by which the more respectable
materials of the national character admit of being
improved, and incorporated into a consistent system
of social felicity ? By what means can a condition thus
formed become secure against the ambitious intermed-
dlings of other powers, consistently with a liberal interchange of social advantages ? And finally, by what
steps might such materials be adopted by those who at
present value nothing so much as original genius in
its free, romantic, and impassioned exercises, without
weakening their mental vigour ? These are problems

of great interest to the citizen of the world, who flat-
ters himself that some Utopian state of society is
within the reach of his species, while he is solicitous
to exclude from his contemplations the reveries of idle
imagination. Such a person can have nothing in
common with those who entertain a bitter animosity
towards the Chinese, and who speak and write as if it
were somewhat unfortunate, that so singular a nation
ever had existence. Yet, a candid wish to acknowledge
their virtues, needs not be suffered to generate a blind
credulity in the ridiculous pretensions which have so
often been urged in favour of this nation."[*]

These sentiments do honour to the enlightened
spirit and sound judgement of this able Geographer,
whose opinion, will not, on this point, be imputed to
prejudice. With regard to the much agitated question, whether China was known to the ancients, the
Author sides with M. Gosselin in maintaining the
negative, supposing the *Serica* of the ancients to have
comprised part of Little Bukharia, Cashmeer, and the
western part of Tibet. The progress of geographical
discovery has, however, tended to confirm the correctness of Ptolemy's details, and to render it highly probable, that the caravans penetrated from Bactriana
into the heart of China, which must, therefore, be regarded as the ancient Serica.[†] Yet, how little was

---

[*] Malte Brun, vol. ii. pp. 607—11.

[†] D'Anville places *Sera Metropolis* at Kan-tcheou, the Kampion
or Kampition of Marco Polo, the chief city of the province of
Tanguth, which now forms a part of the Chinese province of
Shen-si. "A remarkable circumstance in its position is, having
the latitude well ascertained by observation, in our days, to a frac-
tion of a degree the same with that of Sera in Ptolemy."—D'AN-
VILLE, vol. ii. p. 92. See also Marsden's Marco Polo, ch. xl. and
xli. and notes. It is, accordingly, in the provinces of Shen-si and
Shan-si, in the north-west of China, that Gibbon places the original
seat of the Chinese nation. See ch. xxvi.

known of the real situation of the country in the reign of Augustus, may be inferred from the references which occur in the works of the Roman Poets. Horace repeatedly mentions the *Seres* among other Oriental nations, and uniformly as bordering upon the Bactrians, Parthians, and Indians ; * and Virgil, the most ancient writer who expressly mentions the soft wool which the *Seres* combed from their trees, † does not discover a more accurate information of the country, than of its singular production. Pausanias is the first writer who describes the Seric insect. When silk became a Roman luxury, it was brought to them by the Persian merchants who frequented the marts of Armenia and Mesopotamia, and who purchased it of the Sogdian and Bactrian traders. ‡ In the third century, the Chinese empire appears to have extended as far as the neighbourhood of Sogdiana. " Vou-ti, the first emperor of the seventh dynasty, had political transactions with Fergaun, and is said to have received a Roman embassy. In those ages," we are

* Thus, in od. i. 12,
 " *Sive subjectos Orientis oris,*
                        Seras et Indos.'
Again, in od. iii. 29,
      " *Et urbi solicitus times*
      Quid Seres et regnato Cyro
      Bactra parent, Tanaisque discors."
And, in od. iv. 15,
      " *Edicta rumpent Julia, non Getæ,*
      Non Seres, infidive Persæ,
      Non Tanaim prope flumen orti."
In od. i. xxix. the expression, " *sagittas Sericas*" seems to imply that they were classed with the Parthians and Scythians, among the nations formidable in that mode of warfare.
   † " *Velleraque ut foliis depectant tenuia Seres ?*
      Aut quos Oceano propior gerit India lucos,
      Extremi sinus orbis ?"   Georg. ii. 121.
   ‡ See Murray's Discoveries in Asia, vol. i. p. 485, *et seq.*

informed, " the Chinese kept a garrison at Kashgar ; and one of their generals, about the time of Trajan, marched as far as the Caspian Sea."* In the reign of Justinian, the eggs of the Chinese worm were surreptitiously obtained by some Persian monks; and the Romans were taught to emulate the natives of that remote country, in the education of the insect and the manufacture of silk.

Such is briefly the history of the commercial intercourse between China and ancient Europe. Ecclesiastical history furnishes but very scanty and ill authenticated information as to any connexion subsisting in the early ages, between Christian nations and this remote part of the eastern world. The few notices which occur, are thus summed up by a learned Missionary of our own times.

" The first attempts to make known the truths of Christianity in China, were by the Nestorians, who, from the fifth century, when the sect arose, to the end of the seventh century, penetrated through the various countries eastward of Constantinople, to Tatary, where they spread their doctrines, and instituted Christian societies. In the end of the seventh century, they came into China, where, also, they established churches. Little more notice is taken of their proceedings for nearly five hundred years. In the thirteenth century, they are said to have had a flourishing church in the north of China, where it still continued to exist in the beginning of the fifteenth century, after it was nearly extinguished in Tatary.†
In the fifteenth century and the commencement of the

* De Guignes in Gibbon, ch. xiii. (A.D. 286) and xl.

† Mosheim, vol. ii. Seventh Cent. part 1.; vol. iii. Fourteenth Cent. 1.

sixteenth, Nestorianism is thought to have entirely died away in China.

" With respect to the Nestorians in China, two remarks occur. The first is, that no authentic records that I have seen, mention the coming of that sect into China, or of their efforts, doctrines, sufferings, or extinction there. Nor, with the exception of the stone tablet of *See-Gan*,* mentioned by some Romish missionaries, have any monuments, inscriptions, remains of old churches, &c., been noticed by any Chinese writer that I have seen or heard of. The second remark is, that no part of the Nestorian doctrines or ceremonies of worship, seems to have mingled itself with the pagan systems of China. In many other countries, paganism has borrowed from Christianity; and in China, images and pictures of Christ, borrowed from the Roman Catholic religion, are found in some pagan temples, where, at certain times, they are worshipped. There is in the *Shin-seen-tung-keen*, a Chinese mythological history, a brief account of the birth, life, death, resurrection, ascension, and disciples of Christ; an account evidently borrowed from the Roman Catholics. These circumstances, if this view of them be just, are the more remarkable, inasmuch as the Chinese notice every other foreign sect which has entered their country. The Buddhists, the Mohammedans, and the Roman Catholics, are all particularly noticed by them. Moreover, *Choo-foo-tzse*, *Tsang-tse*, and other eminent Chinese writers, lived in or near the time when Nestorianism must, according to the above accounts, have been in its most flourishing state in China. They notice a number of

---

* At Si-ngan-fu, the capital of Shen-si. This monument, found in 1625, is said to record the introduction of Christianity into China by the Nestorians in the seventh or eighth century.

religious sects that existed in the country at that time, but do not mention any sect of Christians. The Nestorians, according to Dr. Mosheim and other ecclesiastical historians, must have been in China during a period of more than eight hundred years ; and it is a singular circumstance, that if they really were there for so great a length of time, Chinese history never mentions them.*

* On the other hand, there seems good reason to believe, that Christianity had established itself in Tatary at an early period. Marco Polo, in his account of the province of Zenduk (near Lake Baikal), says : " The king now reigning is a descendant of Prester John, and named George. He is both a Christian and a priest ; the greater part of the inhabitants being also Christians." " Here," remarks his learned Editor, " we find the assertion circumstantially repeated, that not Ung-Khan (Prester John) only, but all his descendants, to the days of our author," (that is, from the end of the eleventh to the thirteenth century,) " were Christians ; and although it has been common to doubt the fact, no arguments drawn from historical evidence have been employed to disprove it. On the other hand, it is supported by the testimony of the travellers Carpini and Rubruquis, and sanctioned by the authority of Abulfaradj·····. From the Chinese annals, it is true, it receives no confirmation. But so little informed and so incurious have these people been at all periods on the subject of foreigners, and particularly of their religions, which, without discrimination, they hold in contempt, that their silence carries with it no weight····. It may be asked, why there should be so much hesitation to believe, as if it were, in itself, a thing improbable, that, at an early period, the Christian faith (according to the ritual of the Greek church) had spread extensively through Tatary, and penetrated to China ? The fact does not rest upon the evidence of the Catholic friars alone, (who, however, were much more disposed to undervalue, than to exaggerate the successes and political consequence of their rivals,) but is corroborated by the annals of the Nestorian church."—MARSDEN'S *Marco Polo*, c. liii. 364, 365, 450. See also note 507. In a subsequent chapter, the Venetian Traveller, describing the city of Chan-ghian-fu, in the province of Man-ji, says : " There are in this city two churches of Nestorian Christians, which were built in 1274, when his Majesty appointed a Nestorian named Mar Sachir, to the government of it for three years. By him these churches were established *where*

., " In the thirteenth century, the Roman Catholic Church first extended its efforts, rather indirectly, to China. An embassy, composed chiefly of ecclesiastics, at whose head was Johannes à Monte Corvino, was sent from Pope Nicholas IV. to Kublai, Emperor of the Tatars. Their object seems principally to have regarded Tatary; yet, they are said to have erected churches in China also. In the year 1307, the Gospel is reported to have made so great progress in China, that Pope Clement V. erected Cambalu, which some think to be Peking, * into an archbishopric, which was conferred on Johannes à Monte Corvino, above mentioned.†

" Francis Xavier, the celebrated Jesuit, had contemplated the conversion of China to the Christian faith; but, in the midst of his benevolent plans, he was called away by death, while off the coast of that country, in the year 1552. Matthew Ricci, an Italian of the same order, after the death of Xavier, penetrated into China, preached the Catholic faith, and laid the foundation of the Romish Church there. Much stress cannot be laid on any thing done for the Gospel in China before the days of Ricci. In the commencement of the seventeenth century, numbers of Jesuits, Dominicans, Franciscans, and Capuchins entered China, and published part of the Gospel, mixed with

there had not been any before; and they still subsist."—MARSDEN's *Marco Polo, Ib.* c. lxv. The doubts expressed by Dr. Milne, have been also ably met by M. Abel Rémusat.—*Mélanges Asiatiques, tom.* i. p. 31, *etc.*

* Properly *Khan-baligh*, signifying, in one of the Tatar dialects, the city of the khan or sovereign. It was the capital of Khatai, or Northern China, and was afterwards called Yen-king by the Chinese; now, Pe-king.—See MARSDEN's *Marco Polo*, p. 300, note 556.

† This celebrated Italian friar laboured for many years in Tatary, and translated the New Testament and the Psalms of David into the Tatar language.

the superstitions of the Romish Church, and the peculiarities of their respective orders.

" During the reign of the Emperor Kang-he, the Missionaries had less to contend with, and enjoyed more freedom in their work, than either before or since. Several hundreds of Catholic Missionaries, including natives and foreigners, have at different times laboured in China; and it is but justice to say, that many of them appear to have been sincere and single-hearted in their work. Some of them wrote well, where the peculiar errors of their church did not warp their judgement; and several were distinguished for their knowledge of Chinese literature; while, on the other hand, it cannot be denied, that there were among them, some who were tainted with scepticism, and others who loved the honours of a court more than the labours of the Christian ministry. With respect to the doctrines and ceremonies which they taught in China, a fair specimen of the best of these is contained in the Chinese writings of the missionaries. The style of their publications is generally perspicuous, sometimes elegant; but the doctrines which they communicate, are mostly such as were propagated in Europe, in what Protestants call ' the darkest periods of the Church.' Here and there, a beautiful sentiment occurs, well expressed, and supported by appropriate quotations from the Fathers of the Latin Church; but it is often in close connexion with some traditional absurdity. Their Ritual has certainly lost nothing by being transported to the East. The fictions of Chinese paganism, and the legends of the priests of Fuh and Taou, together with imported relations of miracles and wonders, wrought at the shrines of saints, at the tombs of martyrs, or in the caves of hermits, have all contributed to produce considerable additions to the ceremonies of the Church. The virtues attributed to the sign of the cross, to the ringing of bells, to the burning of wax-candles, and the powerful aids said to be afforded by the Virgin Goddess to females in seasons of peculiar solicitude, to sick children, to the aged and poor,—tended very much to render the system acceptable to the lower classes ; especially to females, who, before their conversion, had been accustomed to pray for assistance to two Chinese goddesses. The talents of the Missionaries, their virtues, and their influence (for a time) at court, gained over not a few in the higher walks of life, to the profession of the Gospel. But the rays of Scripture light passing through so clouded an atmosphere, must have been faint indeed. These corruptions are, however, to be attributed to the system, and not to the men themselves. The fear and love of God would have restrained them from corrupting the truth intentionally ; and we find the essential doctrines of Divine Revelation scattered through their Chinese publications. Their stedfastness and triumph in the midst of persecution even to blood, and to death in all imaginable forms of terror, which they endured in Japan, China, &c., shew that the adulterated Christianity which they taught, is to be ascribed to the effect of education, not to design ; and also afford reason to believe, that they have joined the ' noble army of martyrs,' and are now wearing the crowns of those ' who spared not their lives from death, but overcame by the blood of the Lamb, and by the word of their testimony.'

" Of late years, they have been greatly persecuted ; there is, however, reason to believe, that the disputes which took place among the Missionaries themselves, did their cause more real injury than all the persecutions which they endured. The contentions which arose about a term proper to express the Deity, and about the rites of sacrifice usually performed by the Chinese at the tombs of their ancestors, &c., followed by the arrival from Europe of ecclesiastical messengers clothed with secular glory, and invested with spiritual powers to settle controversies, led, in the issue, to the two greatest evils that can ever befall any body of men jointly labouring for the conversion of the Heathen, viz., external disrespect, and internal divisions. The high tone assumed by a legate from Rome, the imperious conduct of individual mission-aries in high ecclesiastical stations, and the inflexible firmness (some have called it obstinacy) of the greater part, who were neither intimidated by the thunders of the Vatican, nor softened by the entreaties of the friends of truth, nor moved from their purpose by the pacific counsels of moderate pagans; all tended to lower their religion and its ministers in the estimation of the Chinese, while the introduction of separate and contending interests divided the Missionaries among themselves. Thus, a very considerable portion of their whole time, strength, and talents was thrown away, in defending the claims, in defining the peculiarities, and in supporting the pre-eminence of the several monastic orders, under the banners of which they had enlisted.

" The Europeans who were the life of the missions, have either died, been banished, or fallen by the hands of their persecutors; and the small number of their converts, partly for want of the holy Scriptures, and partly for want of living teachers, are now falling rapidly back into heathenism.

" There now exists a Greek church in Peking, at which the Russian commercial resident and others from that country attend. The origin of this church is mentioned by Bell, in his account of China. During the reign of Kang-he, in one of his Tatarian wars, some Russians on the river Amour, were taken prisoners, and brought to Peking. That emperor, who was distinguished for many excellent qualities, allowed them to build a 'church, and to enjoy their own religion. The attention of this church has been entirely confined to the foreigners attached to the Russian factory in the capital. The Dutch, though they extended Christianity to the Moluccas, to part of Celebes, and of the island of Formosa, do not appear to have attempted the introduction of the Gospel into China." *

The first attempt, on the part of this country, to open an amicable intercourse with the Celestial Empire, was the mission entrusted to Lord Macartney in 1794. That embassy having failed in its object, (although a gracious audience was vouchsafed to the envoy,) no further official intercourse took place till the recent embassy of Lord Amherst, which was totally unsuccessful; owing to an unfortunate misunderstanding on the part of the Emperor, originating in the gross mismanagement and bad faith of his ministers, the embassy was dismissed from the capital in disgrace, without being admitted to an interview with the *soi-disant* " Son of Heaven." Although little accession to our geographical knowledge has resulted from these embassies, they have thrown fresh light on the manners of the court, and enable us to form a tolerably correct estimate of the rank which this great empire holds in the scale of social existence.

* Milne's " First Ten Years of the Protestant Mission to China."—Malacca, 1820. pp. 7—16. The Russian Mission, composed of six ecclesiastics and four lay-members, is relieved about every ten years.

China, as a country, remains still impenetrable to our travellers;* but our knowledge of the Chinese, as a nation, is daily becoming more extensive and intimate, by means of the outposts occupied by our factories and missionaries. Of the population of Birmah, Siam, and Anam, and the Indian Archipelago, a considerable portion consists of either natives of China or the descendants of natives, speaking the language and retaining the customs and superstitions of their ancestors; and through their medium, under the well-directed efforts of British missionaries, it is probable that European civilization and Christian light will find the readiest and surest' access to the empire. In September 1807, the first Protestant missionary to China sent out from this country, arrived at Canton. This was Mr. Morrison, who has since so highly distinguished himself by his philological labours. In conjunction with his able colleague, the late Dr. Milne, he completed, in 1823, a version of the whole Bible into Chinese: the New Testament, partly their own work, and partly compiled from a manuscript version executed by the Romish missionaries, had been printed and put in circulation in 1814. In the meantime, the Serampore Missionaries had been directing their attention, since the year 1806, to the study of the same language. In 1815, an independent and original version of the New Testament in Chinese was completed at their press, printed with moveable me-

---

* The Editor has received information, that a Scotch gentleman, who speaks the Chinese so well as to pass for a native, succeeded, not long ago, in eluding the vigilance of the local authorities : attended by a native servant, he had made his way about 100 miles into the interior, when he accidentally betrayed himself. His servant was instantly seized and strangled, and the adventurous traveller was himself sent back under guard, to Canton. His narrative would be highly interesting.

tallic characters cut at Serampore; the first of the kind ever attempted. In 1822, the whole of the Scriptures were completed; and this vast undertaking, which cost them the unremitting labour of sixteen years, was achieved under all the disadvantages attendant upon their being deprived of the aid of native assistants. The two translations have since been diligently collated, and a second edition of the Chinese Bible is now in progress at the Serampore press, in which both versions are used for the purpose of obtaining a corrected text. *

Missionaries from three Protestant nations are now unitedly labouring to promote the diffusion of religious knowledge among the Indo-Chinese nations; those of the various British Missionary Societies; those sent out by the Netherlands Missionary Society, and the American Baptist Missionaries. Ever since the year 1813, divine service has been more or less regularly performed, both in English and in Chinese, either at Macao or at Canton. The latter station is occupied by Dr. Morrison. In 1818, the foundation-stone was laid of an Anglo-Chinese college at Malacca,

---

* One of the most accomplished Chinese scholars in Europe, has thus characterised these versions: "Equal praises are due to the respectable individuals whose zeal, patience, and talents have brought to a termination this double enterprise. In paying a just homage to the merit of his coadjutor *(concurrent)*, Mr. Morrison has had the modesty himself to 'point out, how much the MS. ' Harmony of the Gospels,' must have contributed to the perfection of his own work. Mr. Marshman had to supply, by dint of application and labour, the want of foreign aid. If, however, it was wished to characterise the results of the studies of these two interpreters of the sacred books, we might say, that the Serampore version is the more literal, and the Canton one the most conformed to the Chinese taste." Their being alike without note or comment, must, however, the learned Author thinks, render them almost equally difficult and unattractive to the Chinese; a point which experience will decide."—*Mélanges Asiatiques*, par M. Abel Rémusat, *tom.* i. p. 17.

towards the erection of which the learned Missionary himself contributed the sum of £1000 sterling. In this college, there are now twenty-four students. Three missionaries are resident at this important station, at which divine service in Chinese is regularly conducted every Sunday, for the benefit of the students, the Chinese belonging to the printing establishment, and the native boys in the Chinese schools supported by the Mission. Several thousand tracts, containing portions of the Scripture in Chinese, or other useful instruction, have been printed and put in circulation. There are also missionaries stationed at Singapore and Penang. *

* " The English experienced, at the outset, many difficulties in printing their Chinese books. The natives whom they were obliged to employ as translators, revisers, engravers, or printers, aware that they were required to labour in works prohibited by the laws of the empire, demanded a high price for their co-operation. These expenses, and the risks attendant upon them, merit some attention, when it is known, from an exact list given by Mr. Milne, that the total number of copies of Chinese books published in 1818, as well at Canton as at Macao and Malacca, amounted to 140,249; that of Malay books to 20,500; without reckoning the Chinese Grammar of Mr. Morrison printed at Serampore, two Chinese-English Dictionaries, Family Dialogues in Chinese, the Indo-Chinese Gleaner edited by Mr. Milne, the translation of the Sacred Edict by the same Missionary, and the work (' Retrospect of the First Ten Years') from which we borrow these details. Among the Chinese works published in this manner, the Author specifies thirty-two, of which he has given particular notices. In this list, we remark, the Bible almost entire (since completed), an Outline of the Old Testament, History of the Life of Jesus Christ, a Monthly Magazine, a periodical Miscellany in Chinese, a Geographical Catechism with four maps, &c. Thus, we behold an entire literature called into existence at the very extremity of the world, and without our knowledge, by two or three indefatigable men, assisted by a certain number of zealous and liberal persons. These great enterprises of religious zeal have something remarkable in the era in which we live; the more so, as those who direct them, or at least those who execute them, appear, for the

These enterprising and successful labours have drawn the attention and admiration of the literati of Europe, and have extorted commendation from the members of different religious communions. They bid fair, indeed, to break down the great wall which has hitherto intellectually separated this vast section of the world from the rest of the globe, and to achieve, silently, but irresistibly, a mightier revolution than was ever effected by political conquest.

We must now hasten to lay before the reader a brief sketch of the physical geography of the country, preparatory to a description of the capital, with which we shall connect a general view of the national customs, manners, religion, and political condition.

PHYSICAL GEOGRAPHY.

THE conquests of the emperors of the Mantchoo dynasty have extended the Chinese empire northward, over a great part of the countries formerly comprised under the general appellation of Independent Tatary; where, from the neighbourhood of Lake Palcati to the mouth of the river Amour, a line 3000 miles in length,

moment, to be strangers to any political or commercial views." After enumerating the five stations at Canton, Malacca, Penang, Batavia, and Singapore, as they stood in 1819, to which period only the learned Writer had received the Missionary accounts, he concludes the paper with the following remarks: "The Missionaries see, in this concurrence of circumstances, grounds for calculating on the success of their evangelical preaching. There are many of their countrymen who do not participate in all their hopes upon this point; but there is doubtless no one who does not view with lively interest, these proceedings, these literary studies, this abundant harvest of documents of all sorts, which seem to have for their principal effect, if not for their immediate object, to open new markets to their industry, and to prepare the way for their commerce and their policy."—*Mélanges Asiatiques*, tom. i. pp. 43—50.

It is conterminous with the Russian frontier.[*] Lake Palcati, the Alak mountains, and the Beloot mountains, separate the Chinese empire, on the west, from the territories of the Kirguis, Uzbeg, and other independent tribes of genuine Tatars. In a south-westerly direction, it has extended itself over the vast regions of Tibet, and has almost become conterminous with the British possessions to the north of Bengal. Its south-eastern province of Yun-nan brings it into direct contact with the Birman empire; and further eastward, it is bounded by the once tributary states of Anam. Reckoning from the Tongkinese frontier to the mouth of the Amour, it has 3600 miles of coast, washed by the Eastern Ocean.

The extent of China Proper (to which we must now confine ourselves) is far less considerable, and is comprised between about twenty parallels of latitude and as many degrees of longitude, forming an area of about 537,000 square miles.[†] The whole of the empire is generally called *Ta-ts'hing-kwe*, the country of the *Ta-tshing* (the reigning dynasty): the province beyond the Great Wall, formerly denominated Chinese Tatary, bears the name of *Fong-t'hyen-fu*. China is called by the natives *Chung-we*, the central

---

[*] The vast province, north of the Gulf of Peking and the kingdom of Corea, of which Shing-king is the capital, must not be reckoned among those of China properly so called. It comprises the province of Liao-toung, and the ancient country of the Mantchoos and is traversed by the great river Saghalien, or Amour, and its tributaries.

[†] Malte Brun, vol. iv. p. 552. Humboldt assigns to China Proper, a territorial surface of 128,000 square marine leagues, with a population of 150 millions, being 1172 to the square league. The population of the whole Chinese empire is only 377 to the square league.—*Pers. Nar.* vol. vi. p. 337. That of England gives 2524 to the square league.

kingdom; * and, in the reign of Kyen-long, was divided into the following provinces.

	Provinces.	Chief City.	Population, A.D. 1790.
I.	Pe-tche-li or King-se	Pe-king	3,504,038
II.	Shang-tong	Tsi-nan	25,447,633
III.	Shan-si	Taï-ywen	1,860,816
IV.	Kyang-nan		
	i. Kyang-su or Nan-king	} Kyang-ning	28,967,235
	ii. Ngan-hwaï	Ngan-king	1,438,123
V.	Ho-nan	{ Kaï-fong, Tong-king, Si-king, Pyen-king }	2,662,969
VI.	Shen-si		
	i. Shen-si	Si-ngan	257,704
	ii. Kan-su	Lan-cheu	340,086
VII.	Tche-kyang	Hang-cheu	18,975,099
VIII.	Kyang-si	Nan-chang	5,922,160
IX.	Hou-kwang		
	i. Hou-pe	Vu-chang	24,604,369
	ii. Hou-nan	Chang-sha	9,098,010
X.	Se-shwen	Ching-tu	7,789,782
XI.	Fo-kyen	Fo-cheu	1,684,528
XII.	Kwang-tong	Kwang-cheu	1,491,271
XIII.	Kwang-si	Kwei-lin	2,569,518
XIV.	Kwei-tchou	Kwei-yang	2,941,391
XV.	Yun-nang	Yun-nan	3,083,459
			142,638,091
	Fong-t'hyen-fu, or Chinese Tatary	{ Hing-king, Shing-king }	390,714
			143,028,805 †

* This name seems to correspond to the *Medya-b'humi* or Middle Land of the Hindoos. It is also called *Tchon-koo*, the Centre of the World. The Mohammedan travellers of the ninth century give to Southern China the name of Sin, pronounced by the Persians, Tchin. But this appellation is, by D'Anville, with great probability, supposed to belong to Cochin China, which is the *Sinarum Regio* of the ancients. The *Magnus Sinus* which separated that region from Ultra-Gangetic India, he identifies with the Gulf of Siam; and the capital of the *Sines*, he places at Sin-hoa.— Vol. ii. pp. 128, 132. There was, however, another *Sinæ*, contiguous with *Serica*, and far distant from the *Sinæ* beyond the Ganges. " Shen-si, bordering on Serica, comprised, about 800 years before

The surface of the country is very diversified. It contains two distinct mountain regions; one on the south-east, and the other on the north-west. The great southern chain, running from W. to E. between the provinces of Kwang-si, Kwang-tong, and Fo-kyen on the south, and Hou-kwang and Kyang-si on the north, separates the basin of the *Yang-tse-kyang* (Blue river) from that of the *Hon-kyang;* till, on reaching the limits of Fo-kyen, it turns to the N.E., and separates the former river from the sea. Two branches of this chain cut the basin of the *Yang-tse-kyang* transversely. Gneiss and quartz are believed to be the prevailing rocks in this mountain-chain, which has been denominated the *Mangian*, from Mangi, the name of Southern China, and may be considered as rivalling the Apennines, or, perhaps, the Pyrenees.

The mountains of the north-west do not consist so much of regular chains, as of a succession of table-lands. In the western part of the province of Se-shwen, a chain of mountains runs parallel with the river *Ya-lon* from S. to N., till it reaches the Si-fan country; it then turns eastward, and enters the pro-

the Christian era, a kingdom called *Tsin*. This name was preserved by the western people whom commerce brought across Serica."—*Ib.* p. 94. The learned Author thinks, that *Sinæ* might be an ancient generic name for all the nations of Tibet, China, and Indo-China. This is, however, cutting the knot. Northern China or Khataï (Cathay), and Southern China, or Han, appear always to have been distinguished, by whatever names they have been known. The *Sinæ*, of whom Ptolemy had a very imperfect knowledge, were, *perhaps*, the southern Chinese, as the *Seres*, better known to the ancients, were the northern.—See *Ency. Metrop.* art. China.

† Morrison's View, p. 61. Ency. Metrop., art. China. Malte Brun, vol. ii. p. 552. The maritime provinces are six in number; Pe-tche-li, Shan-tong, Kyang-nan, Tche-kyang, Fo-kyen, and Kwang-tong.

vince of Shen-si, running parallel, first with the river *Hoei-ho*, and then with the *Hoan-ho*, and gradually disappearing in the province of Ho-nan. The province of Shan-si is full of mountains, which appear to belong to a chain extending from the banks of the Amour across Mongolia. The province of Shan-tong consists for the most part of a groupe of mountains wholly detached from any other range, and running out towards the N.E. into a large peninsula. These mountains contain coal-mines.

The most extensive plains in China are found in the maritime province of Kyang-nan, which may be described as a Chinese Mesopotamia. The two great rivers, the *Hoan-ho* or *Whang-ho* (Yellow river), and the *Yang-tse-kyang*, each of which has its rise in the great table-land of Tibet, after describing an immense circuit in opposite directions, at a distance of 1100 miles, suddenly approach one another, and, like the Euphrates and the Tigris, wind along the same plain, communicating occasionally by canals and lakes, till they terminate, within a mutual distance of 110 miles, their long and majestic course. Among their respective tributaries are some streams which equal in size the largest rivers of Europe. The *Fuen-ho*, the *Hoei-ho*, and the *Hoay-ho* fall into the Yellow River. The *Ya-lon-kyang* (itself 700 miles in length), the *Tchoo* or *Yan-kyang*, the *La-kyang*, and the *Yuen-kyang*, are tributary to the Blue River, which receives also the waters of several other rivers from the lakes *Ton-ting-hoo* and *Po-yang-hoo*. The former of these lakes, situated in the province of Hoo-kwang (which signifies the country of lakes), is more than 220 miles in circumference, and is one of a series of lakes, almost touching one another, extending northward and eastward, and occupying, in this region, a great part of the basin of the Blue River. The lake *Po-yang-hoo*, in the province of Kyang-si, has a circumference of 90 or 100 miles, and receives four superb rivers. The *Tai-hoo*, a lake to the south of Nan-king, is surrounded with hills, and presents some romantic scenery. Those of *Hon-tse-hoo* and *Kao-yen-hoo*, to the north of that city, are also of vast extent. All these lakes are united by natural or artificial channels, and their tranquil basins are navigable by barks light enough to be portable. They abound with fish, and afford boundless scope for an aquatic sport, which seems intermediate between hawking and fishing. The Chinese pelican is trained for catching fish, a ring being fixed round his neck to prevent him from swallowing his prey.

There are two large rivers which maintain a perfect independence of both these vast reservoirs. The *Pay-ho*, in the north, after receiving the *Yan-ho*, falls into the Gulf of Peking; and the *Hoan-king*, descending from the mountains of Yun-nan, flows eastward through Kwang-si and Kwang-tong, and after a course of 740 miles, falls into the Gulf of Canton.

This multitude of rivers confers on the Chinese nation, incalculable advantages for agriculture as well as for inland navigation. Travellers are astonished at the length, depth, and commodiousness of the canals, which have a stone quay all along their margin, and are sometimes crossed by bridges constructed with singular art. The navigation, however, is slow, as the vessels are generally dragged by men. The most celebrated of these canals is the Imperial Canal, about 1660 miles in length, which forms a communication between Pekin and Canton, with the interruption of only a day's journey in crossing a mountain between the provinces of Kwang-tong and Kyang-si.

The difference of climate in the several provinces, is increased by the influence which the lofty mountains of Central Asia necessarily exert on the one hand, and the modifying effects of the Ocean, on the other, on the maritime provinces. The south of China, near the tropic, experiences heats more intense than those of Bengal, but they are moderated by the monsoons. .The mean heat of Canton is about 76° Fahr. The northern and western parts have a far colder climate than the countries of Europe under the same parallel. The extremes of heat and cold are much greater at Pekin, than at Madrid, although the latitude is much the same. There are, properly, only two seasons there, summer and winter,—the seasons of snow and rain. It freezes daily in December, January, and February, and very often in November and March. The months of June, July, and August are very rainy, attended often by excessive heats. November is the driest month, and one of the pleasantest of the Chinese year.*

The Chinese are eminently an agricultural nation, and no branch of art or industry has been more highly patronized by its government, than the culture of the earth. " It is the most favoured occupation," we are told, " next to learning,† and is considered as the

---

* The mean of the greatest heat is 121°; that of the greatest cold is 63° below zero; the medium heat of the year, 55°. The average number of rainy days in the year is 58.

† " Every one has heard of the honours conferred upon agriculture by the Chinese government. Every year, on the fifteenth day of the first moon, which generally corresponds to some day in the beginning of March," (others say, at the vernal equinox,) " the Emperor in person goes through the ceremony of opening the ground. He repairs in great state to the field appointed for this ceremony, attended by the princes of the imperial family, the presidents of the five great tribunals, and an immense number of

basis of national prosperity. The Emperor is sole proprietor of the soil, and every tenant pays one-tenth of the produce as a rent for the land he holds.* It is a fixed maxim, never to dispossess any landholder who is exact in the payment of this charge; and he is allowed, if he pleases, to underlet his estate. This is commonly done at the rate of one-half of the whole produce, so that the tenant under government makes.

mandarins. These line three sides of the field: the fourth is reserved for the labourers of the province. The Emperor enters the field alone, prostrates himself, and touches the ground with his head nine times, in adoration of *Tien*, the God of heaven. He pronounces with a loud voice, a prayer prepared by the Court of Ceremonies, in which he invokes the blessing of the Great Being on his labour and on that of his whole empire. Then, in the capacity of chief priest of the empire, he sacrifices an ox in homage to Heaven as the fountain of all good. While the victim is offered, a plough is brought to the Emperor, to which is yoked a pair of oxen, magnificently ornamented. The sovereign lays aside his imperial robes, lays hold of the plough, and opens several furrows all round the field. He then gives the plough into the hands of the chief mandarins, who, labouring in succession, display their comparative dexterity. The ceremony concludes with a distribution of money and pieces of cloth among the labourers."—MALTE BRUN, ii. 561, 2. Another account of the ceremony, after stating that a *cow* is offered up in the temple of the Spirit presiding over the earth, adds, that "figures of the same animal, made of clay, are first carried in procession, and then broken and distributed among the people." (*Ency. Metrop.*) After the field has received the necessary dressing, the Emperor commences the sowing with similar ceremonies, which are performed on the same day by the viceroys of all the provinces. The Russian ceremonies of blessing the first verdure of spring, and blessing the waters, present a striking resemblance to these Chinese solemnities.—See MOD. TRAV., *Russia*, pp. 64, 5.

* A land-tax was substituted for the capitation tax by Yongching, who reigned in 1722-1735. This produced in 1777, according to an imperial rescript, 17,260,000*l.*, or nearly three-fifths of the revenue. The other receipts are derived from an assessment on the workshops of artisans, &c., producing about a million and a half sterling, which, with excise and customs, is supposed to form a total of nearly thirty millions.

a clear profit of two-fifths. The land is, on the whole, equally divided; little, except for the emperor's use, is devoted to pleasure-grounds, parks, &c.; and there are no restrictions on the taking fish or game. Famines, however, are very frequent, from drought, inundations, the ravages of locusts, and civil commotions. The government, also, with all its professions, is very improvident; while, on any emergency, the restrictions on external commerce, and the unproductive state of the adjoining countries, cut off all hope of a supply from abroad. The extraordinary diligence of the peasantry in cultivating every inch of soil, so much exaggerated by some of the earlier writers, is no fable with respect to the immediate neighbourhood of towns and cities. There, not a foot of ground is lost; and the hills are formed into terraces, as is the case in Malta and the Pays de Vaud. But banditti, want of cattle, imperfect drainage, and, beyond all, the oppression of men in power, counteract the letter as well as the spirit of the law, and check the cultivation of less favoured tracts to such an extent, that more than one-fourth, perhaps two-thirds, of the whole empire are either swamps or wastes. Any one may, as is the case in Turkey, obtain a grant of waste land, on engaging to pay the stipulated tenth into the hands of the proper officers; but the ignorance and poverty of the great body of the people prevent such speculations from being often attempted. The Chinese are, indeed, ill-adapted to manage land on a large scale; and are more fit for gardeners than for farmers. Their implements of husbandry are singularly defective; and their plough, drawn by a single buffalo, seldom makes a furrow more than four inches deep; new soil, therefore, is never turned up. The ground is never allowed to lie fallow. In some places, two crops of rice are raised in one season ; wheat follows cotton or indigo, and is cut in May or June ; beans are sown *between* the drills of wheat, and ripen after harvest ; *lentils*, sweet potatoes, and yams succeed wheat.

" The want of domestic animals is likewise the source of another evil, the scarcity of manure ; an evil the more felt, as the soil is generally loose and sandy, and therefore soon impoverished. Dung can be procured in small quantities only in the north, where horned cattle are most plentiful. All sorts of excrements are therefore carefully collected and preserved ; slime and mud are dredged up from ponds and ditches ; and even the barbers diligently pocket every hair from the heads and beards of their customers, in order to sell it for the benefit of the soil. Lime, burnt bones, decayed wood and leaves, are mixed with these materials. Manure, in the form of dried cakes, is carried for sale from one part of the country to the other ; and it is conveyed in every state by water-carriage over the whole empire. The combining of different soils is well understood ; and sandy grounds are worked up with marl and clay, as stiff lands are with sand and gravel. Rice is the staple produce ; then, barley ; after that wheat, especially in the north ; buck-wheat, millet (*sorghum*), maize, peas, beans, and other vetches, are the other kinds of grain and pulse most cultivated. Sugar-cane, cotton, hemp, linseed, tobacco, indigo, tea, mulberries, varnish-trees (*rhus vernix*), camphor, tallow-trees (*stillingia sebifera*), and cinnamon, are the trees and shrubs most common in the fields and gardens. Besides our esculent vegetables, a kind of cabbage, called *pe-t'shaï*, earth-nuts (*arachis hypogæa*), yams, and sweet potatoes are raised in large quantities.

THE TCHIN-SHAN, OR GOLDEN ISLAND.

" For ornamental gardening, the Chinese have been extolled as far surpassing every other nation; and certainly, when their style is compared with the formal parterres and ponderous wildernesses of our forefathers, the contrast is striking. The variety, brilliancy, and airiness of the Chinese pleasure-grounds, leave the stiff, monotonous gardens of France and Italy, once so much admired, far behind them; because the Asiatics imitated Nature's beautiful irregularity, while the Europeans strove to force upon trees and greenswards, a symmetry which is entirely out of nature. The defect of the Chinese gardeners is, that they attempt too much. Rocks, forests, plains and valleys, all are to be crowded within the narrow compass of a few acres; while the uncouth forms of their artificial caverns, with an excessive profusion of cascades and pagodas, not only shew the effort of art at every step, but oppress the eye with a superfluity of surprising objects. The grotesque figures of lions, tigers, dragons, and other creatures of a distorted imagination, all from the kilns of the porcelain-manufacturer, are ornaments suggested by the same wretched taste which has peopled the gardens of Versailles and the Tuileries with the heroes and demi-gods of Greece and Rome. The imperial pleasure-grounds of Yuen-min-yuen, near Pĕ-king, occupying nearly 60,000 acres, and comprehending thirty separate palaces, as well as those of Je-hol, beyond the Great Wall, to the north-east of the capital, are magnificent samples of the Chinese taste and skill, well deserving, from their magnitude and constant succession of beauties, the admiration of Europeans as well as natives.

" If the Chinese have little to boast of with respect to the fine arts, their skill in several of those which are more mechanical, is far from inconsiderable. In the construction and use of fire-arms, in printing and engraving, in the manufacture of silk and cotton cloths, and especially in their earthenware, they appear to have taken the lead; and in the two last, still equal, if they do not excel, the Europeans themselves.

" Their sculpture, which is almost all in low relief, is closely allied to the art of engraving; an art probably of great antiquity among them, from their constant use of seals as signatures to all deeds and public documents. Their works of this kind in wood, mother-of-pearl, and ivory, are known to every one; and their hollow spheres, included within each other, are often preserved as curiosities in public collections. Out of one solid ball of ivory, they will carve fifteen hollow globes, all distinct from each other, all moveable by a touch, and ornamented with figures and open work, like the sticks of a fan. Yet, these singular productions of art, which appear to require so much skill and labour, are soon finished, and sold for a trifle.

" From the impressions of their seals, it is probable that the Chinese caught the first idea of the art of printing; an art said to be known to them more than nine centuries before the Christian era, but, like most of their inventions, still in its infancy. It is nothing better than a clumsy kind of stereotype, with all the inconveniences and few of the advantages of that ingenious contrivance. The characters to be printed, are first drawn by a skilful manager of his pencil, on a sheet of thin, transparent paper, which, when dry, is glued on a smooth board. It is then delivered to the engraver, who scrapes out all the spaces between the strokes of the letters, which are thus left in relief, and the paper is carefully washed off. Each board contains two pages; ink, more fluid than that used in writing, is laid on with a hard brush; a sheet of paper is applied, a softer brush is passed over it, and an impression is taken. Four o\ five can be thus thrown off without renewing the ink. The sheets, when printed, are folded back and form two pages. A few moveable types of the most common characters, are sometimes, but very rarely used. All authors who are mandarins, must lay their works before the Emperor, who orders the *Han-lin*, or Royal Society of Pĕ-king, to examine the manuscript; and, if approved, it is printed at the expense of government. Sú-cheu-fú, on the great canal, in the province of Kyang-nan, is a great emporium for books, particularly poetical works; but there are printing-offices in most of the large towns.

" The imitative powers of the Chinese are very great; and it may be in general remarked, that those nations which are least remarkable for original inventions, succeed most readily in arts which are merely imitative. A Chinese at Canton, who had never before seen a watch, made one in every point complete, except in the main-spring; they are therefore capable of imitating our machinery; yet they have scarcely any thing of the kind, their own being extremely clumsy and simple.

" The Jews are the best silk-manufacturers in the empire, and are most numerous in the provinces in which silk-worms are reared ; * it has therefore been

---

* Dr. Morrison was informed, that, at Kae-fung-hoo, in the province of Honan, there were a few families of the *Teaou-kin-keaou*, or sinew-plucking sect ; so called because they take away the sinews from all the flesh they eat. They had a *le-pae-sze*, or temple of worship, and observed the *eighth* day as a sabbath. The person who gave this statement, regarded them as the same with the *Teen-chow-keaou*, or Christians; but they are more likely to be Jews.

conjectured, that the art of weaving silk was introduced by Jewish emigrants after the conquests of
Alexander. This, however, is very inconsistent with
the lofty pretensions of the Chinese, one of whose
historians speaks of brocades as being in use nearly
300 years before our era. The quantity of silk now
produced and manufactured, is almost beyond calculation; it forms the principal article of clothing for
the rich. The province of Che-kyang, between the
twenty-seventh and thirty-first parallels of northern
latitude, is the country from which the finest, softest,
and whitest is brought; but the adjoining province
of Kyang-nan has the greatest number of weavers;
and all articles intended for the emperor's use, are
made there, particularly in its capital, Nan-king. The
productions of the Chinese looms are said to be more
showy than substantial; their brocades are embroidered with gilt paper, and are therefore soon spoiled.
Gauzes, whether flowered or plain, are the manufactures in which they excel; and those most in use, are
a strong, dull satin, called *tú-ngan-tse*, and a close,
grey taffety, which washes well, and is suitable for
drawers, linings, &c. The *kyen-cheú*, spun by an
insect somewhat differing from the silk-worm, and
abounding in the province of Shan-tong, furnishes a
thick, rough material, resembling drugget, and much
valued by the Chinese. The silk goods exported to
Europe are manufactured in or near Canton, and the
raw material is brought from Kyang-nan. That province also produces the crown cotton (*gossypium religosum*), which is manufactured into nankeens; particularly in the city of Nan-king, whence the name of
those cotton cloths is derived. Narrow, stout, and
fine linens are manufactured at Nan-king and in Fŏ-

kyen; they are called *ko-pú* by the natives, and *nunes* by the Portuguese.

" Paper is another article of which the Chinese claim the invention; the first having been made from the bark of a tree (*morus papyrifera*) and old linen, by Tsaï-lun, a mandarin who flourished about a century and a half before Christ. The bark of that tree, and the *Kŏ-ch'hu*, hemp, nettles, straw, the coccoons of the silk-worm, cotton, rags, and the fibres of the bamboo, are the materials now used: from the second of these, the most common sort is made; whence *kú-chú* has become the usual term for paper. The inner bark of the bamboo, after maceration in water, is reduced to a paste by boiling and bruising in a mortar; it is then spread out, on frames of fine bamboo threads, and formed into sheets of various lengths, from three to ten feet. The whitest, softest, and most durable, is made from cotton rags. A size, consisting of seventy-eight parts water, three isinglass, and one alum, is used to prevent the ink from running; but it makes the paper more liable to tear, or be injured by damp and worms. A strong, rose-coloured, transparent paper is used in the windows at Pĕ-king, as a substitute for glass. This kind is brought from Corea.

" That Peninsula is also said to be the country where the Chinese learned the secret of preparing their excellent ink now so univeraally used by our artists under the name of Indian ink. It was not brought to perfection till the ninth century; and is made of the soot deposited by the smoke of pines or oil. This is formed into a paste by a strong solution of isinglass, with the addition of a little musk, to correct the smell. Isinglass prepared from asses-skin and the soot of lamps, which is the lightest kind, make the best ink.

" The delicate painting-brushes, called camel's hair-pencils, were probably invented by the Chinese. The fur of rabbits is that of which they are generally made; and to the natives of China, they are as indispensable as pens to us.

" Almost all trades are itinerant in China, and the tools commonly used are few, clumsy, and unserviceable. The barbers are most active; shaving the whole face, extirpating bristles from the nostrils, adjusting the eye-brows, and plaiting the only lock which the Tatars will allow their Chinese subjects to retain. Carpenters and tailors also ply in the streets; but japanners always work in shops, and even keep their windows shut, as if to conceal the mysteries of their art. The Japanese were the inventors of it, and their neighbours on the continent have never been able to rival their skill. The articles varnished are either made of pasteboard (*papier maché*) or thin wood; black and red are the favourite colours; and the best workmanship is that of Kyang-nan. It is superior to that of Canton.

" Extreme indigence is the lot of thousands, and beggars abound; but charity is not a virtue much practised in China; a thimbleful of rice is all that a beggar can hope to obtain. The tradesmen, however, have associations like our benefit-societies or clubs, for the relief of their distressed brethren.

" The fishermen, a most numerous class, are generally in a very wretched condition, perhaps from living entirely on fish and ducks; though they have some vegetable food, for they raise onions, garlic, &c. on rafts of bamboo covered with beds of earth. They allure fish at night by lights, as is done elsewhere; but their most singular mode of fishing is the employment of a tame water-fowl, of the cormorant tribe, perhaps the *pelicanus aquilus,* or man of war. These birds are carried out on rafts, and have a ring round their necks, which serves for the double purpose of bringing them back, by means of a string, and preventing them from swallowing the fish they have seized. After a certain time the ring is removed, and the bird is allowed to provide for himself. Their ducks also are so well trained, that they return to the boats on hearing their master whistle.

" But, of all the manufactures for which the Chinese have been celebrated, their earthenware is perhaps the most remarkable. Its peculiar excellence made it long an import of considerable value, gave its name to the finer kinds of pottery among ourselves, and rendered it a favourite article of luxury in the courts of Central and Western Asia, long before China was known to Europe. Their materials, and the care with which they are cleansed and prepared, are the real causes of the superiority of the Chinese porcelain over that of most European manufacturers. The forms of their invention, though not always inelegant, have neither the lightness, variety, nor beautiful outline of the Grecian vases; and their designs are wretched when compared with those of European artists, either ancient or modern. The two sorts of earth which are most used in the formation of their porcelain, are called *kao-ling* and *pĕ-tŭn-tsĕ;* the first, a kind of soap-stone mixed with a small proportion of mica; the other a granite in which quartz greatly predominates. The whitest pieces of each are always preferred. The *pĕ-tŭn-tsĕ* is reduced to powder, thrown into a vessel full of water, well stirred up, and then left to settle. A thick cream rises, which is skimmed off and poured into another vessel filled with water. This process is repeated till the cream ceases to rise; and that thrown into the second vessel is allowed to remain untouched, till a crust is deposited below, and the water above is quite clear. The paste thus formed, is dried in moulds, and, before it is completely hardened, is cut into cakes, having nearly the shape and size of a brick, which are sold in the market for so much per hundred. The *kao-ling* receives its name from a hill near King-tĕ-chin, where it is found in large masses under a stratum of red earth. It is subjected to the process just described, and is formed into cakes like those of the *pĕ-tŭn-tsĕ*. For the purpose of making porcelain, these earths are mixed together in different proportions, according to the degree of fineness required; for the best sort in equal quantities; for the second best, four parts of *kao-ling* are added to six of *pĕ-tŭn-tsĕ*; and for the worst, one of the former to three of the latter. A greasy kind of chalk, called *Hwashĕ*, is sometimes substituted for *kao-ling*, after having been prepared in a similar manner; the porcelain thus made, is whiter and more transparent, but more brittle and expensive than the other. *Shĕ-kao*, a kind of gypsum, is likewise sometimes used; but it is not so hard and tenacious as *kao-ling*.

" The mixture, when properly worked up, is thrown into a pit, well paved and plastered with a hard cement; it is then trodden down till it has acquired a sufficient consistency. From this mass, portions are taken and spread upon large slates, on which they are rolled and kneaded till every vacuity and rough substance has been completely removed. The vessel is then formed, if spherical or cylindrical, by a wheel; and is delivered to a second workman, who adds the rims, feet, and other ornaments: a third shapes it on a mould : a fourth pares its edges ; and after passing through twelve or more hands, it is at length fit for the furnace. Figures in relief, spouts, handles, &c. are not formed at the same time as the vessel, but cemented on when nearly dry; the seams being so nicely pared and smoothed as not to appear at all. When sufficiently hardened, the vessel is given to the painters, each of whom has his peculiar province; one to trace circles round the edges, another to draw the landscape, a third to sketch the figures, and so on, till the last applies the colours. Each piece is then put into a separate case, at the bottom of which there is strewed a bed of fine sand, covered with a layer of powdered *kao-ling*. These cases are next placed in the furnace, resting on a floor of coarse sand, and piled one upon the other; first, those containing the coarser wares, then the finer, and lastly, the finest in-grain and colouring, which are nearest to the mouth of the oven. Just room enough is left between the piles to allow a passage for the flame; but, as they have no means of regulating the heat, it often happens that the whole is spoiled and converted into a shapeless mass. The cases are put into the furnace, and removed, when necessary, by means of a kind of iron ladle, with a long wooden handle.

"Porcelain is called *Tsĕ-ki* by the Chinese; and King-tĕ-chin, a village to the east of the Lake Po-yang-hú, in the province of Kyang-si, is the place at which the finest China-ware is made. This is exclu-sively reserved for the Emperor. Blue and white are the ordinary colours; red is one of the most esteemed and expensive; and gilt figures on a black ground are in great request. The gilding is formed by mixing gold-dust, water, and sugar well together; and it is

laid on by a hair pencil first dipped in clear gum-
water, and afterwards into this mixture. When the
vessel has been taken out of the furnace, the gilding is
polished with fine-grained moistened sand.

" A light-brown clay is also much used for making
brown earthenware, in which the Chinese excel, as
well as in porcelain. Jars and vases of every size,
pots, cups, lamps, and spoons, &c. made of this material, are sold for a very small price. Fuller's-earth
is used for making water coolers, and another kind of
clay for vessels which are believed to improve the
taste of the food cooked in them.

" Notwithstanding the perfection of their porcelain,
the Chinese know scarcely any thing about the art of
making glass. Their mirrors are metallic ; a compound, it is said, of zinc and copper. It is dubious
whether there is a single glass-house in the whole
Empire, or any place at which that beautiful and
useful manufacture is carried on, except Canton ; and
nothing more is done even there, than the melting
down old glass, and blowing or moulding it into a new
form.

" Among the minerals, the white copper of Yun-nan
should be noticed as one of the more rare kinds. * It
is naturally brittle, but is rendered ductile by a mixture of zinc. It is, perhaps, the grey copper of Professor
Jamieson. Coal is not uncommon, and collieries are

---

* It is supposed to be a composition of copper, nickel, and iron :
the Chinese call it *pe-tung*. The yellow copper is used for the
current coin. The *tutenague*, or zinc, is found in the province of
Hoo-kwang. Silver mines are said to be abundant, but are not
worked. Gold is obtained from the sands of the rivers in See-
shwen and Yun-nan; and quicksilver is abundant in the latter
province. The lead and tin exported from Canton, come chiefly
from Tibet and Japan.

numerous, particularly near Canton. They are worked by levels cut in the sides of the hills. The coals are charred at the pit, pounded, mixed with earth, and formed into cakes in the shape of bricks. Stones also are hewn and shaped in the quarry, before they are severed from the native rock, as was sometimes done by the Greeks. The torrents descending from the mountains of Yun-nan, Kweï-cheu, and Shen-sí, wash down stones which yield an agreeable sound, and are used for making musical instruments. The stone called Yu is most esteemed. It varies in colour, from the hue of whey to that of a cinder, passing through all the different shades of blue, yellow, red, and green. That which is of a greenish white colour is most valued. It has been erroneously called Chinese Jade, Nephrite, or Prehnite, but is probably undetermined, and nearly allied to axe-stone. Some pieces of it are three feet long, and a foot and a half broad. Marvellous stories are told of their hardness and ponderosity. Another kind, resembling agate, and called ox-fat-stone, is not so hard or heavy, and is found in smaller masses. It is, perhaps, pyritous. Granite and lime-stone are the most common rocks; and no traces of volcanoes, either active or extinct, have yet been found on the main land, though there are many in the neighbouring islands.

" China produces all the European fruits, but some of them do not succeed well. The apples, grapes, and pomegranates are very indifferent; olives, though abundant, are gathered for eating, but not for making oil; a wild apricot, however, which flourishes in bleak tracts and a barren soil, is much used for that purpose. The oil is expressed from the kernels, and the stones are consumed as fuel. There are lemons no bigger than walnuts, and large oranges with an almost solid pulp, which are valued for culinary and medical preparations. The southern provinces are warm enough for most tropical productions, so that the produce both of cold and hot climates is indigenous in China, and it has also many fruits and vegetables peculiar to itself. Such are the *li-chi* (*dimocarpus litchi*), the *long-yan*, dragon's eye (*dimocarpus longan*), *hwâng-pi* (*cookia punctata*), &c. The second is tart and juicy, and more wholesome than the *li-chi*, which it somewhat resembles. The *hwâng-pi* is like an unripe gooseberry. The *shi-tsĕ* (*diospyrus kaki*), called *shi-ping* when dried, is said to taste like a fig, but is a kind of date plum. The *lin-kyo* (*trapa bicornis*) is the fruit, or root, of a water plant, which has a peculiar taste, and is used in soup, or made into a cake with honey. *Pi-tsi*, used as a cooling diet for invalids, is the bulb of the *trapa natans*. A species of *chenopodium* (*beta*) is said to afford much nutritive food; its roots and stem, being dried and pulverized, are made into cakes, and used as bread, while its leaves are either boiled or dressed as sallad. The *pe-tsaï*, or white herb, a kind of mustard (*sinapis brassicata*), is cultivated in large fields, and eaten either fresh or pickled, like the German *sauer-kraut*. Scarcely a lake or morass in the empire but produces the beautiful water-lily, called *nelumbium* by our botanists, and *lyĕn-hwa* by the Chinese. Its seeds, most agreeable to the palate, but least digestible, when green, are as favourite articles of diet with the Chinese as they were with the Egyptians of old; for it is the *cyamus* or Egyptian bean, celebrated by Herodotus, Strabo, and Theophrastus.* Its

* See Mod. Trav., Egypt, vol. i. p. 24.

singular seed-vessel, and shield-formed leaves, which
fold up at night like an Indian screen, figure on most
of the Egyptian sculptures ; and the whole plant,
under the names of *sirisha*, *camala*, and *hô-fú*, is consecrated in the Hindu and Chinese mythologies. The
root, as nutritive and pleasant as the bean, is sometimes pickled and eaten with rice ; at others, ground
into flour, and beat up with milk into a sort of hasty-
pudding. This remarkable plant, which adorns every
ditch and pool in China, resisting equally the cold of the
northern, and the heat of the southern provinces, has
hitherto baffled all attempts to naturalize it in Europe,
and has long since disappeared in Asia Minor and
Egypt ; where we know, from the faithful descriptions
of Dioscorides and Herodotus, it was once so universally cultivated. A kind of *begonia*, called *haï-tang*,
resembling the peach-blossom in colour, is a favourite
subject with the painters and poets of China. It has
dark green leaves and purple branches, from the extremities of which its buds come out in clusters. The
yé-hyàng-hwà, or night-smelling-flower (*pergularia
odoratissima ?*) is a trailing plant, the slender branches
of which must be trained on a frame. Its greenish
yellow blossoms emit a most fragrant and powerful
odour in the night ; and it is so highly valued, that a
fine plant will sometimes sell for nearly ten guineas,
but it is too tender to bear the open air at Peking.
Of all the medical plants in request among the
Chinese, none has obtained such universal repute as
the *jin-seng*. The mountain forests of Eastern Tatary
are the place of its native growth ; and, in 1709,
10,000 soldiers were employed for six months in collecting it for the emperor, whose sole property it is.
Father Jartoux gave so good a description of it in the

Lettres Edifiantes, that Lafitau, another Jesuit, recognised it in the woods of Canada, in 1745 ; and it has, since that time, been imported into China by our merchants. According to the Chinese practitioners, this plant is a sort of panacea, and an infallible remedy for diarrhœa, palsy, and convulsions ; it is therefore naturally an essential ingredient in the immortal beverage dispensed by the priests of Lao-tsĕ ; but the European physicians have not succeeded in discovering its virtues, and have never admitted it into their list of the *Materia Medica*, though it is well known as an umbelliferous plant, and called *panax quinquefolia* by modern botanists.

" Among the trees peculiar to China, the following deserve particular notice ; the *tye-li-mú*, or iron-wood (*baryxylum*), used for making anchor-stocks ; the *nan-mú*, or cedar (*pinus cedrus*), used for beams and pillars ; the *lo-ya-song* (*larix ?*), a deciduous pine, in the timber of which is said to abound a very acrid resin ; and the *syang*, or chestnut (*castanea*), of which the husks contain much of the tanning principle, and are therefore used for fixing colours, while the fruit serves as food for pigs. The *long-ju-tsu* is used for household furniture, and yields a fruit which, when boiled to a jelly, is applied as a preventive against chilblains. The *u-kyeú-mu*, or tallow-tree (*stillingia sebifera*), has bright red, heart-shaped leaves, and bears a fruit, of which the pulp nearly resembles tallow in smell and colour ; it must, however, be softened by linseed oil, in order to reduce it to a proper consistence for making candles. There are likewise two plants on which wax is deposited by insects ; the one a shrub flourishing in a dry rocky soil, called *kan-la-shù* (dry wax tree) by the Chinese ; the other, a tree

which requires moisture, named by them *shwi-la-shù*
(moist wax tree). The wax of the former is white,
shining, and pellucid, and is supposed by the Chinese
to heal and invigorate. The *tong-shu* (*dryandra cor-
data*), yields an oil which, when properly purified, is
called *meng-yeú*, oil of wood, and is used in painting.
The *tsi-shu*, or varnish-tree (*augia sinensis*), exudes,
from incisions in its trunk, a red acrid gum, a solution
of which forms the far-famed vanish of the Chinese.
The trees are let for the season at the rate of three-
pence per foot, and the gum-gatherer must be carefully protected against its pernicious effluvia. *Tse-tan*,
or rose wood, of a dark red and fragrant, is much used
for furniture, as it requires no varnish. The *chang*, or
camphor-tree (*laurus camphora*), grows to a large size.
Its young shoots, when boiled and strained, yield camphor, which is purified by being laid on beds of pul-
verised earth, and then exposed to a moderate heat.
The bamboo-cane, which forms so elegant an ornament in the landscapes on the Chinese screens and
earthen-ware, is as useful as it is ornamental; and
from the numberless variety of purposes to which it
can be applied, deserves to be noticed, though not
peculiar to China. Its tender shoots are brought to
table; its fibres are used as the wick of candles; its
macerated wood is converted into paper; and its stems
serve for almost every object of the carpenter, wheel-
wright, and cabinet-maker.

" But the vegetable production which is now most
peculiarly the exclusive property of China, is Tea.
The shrub, from the leaves of which this beverage is
prepared, is considered by some writers as a native of
the mountainous tracts between the Burman and
Chinese empires; but it has long been naturalized

in the latter ; and the art of drying and preparing its
leaves, seems to have indisputedly originated with the
Chinese. The plant is by them called *ch'ha*, and, in
some dialects, *chè* or *t'hé*, whence its European names
have been borrowed.   Yun-nan and Sŭ-chwen in the
south and west ; Hú-kwang and Kyang-nan in the
centre ; and Che-kyang, with Fŏ-kyen on the south-
eastern side of the empire, are the provinces in which
it is raised in the greatest quantities. The green
teas (*súng-lo*) are brought chiefly from Kyang-nan ;
the black (*vú-í*) or boheas, from Fŏ-kyen, called the
Bohea country by the Supra-cargoes at Canton. Os-
beck, however, conjectured, and the Chinese affirm,
that the difference between those kinds of tea is
occasioned entirely by a difference of soil and prepa-
ration.   The flavour and quality appear to depend
upon the age of the leaf, rather than upon any specific
difference in the plants ; and in fact, the distinctions
between the *bohea* and *viridis*, established by Lin-
næus, are so trifling and liable to variation, that they
have been disregarded by many botanists.

" China has scarcely any animals which are not
common to other countries, except we give credit to
a work on Natural History, published by authority of
K'hang-hi, in which gigantic rats, scaly tigers, and
dragons, the favourite emblems of power and majesty,
are described and figured.   The musk-deer is among
the valuable quadrupeds which China possesses ; its
buffaloes are usually grey, instead of black ; and its
pigs so cleanly, as to be petted in the house as domestic favourites.*

* " Elephants are common in the south of China, and are found
as high as the 30th parallel in the provinces of Hiang-nan and
Yun-nan. The unicorn rhinoceros frequents the marshes in

" The *haï-tsing*, a kind of hawk, found only in Shensí, is called the king of birds, and is reserved for the emperor's exclusive use. Small birds of beautiful plumage and water-fowls abóund, among which the Mandarin duck (*anas galericulata*) merits particular notice on account of its singular beauty, and the value set upon it by the great. The eggs of ducks, a favourite article of diet, are hatched in sand-baths, as the Egyptians hatched chickens in ovens.

" Besides the fish common in Europe, the Chinese have many unknown to us; as the *sho-kya-yu*, or fish in armour (*tetrodon*), which tastes like veal, and is covered with spines; a kind of cod, caught and salted on the shores of Fŏ-kyen; *haï-seng*, an unpalatable kind of blubber (*medusa*), which is eaten by the common people ; and *kin-yu*, or gold-fish (*cyprinus auratus*), a constant ornament in the ponds and reservoirs in their pleasure-grounds.* The *pi-mú-yú*, of which absurd tales are told, is a kind of flat-fish ; and the *ming-fú-yu*, or bright belly, is a *molluscum*, probably one of the *polypus* tribe.

Yun-nan and Quan-si. The lion, according to Duhalde and Trigault, is a stranger to China; but the animal figured by Neuhof, under the name of the tiger, seems to be the maneless lion known to the ancients, and seen by M. Olivier on the Euphrates. Marco Polo saw lions in Fo-kyen. The true tiger probably shews himself in the more southerly provinces, where there are also various kinds of monkeys (the *simia longimana, simia influens,* and *simia sylvana*). The musk-animal, which seems peculiar to the central plateau of Asia, sometimes goes down into the western provinces of China. The deer, the boar, the fox, and other animals, some of |which are little known, are found in the forests."—MALTE BRUN.

* The Chinese gold-fish is said to be a native of a lake at the foot of the high mountain of Tien-king, near the city of Tchang-hoo, in Tche-kyang; whence it was taken to all the other provinces, and to Japan. It was first brought to England in 1611.

" The splendid butterflies and multitudes of singular insects peculiar to China, are well known as favourite subjects of the Chinese artists ; but that country has one insect not so commonly known, which produces a substance called *U-pweï-tse*, (*i. e.* nests filled with eggs,) which has all the appearance of a gall-nut, and is filled with a fine and exquisitely bitter powder.

" The valuable productions of their soil, together with the many arts and manufactures successfully carried on by the Chinese, furnish materials for an extensive commerce. But foreign trade receives no support from the government; it is barely tolerated ; for it is always at variance with that jealous policy which draws a line of perpetual demarcation between China and the rest of the world. Internal commerce, on the other hand, as it excites no apprehension of a dangerous rivalry, is not an object of distrust, but has met with some encouragement. In the construction and management of their boats, the Chinese shew much ingenuity : those designed for pleasure or parade are highly ornamented, as well as light and elegant in their forms. A projecting gang-way of broad planks, on each side, serves as a deck, on which the sailors can manœuvre the vessel without incommoding the passengers ; and the large oars of bamboo, at the stern or near the bow, by which the boat is impelled against a contrary wind and current, are so well managed, as never to interfere with those of other boats passing close by them, in the same or an opposite direction.

" But it is only in their rivers and canals, that the Chinese are good sailors : at sea, they are awkward, unskilful, and cowardly ; and their ships are as ill-constructed as their seamen are clumsy in managing them ; the long voyages, therefore, of which their historians speak, could have been nothing more than excursions in the eastern Archipelago, magnified by Chinese bombast and exaggeration. When at sea, they keep no reckoning, and steer from point to point, as the Greeks and Romans did, never, voluntarily, losing sight of land. Their compass is so imperfect as to be of little use, and is, therefore, rarely looked at. The discovery of that peculiar property of the magnet, by which it causes the needle to point northward, has indeed been ascribed to the Chinese; but, if they were the inventors of the mariner's compass, they have been no improvers of it. A shrine, altar, and spiral taper, kept constantly burning, are usually placed behind the compass, to which the sailors pay a kind of adoration.

"Their trading vessels, called *ch'hwén*, (and by us *junk*, from the Malay word *ajōng*,) are so ill-built and unfit for sea, that it is surprising how they can ever reach the Moluccas and New Holland, the most distant voyages they attempt. With a square bow, no keel or bow-sprit, thick masts of one piece, single sails of bamboo-matting, folded like a fan, heavy and unmanageable, and a moveable, unsteady rudder ; these crescent-shaped vessels, adorned with dragons' mouths, frightful heads, and goggle eyes, are almost ungovernable in rough weather, and frequently upset from press of sail ; for their seamen are often too lazy or too cowardly to take in sail while they have time ; not being willing to climb the shrouds, and press the folds of the sails down with their feet, when the vessel labours. Instead of pitch, they use a compound of gum, lime, and bamboo-threads, (called *tong yeú*,) which is said to become, by exposure to salt water, hard and impervious to moisture. The hold is subdivided by thick partitions well calked, a precaution of great service in case of leaks. These vessels draw little water, and are calculated for shallow seas. They sometimes carry as much as 1000 tons; but from 200 to 600 is their usual burden. They have occasionally 100 different owners, each of whom has his own birth, and portion of the vessel, in which his goods are stowed, and placed under the charge of himself or one of his family.

" The military profession is one which the Chinese peasantry are eager to embrace, notwithstanding their cowardice; for the soldiers, who are rarely, if ever, removed from the province in which they are enrolled, are seldom called into actual service. But so decided a preference is given by the Government to its civil servants, that none who can obtain the education requisite to qualify them for a civil post are willing to enlist; the soldiers are therefore drawn from the lowest and poorest classes of the people. The Tatars, who are almost considered as soldiers from their birth, take the lead in this, as in every other department. The protection of the northern frontier and conquered provinces, is intrusted to the Tatar cavalry; and the regiments of Tatar infantry garrison all the great cities of the empire. The smaller towns and villages are occupied principally by Chinese troops. The ordinary pay of a horse-soldier may be estimated at about ten-pence per diem, including his rations; that of a foot soldier, at seven-pence; but each man has a house and garden of his own, and is allowed to work at his trade when not on duty. In time of war, six months' pay in advance is allowed; and a deduction is made

A CHINESE MILITARY POST.

by Government for the support of a soldier's family, as long as he is absent from home.

" The dress of the military varies in different provinces; blue jackets, bordered with red, being worn in some, brown and yellow in others; but sugar-loaf caps, terminated by a spike and long tufts of scarlet hair, seem to be the proper distinction of a soldier, just as the bead on his bonnet marks the rank of a Mandarin. From each side of these conical helmets, long flaps hang down on the shoulders, and are tied by a riband under the chin : divers, also, are the materials of which these head-dresses are made, from gilt pasteboard to glittering steel. Cuirasses of quilted cloth, thickly studded with brass knobs, are worn in some districts, especially by the archers. Shields of basketwork, 2 feet long, and painted to look like the heads of dragons, are used by a corps called *the Tigers of War;* but the fans and umbrellas, which are a part of the equipment of every Chinese soldier, remind the European of that formidable corps, the Pope's bodyguard. Their arms are swords, pikes, matchlocks, and bows; except when, acting as police-men, they exchange these for a more offensive weapon, the whip. Matchlocks are preferred to muskets, and are provided with a sort of stand, upon which they can be fixed when discharged: a pouch for balls, a powder-horn, and a match-bag fastened to his sleeve, complete a soldier's accoutrements. They estimate the power of a bow by the weight requisite to bend it; fifty pounds being the lowest, and eighty pounds the ordinary rate of the bows used by the army. The archer's thumb is guarded by a thimble of horn or agate. The form of their arrows is very various; some are barbed with small hooks, and others have cavities in which letters may be conveyed clandestinely into the enemy's rank.

. "Their tents are either made of coarse linen, and fixed on a wooden frame, 14 feet long and 5½ feet high, or they are round and covered with grey felts. The latter are peculiar to the Tatars. Five soldiers oc‑ cupy each tent, together with two camp-followers, whose duty it is to pitch and dismantle it.

"Each company consists of twenty-five men, and has its own standard, which is triangular and about 6 feet high : hence, the Chinese army is estimated by the number of banners ; but, in the Tatar army, each company has 100 men, according to the Mancheu au‑ thorities quoted by Mr. Huttmann (*Annals of Orient. Lit.* 153). The colours of these banners vary in the Tatar regiments, being either white, yellow, red, or blue, with or without borders : among the Chinese, they are usually green. The Tatars and Chinese of the northern provinces form the most serviceable part of the army, which does not inspire a European with any exalted idea of its military skill or prowess. The Tatars, indeed, accustomed to the management of horses and to the use of arms from their infancy, are not deficient in spirit and enterprise ; but their fa‑ vourite proverb, ' that the neighing of a single Tatar horse would put the whole Chinese cavalry to flight,' shews the contemptible opinion which they entertain of the valour of their subjects. Great pains are taken by the Government to keep up this spirit ; and no one who distinguishes himself in the field, is left unnoticed or unrewarded.

"Among the inventions ascribed to the Chinese, are the arts of manufacturing gunpowder, guns, and fire-works. The soil and climate in Tatary and China, as well as in India, are favourable to the spontaneous production of nitre; it is, therefore, not unlikely, that its explosive power, when combined with sulphur and charcoal, may have been discovered by the natives of those countries long before it was known in Europe. This, however, seems very doubtful; and it is equally probable, that the art of making gunpowder, together with the use of fire-arms, was introduced into China by the Tatars in the latter half of the thirteenth century. But, whatever may be their claim as inventors, it is certain that the Chinese have made no progress in the art. They have neither any public powder-mills, nor any fixed rules for proportioning the ingredients. One part sulphur, one charcoal, and two nitre, are the quantities used by some, while others add two-thirds, or even five parts of nitre; which is, moreover, often employed in so impure a state, as speedily to attract moisture and render the powder useless. Having no method of granulating their powder, it is likewise very liable to cake into a solid mass. If they were ever acquainted with the use of artillery, they had forgotten it before the Missionaries entered the country, in the sixteenth century; and though they admired and imitated the cannons presented to the Emperor by the King of Portugal, in 1621, they have never been able to mount a park of artillery. Nor can any thing be more wretched than the condition of those Chinese batteries which have fallen under the notice of modern travellers. The petards with which they, fire salutes, have a bore not larger than that of a pistol-barrel; they are stuck perpendicularly in the ground, and discharged by a train communicating from one to the other. Their fire-works are really excellent, and excited the admiration of Lord Macartney almost as much, at the close of the last century, as they astonished the Jesuits two hundred years earlier.

" The Chinese have many fortresses; but they are calculated as a protection against robbers, rather than as a check upon the progress of a regular force. Besides their castles on exposed points, their cities are all fortified by a broad rampart, sometimes flanked with square towers at intervals, faced with stone or brick, as well as protected by a ditch. These ramparts are usually 20 or 25 feet in breadth at their base, and from 25 to 30 feet high; their breadth at the top being 10 or 12 feet; the road to which is so gradual, that a man on horseback can ascend them with ease. Little attention is paid to the guns, but the gates are constructed and guarded with much care. The single gates are a simple passage through the wall: in the double gates, this passage is faced by a semi-lunar outwork, the entrance to which is placed obliquely with respect to that which passes through the wall. The triple gate is the most uncommon, and differs from the double one by a returning passage between the outwork and the city wall, so that the first and third gates are nearly on a line. The gateway is seldom ornamented, but sometimes surmounted with small towers, and provided with a few small cannons laid flat on blocks of stones.

" The ornamental architecture of the Chinese is principally remarkable for its airiness and singularity. Some of their pagodas are from 80 to 160 feet in height, and have as many as nine stories, but always an uneven number. They seem to be intended merely for ornament, and, though occasionally attached to temples, are never, it is said, used as places of worship. They do not appear to suit the taste of the Tatar sovereigns, for there are none of modern date, and most of them are in ruins. Such splendid ones as the tower of Nanking are rare: the greater number have only two or three stories, and few can rival that which adorns Kew-gardens.

" Their numerous triumphal archways have all the same form, and seldom exceed 25 feet in height. They are often sculptured with flowers and other figures, but are generally ill-proportioned and heavy. In their sepulchral monuments, a great diversity of taste is indulged. * Diminutive dwelling-houses, ornamented vaults of various shapes and sizes, and a series of terracés, within the highest of which the corpse is deposited, are some of the singular expedients which they have adopted in order to soothe the spirit of the deceased. Figures of his favourite slaves, dogs, and horses, are dispersed over the terraces, to remind him of his former pleasures and attachments. Cylindrical or angular columns are also usually erected over the graves.

" The bridges of the Chinese are not less light and elegant than their pagodas ; but they are seldom either solid or durable, often unprovided with side-rails, and frequently in such a dilapidated state as to be dangerous. As wood is the usual material, the builder can indulge in every variety of arch or ornament which his fancy may suggest, from a flat causeway on a line with the level bank of the stream, to an arch of such a span that a vessel of 200 tons can pass under it in full sail. The arches of stone are occasionally formed like ours, but are more frequently constructed of stones five or ten feet long, hewn into seg-

* On a mountain in the neighbourhood of Taï-yuen, the capital of Shan-si, are found the royal sepulchres of the *Tai-ming-chao* dynasty; consisting of monuments of stone or marble, triumphal arches, and statues of men and animals, interspersed through a grove of cypresses. Tsi-nan, the capital of Shan-tong, was also the residence of a dynasty of sovereigns, whose tombs form a conspicuous object on the neighbouring mountain.

ments of the arch required; and instead of a key-stone,
ribs of wood are fitted to the convex part, and bolted
into the stones by iron bars. In other cases, the curved
stones are mortised into long transverse blocks, running along the whole width of the arch. Some of these
bridges are of great magnitude. That at Tsŏ-cheu,
600 feet long, is adorned with well-executed sculptures; and one was noticed by Lord Macartney's suite,
which had ninety arches, the central ones being thirty
feet high and forty wide.

"But of all the architectural monuments in China,
the Great Wall is certainly the most remarkable. A
large bulwark or pile of stones thrown up on the edge
of the Hwang Haï, or Yellow Sea, at the boundary of
Lyao-tung, (nearly in lat. 40° N. and long. 119° 30′ E.)
forms one extremity of this vast work. From that
point, it proceeds westward, with various curvatures,
along the borders of the northern provinces, Pĕ-chŏ-li,
Shan-sí, and Shen-si, to the mountains north-west of
Ling-tao, (37° 20′ N. 103° 30′ E.) where almost im-
passable rocks and extensive deserts of sand afford a
sufficient protection against an invading army without
any artificial defence. It is called by the Chinese
Wan-li-chang-ch'hing, ' the Long Wall of 10,000 li,'
of which sixteen make a league. The sum of these
would amount to nearly 1900 miles; and, in point of
fact, including all its windings, it cannot be estimated
at less than 1500. The only interruptions of its con-
tinuity, are a ridge of lofty mountains near Suen-hao,
in Pĕ-chĕ-li, and the stream of the Whang-ho, which
crosses it twice. It is carried by means of arches over
smaller streams, and continued through valleys and
morasses, as well as over all but inaccessible mountains. It consists of an embankment of earth, raised
upon a foundation of large square stones, cased with the

same materials or brick, and paved with flag-stones.
The space between the inclosing walls is in many
places broad enough for six horsemen abreast. Its
height varies; but, in valleys and plains, it is not less
than thirty feet. In such places, it is strengthened by
square projecting towers, at the distance of a bow-shot
from each other. It is said to be a mere mound of
earth near its western extremity, and was probably
never quite completed in that direction. Its magnitude
is such, that a calculation has been made, by which it
appears that its materials, supposing it were a solid
mass of masonry, would be sufficient to surround the
earth, on two of its great circles, with a wall six feet
high and two thick. There are gates in it at intervals,
strongly fortified and garrisoned. It was probably
begun as early as two centuries and a half before the
commencement of our era, under the Princes of Chao
and Yen, petty states on the northern frontier; but
was completed, according to the Chinese historians,
(Martinii, *Hist. Sin.* 237—239,) in the thirty-third
year of the reign of Shi-hwang-ti, (B. c. 215,) under
the direction of Mung-tyen, who had been sent at the
head of 300,000 men, to disperse the Tatars and desolate their country. It was finished, say the same authorities, in the space of five years; every third man
in the empire, capable of such labour, being pressed
into this service. When they add, that the greater
number sank under the pressure of such severe fatigue,
their account is more credible; but the whole appears
to have been much misrepresented and exaggerated;
and it is more probable, that this stupendous undertaking was the work of several generations, than of
one prince, who had scarcely united the whole empire
under his own authority.

" The *Yun-ho,* or Great Canal, is another of those

vast undertakings which exceed the power of almost
any but an absolute sovereign, and which, from its
extensive utility, may be considered as a sort of com-
pensation for the injuries occasioned by its compulsory
construction.   It was completed in about 120 years,
between 1289 and 1409, and unites the waters of the
Weï-ho with those of the Hwang-ho and Yang-tsĕ-
kyang, terminating at the city of Han-cheú-fú, a
course of almost 1000 miles.   It commences near a
small town called Lin-tsin, (nearly in 37° N. and 116°
E.) crosses the province of Shan-tong, and a part of
Kyang-nan, and enters the river Hwang-ho at the
town of Yang-kya-yn.   It passes by Yang-cheú-fú,
enters the Yang-tsĕ-kyang at Kwa-cheú, and resum-
ing its course at Ching-kyang-fú, continues till it
reaches Han-cheú-fú, on an arm of the Tung-haï or
Eastern Sea; 'supplied, in the greater part of its
course, through a flat and probably alluvial country,
by innumerable streams and pools.   Strong dikes,
formed of alternate layers of earth and straw, and
sometimes cased with stone, prevent its waters from
overflowing wherever the country is low and swampy;
the level of the soil being sometimes as much as 20
feet below that of the canal.   In other places, a bed
has been excavated to the depth of 60 or 70 feet, and
the whole has a width of about 200 feet.   The slope
of the country through which it passes, is from north
to south, and its current moves at the rate of about
three miles in an hour.   There are no locks but flood-
gates; and in hilly tracts, inclined planes interrupt and
regulate the rapidity of the stream.   So slight are the
materials of which public works are constructed in
China, that, excepting those just mentioned, there are
scarcely any monuments to be found, the age of which
exceeds three or four centuries.

" A tent suggested the first idea of a Chinese house, as is obvious from the upright posts which support its projecting and slightly inclined roof. This moreover shews what were the ancient habits of the people. High enclosures and a wider area are the principal points which distinguish the habitation of a grandee from that of an ordinary individual. The poor live in wretched huts : a small court, with two or three low apartments, is sufficient to lodge a whole family of the middle rank. Brick and wood are the common materials; rarely stone. The ground floor, the part principally inhabited, is raised a foot or two above the soil, to guard against damps, and is paved with tiles. The upper chambers are used for store-rooms'; and the staircases are mere ladders. The houses of the great occupy much space, are built round several courts, many of which contain three or four separate habitations, raised on stone terraces three or four feet high, and communicating by corridors with wooden pillars painted red. Oiled paper, horn, gauze, or mother-of-pearl, are the substitutes for glass in the windows. The rooms are sometimes heated by flues in the walls and under the floor. A table, some clumsy chairs, porcelain vases containing fragrant shrubs, copper chafing-dishes for perfumes, and ornamented lanterns of various materials, are the principal articles of furniture. The rich have splendid bed-steads with gauze or silk hangings : persons of moderate fortune use benches formed in the walls of the house, which are heated by a stove in winter. A mat in the southern, and a mattress in the northern provinces, with a coverlid of felt, and a wooden cylinder covered with leather for a pillow, are the articles of bedding commonly used. The ornaments of their internal courts, flowering shrubs, vases filled with

gold and silver fish, artificial rocks, &c. are well
known from their screens and porcelain dishes. The
principal entrance is generally splendid ; and of the
three gates, the central one is never opened except for
strangers of distinction. Even within the palace of
the Emperor, many of the apartments are wretchedly
furnished and miserably out of repair ; and the hall
of audience itself has little of the splendour, and less
of the luxury, of the dwellings of most Asiatic princes.
Larger dimensions, and a greater abundance of painting and gilding, are the only points in which the
imperial residence surpasses any other." *

In their physiognomy and the general conformation
of the head, the Chinese approach the Mongol race.
The head is almost quadrangular, the nose short,
without being flattened, the complexion yellow, the
beard thin. The oblique direction of the eyes is more
particularly characteristic of the Chinese, and of their
neighbours, the Japanese and the Coreans. " There
is, undoubtedly," M. Malte Brun remarks, " a great
difference between the Southern and the Northern
Chinese ; between the inhabitants of the mountains,
those of the plains, and those of the maritime districts.
In colour, we know there are great varieties ; but we
have not sufficient information to enable us to trace
the successive shades by which the rude Kalmuck is
separated from the polished inhabitant of Canton."†

* For the preceding details relating to the Arts, Manufactures,
Productions, and Public Edifices, we are indebted to a very able
article in Part xiii. of the Encyclopædia Metropolitana ; a work
which deserves particular praise for the pains and talent employed
in drawing up the geographical articles.

† " The Chinese, in general, are of a middle stature. Their
limbs, especially their hands and feet, are very small. Those of
the northern provinces are much fairer and taller than those of
Kiang-si and Kwang-tong.... The difference between the Chinese

A difference has also been remarked in the national character of the inhabitants of the northern and those of the southern provinces; the latter being more supple, lively, and acute, and consequently more inclined to literary pursuits than the former, who, though excelling them in bodily strength and courage, are inferior in intelligence. A Chinese woman becomes vain of her beauty, in proportion to the smallness of her eyes, the protuberance of her lips, the lankness and blackness of her hair, and the unnatural smallness of her feet. "The size of the foot determines the value of the bride." Almost as soon as they are born, the nurse sews up the feet of the female infant very tight in stiff leather; and they are afterwards swathed with bandages to prevent their growing, so that the pointed foot seems to have but a single toe. Including the heel, it is seldom more than five inches in length. Their handsome embroidered shoes only render the deformity more striking. The feet are extremely thick at the instep; a defect which is partly concealed by silk trowsers adorned with fringe. This absurd custom, whatever may have been its original design,* effectually deprives the women of the power of walking with ease: they totter, rather than walk. The country women compress their feet, but much less than the rich ladies,

and the Mantchoo is almost imperceptible; the latter, however, are fatter and more robust."—TIMKOWSKI's *Travels*, vol. ii. p. 189.

* Excessive jealousy, it has been thought, can alone have introduced so cruel a custom. The affectation of rank, as indicated by their not being required to use their feet in so vulgar an exercise as walking, is more likely to have given rise to it, as the ladies pride themselves on this genteel deformity. There is some reason to suppose that this barbarous custom is not very ancient, as Marco Polo, who describes the dress of the Chinese ladies, does not mention it.

who are scarcely able to cross the apartments of their magnificent prisons. The Mantchoo women, however, M. Timkowski says, let their feet grow to their natural size; but they wear a singular shoe with a wooden sole five inches thick, which hinders them from moving freely, and gives loud notice of their approach. M. Timkowski supposes that they have adopted it, to imitate the tottering gait of the Chinese. Among the Mantchoo ladies, more especially, individuals may be found, of as fair complexion as any European women, " without the aid of white paint and rouge, of which many of them make an immoderate use." Their small, though black and brilliant eyes, have not, to a European, a pleasing expression. Among the men, corpulence, as an indication of an easy life, commands a certain degree of respect, and a spare form passes for a sign of want of talent. People of quality, moreover, allow their nails to grow. The hair of the head and beard are stained black.

The Chinese have been characterized with some justice by M. Malte Brun, as a nation of subjugated and well disciplined barbarians. " A despotism of the most absolute kind has either acquired or preserved for China the external forms of patriarchal government;" but, since the country fell under the yoke of the Mantchoos, " the whip of the Tatar has been conjoined with the paternal rod by which China was previously governed." " The Emperor is styled the sacred son of heaven, sole ruler of the earth, the great father of his people. Offerings are made to his image and to his throne; his person is adored; his people prostrate themselves in his presence; the noblemen of his court, when addressed by him and receiving his orders, must bend the knee. When this demigod

goes abroad, all the Chinese take care to shut themselves up in their houses. Whoever is found in his
way, is exposed to instant death, unless he turns his
back, or lies flat with his face to the ground. All the
shops by which the Emperor is to pass, must be shut;
and this prince never goes out without being preceded
by two thousand lictors, carrying chains, axes, and
various other instruments characteristic of eastern
despotism.

" The power of the mandarin is fully as absolute as
that of the sovereign from whom he derives his authority. An officer of this description, on entering a
city, can order any person whom he chooses to be
arrested, and to die under his hand; and no one can
venture to undertake his defence. He is preceded by
a hundred executioners, who, with a sort of yell, announce his appproach. Should any one forget to retire
to the side of the wall, he is mauled with whips of
chains or rods of bamboos. The mandarin himself,
however, in his turn, is not secured against the
punishment of flogging. For the slightest prevarica-
tion, the Emperor will order the bastinado....In short,
all the notions of a Chinese, from his infancy, are
directed to a single point, obedience. The sacred nature of social rank is perpetually impressed on his
mind by innumerable ceremonies. At every step he
makes a bow; every phrase that he utters, must be a
compliment; not a word can he address to a superior, without calling to mind his own utter insigni-
ficance."

" But the great secret of Chinese policy," continues
M. Malte Brun, " and the very basis of the empire,
is to be found in an institution which in some measure deprives the inhabitants of the power of forming
new thoughts, by depriving them of the liberty of

expressing them by means of external characters corresponding to the words of their language. Such is
the effect of the Chinese mode of writing. It has
been compared, though not with much propriety, to
the hieroglyphical or figured language of the Egyptians.
It can only be compared to those systems of pasigraphy
or universal character, by which some wrong-headed
persons in Europe have brought on themselves universal ridicule....This institution, not singular in the
end at which it aims, but altogether unique in its
method of proceeding, perpetuates that eternal infan-
tine imbecility of intellect by which the Chinese are
degraded. The spoken language, in the first place, is
left in a deficient state. The ideas of the people
receive no enlargement, because the higher classes
cannot express their thoughts except in a language
totally distinct, and understood only by the select few.
The information of the privileged class has no means
of becoming disseminated by speech, where the signs
for representing ideas have no corresponding words.
This information must become obscure or utterly extinct, even among those to whose care it is confided."[*]

The radical and incurable defect of such a written
medium is, that while it may serve to call up ideas, to
suggest and convey simple sentiments and a certain
degree of information, it affords no facilities for the
acquisition of new ideas. It is knowledge in stereotype: the impression may be indefinitely multiplied,
but the characters are fixed. The language is the
mould of the ideas received into it, rather than the
body which they assume, and through which they
develop themselves; and thus, it makes no provision
for the expansion of the national mind. It depends,

* Malte Brun, vol. ii. pp. 592—5.

for being understood, upon certain 'fixed associations
of ideas, and is all but absolutely impotent to express
new and foreign associations. It gives us language
in its crude state, in which the only mode of expressing ideas relating to immaterial objects, is by palpable
metaphor. For the next stage in the progress of
language, in which metaphorical terms become the
simple signs of abstract ideas, such a system of sym-
bols is wholly unsuitable. The difficulty of translating
Chinese poetry into a foreign language, is all but
insuperable; and a verbal translation would be unin-
telligible, because it would not express the allusion
on which the meaning depends. What must be the
difficulty of transfusing into such a language, European notions and Christian ideas ?

The colloquial medium of the Chinese, which has
no connexion whatever with the written character,
has all the meagreness of a monosyllabic language;
the same term being made, by various inflections of
the voice, to express the most different objects. It has
been asserted, that the vernacular Chinese scarcely
contains 350 terms which the unpractised ear of a
European can distinguish from one another. Such a
language may be melodious, and even expressive of
the passions of the speaker; but it must lie under
the disadvantages inseparable from an unwritten
dialect; it must be at once defective and ambiguous,
totally destitute of the precision necessary for conducting any process of reasoning, and incapable of
being made the medium of any wide range of ideas.
All unwritten languages are liable to the endless
diversification of provincial dialect. Accordingly, the
oral dialects of China are very numerous, and the
inhabitants of neighbouring provinces are frequently
unable to carry on a conversation of any length,

without having recourse to writing. Various are the
contrivances which the natives themselves employ, in
order to obviate the extreme ambiguity of their oral
language. Expressive gestures, signs made in the air,
contortions of the features, are all continually called
into action. But the addition of synonymes is the
most common expedient ; and double words, thus
compounded of synonymous verbs or substantives,
have so far become integral parts of the language as
to render it in some degree polysyllabic. A similar
process has apparently taken place in some of the
Indo-Chinese dialects, which were originally monosyllabic. By whatever process the change is brought
about, a language must cease to be monosyllabic, by
the introduction of the finer mechanism of inflection
and declension, long before it can become available as
the vehicle of any thing deserving the name of philosophy or literature.

The ancient religion of China appears to have been
a species of Sabianism; but it has been smothered
under the numerous sects which have been grafted
upon it. Buddhism, under the name of the religion
of Foh, was introduced from India about A.D. 65,
and has become the creed of the majority of the
Chinese.* The religion of the Mantchoo dynasty is
that of the Dalaï Lama. Perhaps it may be said, that
the worship of the Emperor is the religion of their
subjects.

We must now proceed to give a brief description of
the capital.

* See our history of Buddhism in Mod. Trav., Birmah, pp. 91—
116. A valuable account of the Chinese sects is given by Dr. Milne,
" Retrospect," &c. Sec. 2.

ONE OF THE WESTERN GATES OF THE CITY OF PEKIN.

London. Published by J. Duncan Paternoster Row, Nov.r 1827.

PEKING.

PE-KING (the court of the north), otherwise called *Chun-thian-fou*,[*] the present metropolis of China, is situated in the northern part of the province of Pe-tche-li, about 26 miles to the south of the Great Wall, in lat. 39° 42' 15" N., long. 114° 5' 30" E. (Paris.) It stands in a sandy, arid plain, destitute of all vegetation, bounded, westward, by a chain of lofty mountains extending from N.E. to S.W. From these mountains issue several small rivers, which water part of the plain. One of these enters the city on the north, and dividing into several arms, surrounds the imperial palace, forms some artificial lakes, and again uniting its waters, falls into the Pe-ho, about 20 miles E. of Pe-king. The city is divided by a high wall into two parts. The northern quarter, which forms nearly a perfect square, is called *King-tching*, or the City of the Court: this is the Mantchoo town, and contains the imperial palace. The southern quarter, or Chinese town, is called *Vai-tching:* it is in the form of a parallelogram. Both together occupy an area seventeen miles in circuit, inclosed with walls built of brick. Those of *King-tching* are 40 feet in height, and 20 feet thick, forming a rampart broad enough for horsemen to ride on the top : for this purpose, a gentle slope is made at intervals, by which cavalry can ascend with ease. The walls of the Chinese quarter are less massive. The gates are sixteen in number. Those of the Mantchoo town are lofty and strongly vaulted : above them rise towers nine stories high, with embrasures, and their commanding height gives them at a distance an air of grandeur.

* This is interpreted, " city of the first order, obedient to heaven." It is said to have been founded by Kublaï, the grandson of Tchengiz Khan.

Before each gate is a walled space about 360 feet square, forming a parade. The walls are besides flanked with small square towers, at intervals of 40 yards, and with larger ones at the angles.

The streets of Pe-king are, for the most part, broad, and in straight lines; the largest is sixty yards in width, and nearly three miles in length, running from E. to W. They are unpaved, but clean and well kept. The houses are very low, often of only one story; built of brick and tiled. The shops are handsomely ornamented, and the brilliancy and variety of the goods exposed to sale, give them a gay appearance. The courts of justice and the palaces of the princes have a lofty basement story and handsome entrances. The latter are covered with varnished green tiles. The finest buildings in Pe-king are the temples, which are spacious and magnificent, adorned with columns and staircases of fine white marble. The streets and houses in the Chinese town are very inferior to those in *King-tching*. Besides these two towns, Pe-king has twelve large suburbs, which altogether form a very large city. Half of the Chinese town, however, according to Father Gaubil, is uninhabited; and a large part is occupied with temples, cemeteries, fields, and gardens. In the Mantchoo town, besides the Imperial palace and park, there are several other palaces, and various public edifices, powder-magazines, temples, and lakes, occupying above half of the city. The breadth of the streets and lowness of the houses must also be taken into consideration in estimating the population. Many of the Chinese, on the other hand, will herd together in a room; so that the population of the city and suburbs may, perhaps, amount to two millions of souls.*

* This is the estimate of Father Gaubil as cited by Mr. Tim-

. The magnificence of the Imperial palace, we are told, does not consist so much in the imposing elegance of its architecture, as in the multitude of its buildings, its courts, and its gardens. The walls of the palace comprehend a little town, inhabited by the great officers of the court, and a great quantity of mechanics, all in the Emperor's service. Father Artier, a French Jesuit who obtained permission to visit the palace, says, that it is a league in circumference; that its front is embellished with paintings, gilding, and varnished work, and that the furniture and ornaments of the interior comprise every thing that is most rare and valued in China, India, and Europe. The gardens of the palace form a vast park, in which, at proper distances, mountains rise twenty or sixty feet in height, separated from one another by little valleys, which are watered with canals; these waters unite to form lakes and broad ponds, which are navigated by magnificent pleasure-boats, and their banks are adorned with a series of buildings of which no two are alike. Each valley contains a summer-house or villa, sufficiently spacious to accommodate one of the first noblemen of Europe, with all his attendants. The cedar of which these houses are built, is not found within a less distance than 1400 miles from Peking. In the midst of a lake which is a mile and a half broad, there is a rocky island, crowned with a superb palace, containing more than a hundred apartments. The mountains and hills are covered with trees and fine aromatic flowers; the canals, skirted

howski, confirmed by that Traveller's own observation. M. Malte Brun says: " The English make the number of inhabitants amount to three millions; an estimate ridiculously extravagant." He is even disposed to bring down the estimate to 6 or 700,000 inhabitants.

with rocks, so artfully arranged as to be a perfect imitation of nature in her wildest and most desolate forms. The whole has an air of enchantment. On the summits of the highest mountains, tall trees encircle pavilions and kiosks consecrated to retirement and pleasure.

The air of Peking is deemed salubrious. Epidemic disorders are very rare. The heat is very great in summer, attended by abundant rains. Sometimes, the torrents, pouring down from the mountains, do great damage, destroying whole villages. From the middle of December to March, the water is frozen. The autumn is the pleasantest season; the air is then mild and the sky serene.

To this general description of the city, may be added, from the recent publication by M. Timkowski, the following details and observations.

"Peking is distinguished from other capitals and great cities of Asia by the peculiar style of its buildings, and the order which reigns in its interior. We must not look for houses of four or five stories in height; there are no fine quays, no foot-pavements, nor are the streets lighted at night. Every thing, however, in the Chinese capital indicates a country that has long been civilized. The tranquillity of the inhabitants is secured by moral institutions, by stable regulations, and by an active police. There are constantly in the streets, soldiers with swords at their sides and whips in their hands, ready to strike those who are disposed to create any confusion. They take care that the streets of King-tching are kept perfectly clean, and in case of need, put their hands to the work themselves. They keep watch during the night, and allow nobody to go in the streets unless with a lantern, and for some necessary business, as to fetch a physician. They even question those who may be charged with commissions from the Emperor, and a satisfactory answer must always be given them. They have a right provisionally to arrest any person who resists them, or is thought suspicious. The governor of the city often makes visits when they are least expected. The officers of the guard are bound to be extremely vigilant with respect to the soldiers under their command. The slightest negligence would be punished, and the officer cashiered the following day. These police soldiers are Chinese infantry belonging to the regular troops.

" There is besides at Peking, a body of cavalry said to amount to 80,000 men. Their principal business is to do duty at the gates and on the walls, and to be ready to march on the shortest notice.

" One of the principal duties of the police at Peking is to prevent famine. In the city, as well as in the suburbs, there are numerous granaries, where a great quantity of rice is warehoused against seasons of scarcity. The regulations respecting these granaries are faithfully executed in the vicinity of the court; if they were equally well observed in the provinces, there would be no famine; but this calamity frequently occurs through the negligence of the mandarins. Besides those granaries, the Emperor has others, which are filled with wheat, pulse, and fodder for the beasts of burden.

" At Peking, we rarely hear of dissensions in families. The maxims of the religion of Confucius, and the principles of the education of youth, which are impressed on the memory of the Chinese, serve them as guides on all occasions throughout their lives. The unlimited submission of children to their parents regulates the conduct of each towards his fellow-citizens.

It is this principle which leads the Chinese to obey the orders of the government, and to respect and venerate its civil and military agents.

" On the other hand, the Chinese, like all other nations, have their failings and their vices. They are indifferent not only to strangers, but also to their own countrymen: this is one of their greatest defects. They are proud, vindictive, interested, jealous, very distrustful, and very cunning. The poverty which is very common in all classes, obliges them to employ address which often degenerates into roguery. The population is so considerable that the national wealth, though very great, cannot be properly distributed. A Chinese officer having the rank of colonel, has less to live upon than one of our inferior officers; that is, if both have no other income than their pay.

" In general, the Chinese are inclined to a dissolute way of life. The rich, besides their lawful wife, have a harem; yet, yielding to bad example, they visit women of ill fame, and even indulge in still greater depravities.

" The principal class of inhabitants in Peking is composed of the Mantchoo troops: the officers, who are at the same time members of the civil tribunals, but too indolent to employ themselves in investigating the causes brought before them, leave the management of business to their Chinese secretaries. When the Mantchoos took possession of Peking, the officers and privates had for their share, the houses of the inhabitants in the southern cities. But these Mant- choos have long ceased to be any thing more than the tenants of the houses, and the lands which have been granted to them; they have consumed their property, and the estates have fallen into the hands of Chinese merchants. The military, who are in good circum-

stances, possess houses and shops which bring them in
a considerable income.

"The merchants and artisans compose the second
class of inhabitants; the former principally live in the
Vai lo tching: the great population of the empire
deprives many of the inhabitants of the means of supporting themselves by agriculture. A great number
of people resort from all the provinces to the capital,
to gain their livelihood; but they do not always succeed, the class who have need of workmen being very
moderate in their desires. It is said, that there are
in Peking fifty thousand persons, who, being without
employment, have recourse to robbery and cheating.
The vigilance and the severity of the police, however,
keep them in good order; for, during a residence of
about six months at Peking, I did not hear of a single
robbery of importance. As the Chinese are extremely
distrustful of the poor, and beggars always meet with
a decided refusal, it is but seldom that a poor individual has recourse to this easy means of gaining a livelihood. The poor are employed in cleaning and watering the streets and gardens, and cultivating the
ground; they also do the business of porters, and
increase or compose the groupes which follow the processions at marriages, funerals, &c. I have often met
some of these poor creatures, who had scarcely clothes
to cover them, wearing cloaks of ceremony, and caps
with red feathers, accompanying the funeral of some
rich man. When a tradesman employs a man of this
class to carry the goods which he has sold to any body,
the porter faithfully delivers them, and contents himself with a remuneration of about three pence, even if
he has worked for two hours.

" Wherever two streets meet, and at every bridge,
there are two-wheeled carriages, answering the same

purposes as hackney-coaches in Europe. They are
lined with satin and velvet, and drawn by mules or
horses; the first of which in particular are very active. The great people, and especially the ladies, use
sedan chairs, but they must first obtain permission
from the Emperor. Persons in office prefer riding on
horseback, which, on account of the unevenness of
the streets and the great crowd, is the most conve-
nient and expeditious mode of conveyance, as I know
by experience. There are many officers in Peking
who have their own carriages and horses; but, notwithstanding this, the owners of the above-mentioned
coaches or chaises carry on a very lucrative business.

" The inhabitants of Peking receive every thing
from the southern provinces. In Peking itself, there
are no good manufactories, except of coloured glass.
Precious stones are also cut and polished in the capital. The inhabitants of the city, and the Chinese
in general, prefer pork, which is here better fla-
voured, and more easy of digestion than in Russia.
The Mantchoos and Mongols eat mutton, and the
latter, beef. Mutton and beef are not very good
in China, because the cattle coming from Mongolia
are too much exhausted, and are not properly attended
to after they reach the capital. Butter, especially
made of sheep's milk, comes from Mongolia. The
Chinese prefer hogs' lard, and cannot bear even the
smell of butter made of cow's milk. The most common domestic fowl are geese, ducks, and chickens.
The first 'are indispensable at grand entertainments.
The physicians forbid patients to eat poultry, as indi-
gestible and unwholesome. A species of duck called
ya-tsu is a very favourite dish on grand occasions,
and is dressed in more than thirty different ways.
The ducks of Peking are very large, very fat, and

juicy. In the winter, there are partridges, pheasants, and game of all kinds. But it is necessary to be very careful in purchasing provisions, for the Chinese dealers mix plaster or sand in the flour to increase the weight. Often they sell the flesh of animals that have died of some disorder, or of such as are not generally used for food; for instance, asses, mules, camels, &c. They improve the appearance of ducks and chickens by blowing the air between the skin and flesh, which makes them look very white and plump.

" The Chinese have but little inclination for gymnastic exercises. It seems that they are not well fitted for amusements of this description, on account of their weak constitutions, arising partly from the heat of the climate, and partly from the bad quality of their food. The soldiers, especially the Mantchoos, are obliged to ride a great deal, to exercise with the bow and arrow, &c. The Chinese have no dances except a very imperfect kind of pantomime, which is executed by the actors on the stage."*

One of the darkest-traits in the national character of the Chinese is, the prevalence of at least *female* infanticide. With regard to the extent to which this is systematically practised, authorities are at variance, and we do not, therefore, venture upon specific details. Dr. Morrison, while he gives the Chinese credit for their mildness and urbanity, their docility and industry, their subordination to authority, and reverence for age, and those virtues which are enforced by public opinion,—is compelled to place to their account, on the darker side, insincerity and jealousy, an atheistic spirit, ill concealed by a little frigid ratiocination, cold-blooded selfishness, and inhumanity. †

* Timkowski's Travels, pp. 141—191.
† Morrison's View, pp. 124, 5.

" Since the union of China to Mantchoo Tatary," remarks Dr. Milne, " there have been two national characters in the Empire, of a very opposite kind, affecting each other by a mutual re-action. The ruder qualities of the Tatar have been softened by the more mild and polished ones of the Chinese. The cowardly imbecility and the slow, calculating prudence of the Chinese, have been improved by the warlike spirit and elastic activity of the Tatar. The intrigue and deceit of the Chinese, and the rude courage of the Tatar, unite in what may be considered as the present national character."*

Such, alas ! are the fruits of the boasted wisdom and civilization of this enigmatical nation ! The country itself may deserve the investigation of the naturalist ; but, to use the words of the learned Author of the " View," " abstract science and the fine arts can learn nothing from China ; and, perhaps, as much is already known, as can be known, to aid the general philosopher in his reasonings."

* " Retrospect," &c., p. 23.

THE END.

LONDON :—PRINTED BY W. CLOWES, STAMFORD STREET.

www.ingramcontent.com/pod-product-compliance
Lightning Source LLC
Chambersburg PA
CBHW051313060726

PP18533700001B/9